The Penguin Book of
Australian Bush Writing

John Ross was a newspaper journalist with *The Age* and Editor of *Walkabout* magazine before becoming a book publisher and writer. He joined Lansdowne Press as Managing Editor and subsequently became Publishing Director at Macmillan Australia and then Managing Director of Currey O'Neil Ross. He then began his own book production company and consultancy. He was Editor-in-Chief of *Chronicle of the 20th Century*, *Chronicle of Australia*, *100 Years of Australian Football* and co-editor of *200 Seasons of Australian Cricket*. He has written, among some twenty books, *Every Picture Tells a Story*, *Country Towns*, *Voices of the Bush*, *One People: One Destiny* and *The Sound of Melbourne*.

The Penguin Book of

Australian
Bush
Writing

Edited by
JOHN ROSS

VIKING
an imprint of
PENGUIN BOOKS

VIKING

Published by the Penguin Group
Penguin Group (Australia)
250 Camberwell Road, Camberwell, Victoria 3124, Australia
(a division of Pearson Australia Group Pty Ltd)
Penguin Group (USA) Inc.
375 Hudson Street, New York, New York 10014, USA
Penguin Group (Canada)
90 Eglinton Avenue East, Suite 700, Toronto, Canada ON M4P 2Y3
(a division of Pearson Penguin Canada Inc.)
Penguin Books Ltd
80 Strand, London WC2R 0RL, England
Penguin Ireland
25 St Stephen's Green, Dublin 2, Ireland
(a division of Penguin Books Ltd)
Penguin Books India Pvt Ltd
11 Community Centre, Panchsheel Park, New Delhi – 110 017, India
Penguin Group (NZ)
67 Apollo Drive, Rosedale, North Shore 0632, New Zealand
(a division of Pearson New Zealand Ltd)
Penguin Books (South Africa) (Pty) Ltd
24 Sturdee Avenue, Rosebank, Johannesburg 2196, South Africa

Penguin Books Ltd, Registered Offices: 80 Strand, London WC2R 0RL, England

First published by Penguin Group (Australia), 2011

10 9 8 7 6 5 4 3 2 1

Design by John Canty © Penguin Group (Australia)
Cover image: Arthur Streeton 'The selector's hut (Whelan on the log)' 1890
National Gallery of Australia, Canberra
Typeset in 12/16.5 Adobe Garamond by Post Pre-press Group, Brisbane, Queensland
Printed and bound in Australia by McPherson's Printing Group, Maryborough, Victoria

National Library of Australia
Cataloguing-in-Publication data:

The Penguin book of Australian bush writing / edited by John Ross.
9780670076413 (pbk.).
Australian literature. Australia–Fiction.

820.80994

penguin.com.au

Contents

Introduction

The Australian bush – sometimes referred to as 'the great emptiness' – has been a rich topic for generations of Australian writers. Literary evocations of the land and its people – of struggle and humour, of hardship and hard labour, of make-do and mateship – have done much to foster our understanding and love of country.

As Australians we carry a certain vague longing for the bush, a feeling often inculcated by story and song rather than deep experience.

Australians overseas can become genuinely emotional over a whiff of gum leaves, and expatriates in 'cities pent' can be transported by a glimpse of country on the ABC news. And all of us are moved by words written – yesterday or long ago – about the experiences of the bush.

A recent study of national characteristics found that there are geographic triggers of patriotism from country to country – for Russians it is the vast sweep of the Steppes from Moscow to Siberia, for Italians the crowded life of the village square, for the Scots the mountain crags and glens of the highlands. For Australians it is simply the bush, that ill-defined territory more country than town.

It is in places of dry farmlands and big mobs of cattle and sheep; it is in parched watercourses and lazy rivers. These were the places of bush itinerants – shearers, drovers, workers, battlers – that gave rise to the Australian qualities of strength, stoicism and the fair go that are now mostly seen on sporting grounds and battlefields.

The bush can be far away in the backblocks of all of the states, or just down the road, only a short journey from any of our capital cities.

Picture big gum trees and low hills of pasture, moving through shades of grey to green with the seasons, with bones of rocks and boulders protruding here and there. There are the skeletal remnants and shards of fallen timber, and, in the haze of the blue mountain or the forest in the distance, there is the natural and original vitality of the land.

There are other country scenarios, of course – rainforest and plain, snowfield and coastline, and the great and still-mysterious inland. The desert as the last frontier holds a singular magic, as the pall of nothing but sand and scrub for thousands of kilometres can be suddenly arrested by the emergence of the thrall of escarpments, gorges and hidden valleys, all laid down by time and the workings of nature on ancient tablelands.

The Penguin Book of Australian Bush Writing will transport you into those inland depths. You will be in the company of great characters and surprising dramas, and fall under the spell of many Australian writers. The stories range through time and place, but are always somewhere in the heartland.

Many writers demand their inclusion, and we may be allowed to bask a little in the contributions of the early giants Henry Lawson and A.B. 'Banjo' Paterson. Lawson's reportage seems so easy and is so rich in atmosphere and variety. He gives us a brisk lesson on itinerant life in 'The Romance of the Swag', which contrasts with the sombre note of 'In a Wet Season', when he takes an agonisingly slow train journey through sodden country. And Paterson's masterly observations bring all the greatness of our pastoral past into focus with his reflections on 'The Trouble with Merinos'.

Not far behind Lawson and Paterson is Edward S. Sorenson, who had a wry look at Bushman Junior in the analogously titled story from his book *Life in the Australian Backblocks*.

There is danger and drama in many journeys across the vastness of the land, as latter-day explorers attempt some pretty hard assignments. That most intrepid solo walker G.E. 'Chinese' Morrison goes for a solitary ramble from Darwin to Melbourne in 'A Transcontinental Ramble'. C.T. Madigan seeks to conquer the last unknown inland as he leads his team into the Simpson Desert in 'Crossing the Dead Heart'. Geoffrey Dutton's father is determined to be the first across the continent by motor car in 'Across Australia by Car'. Alan Marshall travels in a horse-drawn caravan, while Jonathan Green and family make it around Australia in eighty days, and Green writes his newspaper column as well, despite getting trapped in Borroloola.

As faraway places go, Keith Willey finds that Borroloola is at the end of the line, but there are other people looking around elsewhere. D'Arcy Niland explores the first inland city in 'Bathurst', and Alan Frost travels the cane fields of the tropical north. And the drama is immediate in two classic newspaper features: in 'Cheating the Flames of Death', Gary Hughes fights for survival in the Black Saturday bushfires, and in 'An Angel in the Queensland Floods', Tony Wright relates an all-night struggle for life in the Grantham flood surge.

And among the other adventures there is 'Walking on Water', in which tour leader Bill King has snakes in the camp and crocodiles upsetting boats on the Roper River. The wonders of wild Australia are superbly explored in 'Close to Nature' by John Landy, in 'Wilderness – A Personal Account' by Tasmanian Chris Bell, and by such great names as Les Murray, Eric Rolls, Edna Walling and Henry G. Lamond.

The land of Australia and the lives of its country people are ever present – explored in such contributions as Tom Cole's 'Head Stockman at Wave Hill', Patsy Adam-Smith's 'The Waaia Races' and Brian Taylor's 'The Brumby Mare'.

The stories mentioned here are but a sample of this collection of bush writing. And the complete collection leaves behind a host of good material which space would not allow – this time. It has been a joy and a privilege to read and assemble all these works, and to revisit the far reaches of Australia.

– John Ross

The Landscape
of the Imagination

Gerald Murnane

Gerald Murnane muses, in a preface to the art book Wimmera, *on the existence in his imagination of the landscape of his award-winning novel,* The Plains.

Whenever I have written fiction, I have looked often at what I call, for convenience, images-in-my-mind, rarely troubling myself as to whether those images come from memory or from that other equally vague and remote locality, the imagination. One image prominent while I wrote the book named after level countryside was a simple image with its source near at hand. I was writing in a room in the shaded, southern side of a house in a northern suburb of Melbourne, but I saw often an image of a rectangular window-blind, brown-gold in colour and drawn down over a window that looked northwards. On either side of the blind was a strip of bright sunlight from outside the window. Such a blind was sometimes drawn in a room of the house where I was writing, and I made sure to look at it on hot, bright days, but only so that I could see more clearly in my mind certain other images. One of these was of a blind that was kept drawn for day after day during every summer of the four years that I spent as a child in Bendigo. The worn fabric of that blind was suffused with orange-gold light from outside, and the gaps around the ill-fitting rectangle were zones of yellow-white. The window behind the blind rattled all day when the hot wind blew from the north.

There was another image of a drawn blind with dazzling sunlight behind it. This image came from my memories of summer holidays in the south-west of Victoria, where the forebears of both my parents had lived since the 1860s. One of my grandfathers owned a farm on the very edge of the Southern Ocean. On many days you could hear from every room of the spacious farmhouse the breaking of waves against rocks and cliffs. My lasting memories are not of sea or cliffs. The window where the blind was always drawn in the image in my mind faced away from the coast and inland, across the yellowed pad-docks where the grass leaned in the north wind on hot days.

I have learned little from staring at things, not even at images in my mind. I have learned much more from details that have appeared at the edges of my vision. I prefer to look out from the sides of my eyes until one or another detail winks at me. I use the word *winks* advisedly. A detail within view of my eyes or at the edge of my mind, being almost always something other than a human face, has no eye with which to wink and must signal to me by a sort of flickering or nodding or trembling. Even so, I describe as *winking* this primitive signalling to me from some patch of colour or some shape within my sight. I so choose because my seeing the signal never fails to make me feel reassured and encouraged as many a person must feel after hav-ing been winked at by another person. And I choose the word *winks* because a wink from one person to another often signals that the two persons share a secret knowledge, and I often feel, after some detail in my view or in my mind has winked at me, that the visible world wants me to learn its meaning or that the farthest places in my mind are well-disposed towards me.

Even as a child looking at the drawn blind in front of the rattling window in Bendigo, I suspected that the true meaning of that sight lay far away behind it or to one side of it. I was led to imagine level countryside in a vague region inland from Bendigo, but I could not guess what it might portend. Likewise when I stared at the drawn blind in the house on the coast, the limits of my imaginings were level vistas vaguely to the north.

I believe I am barely capable of abstract thought. I can only think by considering images. The meaning of my book, *The Plains*, appears to me now as part diagram and part map. From the room in the suburb of Melbourne where I wrote my book, two straight lines extend to form almost a right angle. One of the lines extends through Bendigo and then, like all straight lines, onwards to infinity. The other straight line extends towards infinity by way of the district south-east of Warrnambool. In the angle between these lines as they cross the western half of the state of Victoria a variety of landscapes lies, but this variety is wholly obscured beneath a floating or hovering vista of level grassy countryside with a few trees in the far distance and among those trees an iron roof winking in the sunlight.

The contents of my book appear to me in a place that was often previously at the edges of my vision, but that place is on no known map. Under the winking roof might be a library of ten thousand volumes or a painter's studio or a puppeteer's workshop. The scholar in the library, the painter in the studio, or the puppeteer in the workshop works behind drawn blinds, trying to find the meaning of what lies on the other side of those blinds; what ought to be clear to view but instead resists inspection. The central image in my book seems to me that of a person peering at some representation of plains in the inmost room of a large house surrounded by a level landscape under a cloudless sky.

I have never travelled more than a thousand kilometres from my birthplace. I have found enough hints of strangeness in my native territory without having to look elsewhere. For almost 50 years, I had seen myself as settled in the northern suburbs of Melbourne while noticing sometimes from the sides of my eyes the gravelly hills of Bendigo to the north-west or the grassy paddocks of Mepunga to the south-west or the fictional landscapes between. Then, three years ago, I was invited to make use of an empty house on the far side of the Wimmera. For the first time in my life, I drove past Ballarat to Horsham, and then still further. Since then, I have travelled the same route every few months and stayed for days at a time on the edge of the Little Desert.

I do not stare at the Wimmera as I pass through. I watch from the sides of my eyes, especially on hot and cloudless days. The house where I stay has walls of thick stone and deep-set windows, one of which faces east. I have not yet begun to understand the Wimmera, but I have already glimpsed in my mind an occasion when something of meaning will be revealed to me.

On that occasion, the morning will be hot. I will already have drawn the greenish blind in the east-facing window. The room where I sit will be shaded like the rooms where the characters in *The Plains* brooded and speculated, themselves wholly imaginary on the site of an imaginary Wimmera. Late in the morning, I notice at one side of my vision a patch of sunlight on a surface. The light from the direction of the Wimmera lies on the open page of a certain book on a table near the window. On the page is a reproduction of a painting from a series of paintings to do with a district of plains. A detail from the page seems to wink in my direction.

The Romance of the Swag

Henry Lawson

Henry Lawson gets out on the track and among the itinerants of an old Australia as he explains the intricacies of the swag and its contents.

The Australian swag fashion is the easiest way in the world of carrying a load. I ought to know something about carrying loads: I've carried babies, which are the heaviest and most awkward and heartbreaking loads in this world for a boy or man to carry, I fancy. God remember mothers who slave about the housework (and do sometimes a man's work in addition in the bush) with a heavy, squalling kid on one arm! I've humped logs on the selection, 'burning-off,' with loads of fencing-posts and rails and palings out of steep, rugged gullies (and was happier then, perhaps); I've carried a shovel, crowbar, heavy 'rammer,' a dozen insulators on an average (strung round my shoulders with raw flax) – to say nothing of soldiering kit, tucker-bag, billy and climbing spurs – all day on a telegraph line in rough country in New Zealand, and in places where a man had to manage his load with one hand and help himself climb with the other; and I've helped hump and drag telegraph-poles up cliffs and sidings where the horses couldn't go. I've carried a portmanteau on the hot dusty roads in green old jackeroo days. Ask any actor who's been stranded and had to count railway sleepers from one town to another! he'll tell you what sort of an awkward load a portmanteau is, especially if there's a broken-hearted man underneath it. I've tried knapsack fashion – one of the least healthy and most likely to give a man sores; I've carried my belongings in a three-bushel sack slung over my shoulder – blankets, tucker, spare boots and poetry all lumped together. I tried carrying a load on my head, and got a crick in my neck and spine for days. I've carried a load on my mind that should have been shared by editors and publishers. I've helped hump luggage and furniture up to, and down from, a top flat in London. And I've carried swag for months out back in Australia – and it was life, in spite of its 'squalidness' and meanness and wretchedness and hardship, and in spite of the fact that the world would have regarded us as 'tramps' – and a free life amongst *men* from all the world!

The Australian swag was born of Australia and no other land – of the Great Lone Land of magnificent distances and bright heat; the land of self-reliance, and never-give-in, and help-your-mate. The grave of many of the world's tragedies and comedies – royal and otherwise. The land where a man out of employment might shoulder his swag in Adelaide and take the track, and years later walk into a hut on the Gulf, or never be heard of any more, or a body be found in the bush and buried by the mounted police, or never found and never buried – what does it matter?

The land I love above all others – not because it was kind to me, but because I was born on Australian soil, and because of the foreign father who died at his work in the ranks of Australian pioneers, and because of many things. Australia! My country! Her very name is music to me. God bless Australia! for the sake of the great hearts of the heart of her! God keep her clear of the old-world shams and social lies and mockery, and callous commercialism, and sordid shame! And heaven send that, if ever in my time her sons are called upon to fight for her young life and honour, I die with the first rank of them, and be buried in Australian ground.

But this will probably be called false, forced or 'maudlin sentiment' here in England, where the mawkish sentiment of the music-halls, and the popular applause it receives, is enough to make a healthy man sick, and is only equalled by music-hall vulgarity. So I'll get on.

In the old digging days the knapsack, or straps-across-the chest fashion, was tried, but the load pressed on a man's chest and impeded his breathing, and a man needs to have his bellows free on long tracks in hot, stirless weather. Then the 'horse-collar,' or rolled military overcoat style – swag over one shoulder and under the other arm – was tried, but it was found to be too hot for the Australian climate, and was discarded along with Wellington boots and leggings. Until recently, Australian city artists and editors – who knew as much about the bush as Downing Street knows about the British colonies in general – seemed to think the horse-collar swag was still in existence; and some artists gave the swagman a stick, as if he were a tramp of civilization with an eye on the backyard and a fear of the dog. English artists, by the way, seem firmly convinced that the Australian bushman is born in Wellington boots with a polish on 'em you could shave yourself by.

The swag is usually composed of a tent 'fly' or strip of calico (a cover for the swag and a shelter in bad weather – in New Zealand it is oilcloth or waterproof twill), a couple of blankets, blue by custom and preference, as that colour shows the dirt less than any other (hence the name 'bluey' for swag), and the core is composed of spare clothing and small personal effects. To make or 'roll up' your swag: lay the fly or strip of calico on the ground, blueys on top of it; across one end, with eighteen inches or so to spare, lay your spare trousers and shirt, folded, light boots tied together by the laces toe to heel, books, bundle of old letters, portraits, or whatever little knick-knacks you have or care to carry, bag of needles, thread, pen and ink, spare patches for your pants, and bootlaces. Lay or arrange the pile so that it will roll evenly with the swag (some pack the lot in an old pillowslip or canvas bag), take a fold over of blanket and calico the whole length on each side, so as to reduce the width of the swag to, say, three feet, throw the spare end, with an inward fold, over the little pile of belongings, and then roll the whole to the other end, using your knees and judgment to make the swag tight, compact and artistic; when within eighteen inches of the loose end take an inward fold in that, and bring it up against the body of the swag. There is a strong suggestion of a roley-poley in a rag about the business, only the ends of the swag are folded in, in rings, and not tied. Fasten the swag with three or four straps, according to judgment and the supply of straps. To the top strap, for the swag is carried (and eased down in shanty bars and against walls or veranda-posts when not on the track) in a more or less vertical position – to the top strap, and lowest, or lowest but one, fasten the ends of the shoulder strap (usually a towel is preferred as being softer to the shoulder), your coat being carried outside the swag at the back, under the straps. To the top strap fasten the string of the nose-bag, a calico bag about the size of a pillowslip, containing the tea, sugar and flour bags, bread, meat, baking-powder and salt, and brought, when the swag is carried from the left shoulder, over the right on to the chest, and so balancing the swag behind. But a swagman can throw a heavy swag in a nearly vertical position against his spine, slung from one shoulder only and without any balance, and carry it as easily as you might wear your overcoat. Some bushmen arrange their belongings so neatly and conveniently, with swag straps in a sort of harness, that they can roll up the swag in about a minute, and unbuckle it and throw it out as easily as a roll of wall-paper, and there's the bed ready on the ground with the wardrobe for a pillow. The swag is always used for a seat on the track; it is a soft seat, so trousers last a long time. And, the dust being mostly soft and silky on the long tracks out back, boots last marvellously. Fifteen miles a day is the average with the swag, but you must travel according to the water: if the next bore or tank is five miles on, and the next twenty beyond, you camp at the five-mile water to-night and do the twenty next day. But if it's thirty miles you have to do it. Travelling with the swag in Australia is variously and picturesquely described as 'humping bluey,' 'walking Matilda,' 'humping Matilda,' 'humping your drum,' 'being on the wallaby,' 'jabbing trotters,' and 'tea and sugar burglaring,' but most travelling shearers now call themselves trav'lers, and say simply 'on the track,' or 'carrying swag.'

And there you have the Australian swag. Men from all the world have carried it – lords and low-class Chinamen, saints and world martyrs, and felons, thieves, and murderers, educated gentlemen and boors who couldn't sign their mark, gentlemen who fought for Poland and convicts who fought the world, women, and more than one woman disguised as a man. The Australian swag has held in its core letters and papers in all languages, the honour of great houses, and more than one national secret, papers that would send well-known and highly-respected men to jail, and proofs of the innocence of men going mad in prisons, life tragedies and comedies, fortunes and papers that secured titles and fortunes, and the last pence of lost fortunes, life secrets, portraits of mothers and dead loves, pictures of fair women, heart-breaking old letters written long ago by vanished hands, and the pencilled manuscript of more than one book which will be famous yet.

The weight of the swag varies from the light rouseabout's swag, containing one blanket and a clean shirt, to the 'royal Alfred,' with tent and all complete, and weighing part of a ton. Some old sun-downers have a mania for gathering, from selectors' and shearers' huts, and dust-heaps, heartbreaking loads of rubbish which can never be of any possible use to them or anyone else. Here is an inventory of the contents of the swag of an old tramp who was found dead on the track, lying on his face on the sand, with his swag on top of him, and his arms stretched straight out as if he were embracing the mother earth, or had made, with his last movement, the sign of the cross to the blazing heavens:

Rotten old tent in rags. Filthy blue blanket, patched with squares of red and calico. Half of 'white blanket' nearly black now, patched with pieces of various material and sewn to half of red blanket. Three-bushel sack slit open. Pieces of sacking. Part of a woman's skirt. Two rotten old pairs of moleskin trousers. One leg of a pair of trousers. Back of a shirt. Half a waistcoat. Two tweed coats, green, old and rotting, and patched with calico. Blanket, etc. Large bundle of assorted rags for patches, all rotten. Leaky billy-can, containing fishing-line, papers, suet, needles and cotton, etc. Jam-tin, medicine bottles, corks on strings, to hang to his hat to keep the flies off (a sign of madness in the bush, for the corks would madden a sane man sooner than the flies could). Three boots of different sizes, all belonging to the right foot, and a left slipper. Coffee-pot, without handle or spout, and quart-pot full of rubbish – broken knives and forks, with the handles burnt off, spoons, etc., picked up on rubbish-heaps; and many rusty nails, to be used as buttons, I suppose.

Broken saw blade, hammer, broken crockery, old pannikins, small rusty frying-pan without a handle, children's old shoes, many bits of old bootleather and greenhide, part of yellow-back novel, mutilated English dictionary, grammar and arithmetic book, a ready reckoner, a cookery book, a bulgy anglo-foreign dictionary, part of a Shakespeare, book in French and book in German, and a book on etiquette and courtship. A heavy pair of blucher boots, with uppers parched and cracked, and soles so patched (patch over patch) with leather, boot protectors, hoop-iron and hobnails that they were about two inches thick, and the boots weighed over five pounds. (If you don't believe me go into the Melbourne Museum, where, in a glass case in a place of honour, you will see a similar, perhaps the same, pair of bluchers labelled 'An example of colonial industry.') And in the core of the swag was a sugar-bag tied tightly with a whip-lash, and containing another old skirt, rolled very tight and fastened with many turns of a length of clothes-line, which last, I suppose, he carried to hang himself with if he felt that way. The skirt was rolled round a small packet of old portraits and almost indecipherable letters – one from a woman who had evidently been a sensible woman and a widow, and who stated in the letter that she did not intend to get married again as she had enough to do already, slavin' her finger-nails off to keep a family, without having a second husband to keep. And her answer was 'final for good and all,' and it wasn't no use comin' 'bungfoodlin'' round her again. If he did she'd set Satan on to him. 'Satan' was a dog, I suppose.

The letter was addressed to 'Dear Bill,' as were others. There were no envelopes. The letters were addressed from no place in particular, so there weren't any means of identifying the dead man. The police buried him under a gum, and a young trooper cut on the tree the words:

SACRED TO THE MEMORY OF
BILL
WHO DIED.

Land of the Delicate Scrub

C.E.W. Bean

The superficial view of the Australian bush as a monotony of gum trees was given the lie by C.E.W. Bean in his book On the Wool Track *(1910) as he looked at the country of western New South Wales, where he saw a bewildering variety of trees and exquisite, wonderful plant life.*

When European writers, and some Australians too, speak of the monotony of the Australian scrub – gum-trees, and gum-trees, and gum-trees still beyond that – they doubtless describe conscientiously what they have seen, which is usually a strip of Australia along the coast. But few of them have any right to speak of Australia as a whole; for the greater part of Australia is the part that most of them have not seen, and the chief mark of the scrub which grows in that part is the bewildering variety of trees . . .

The truth is that there exists inside coastal Australia a second Australia – the larger of the two – of which most of our people know very little more than do the Londoners.

It is the land of those astonishing grasses which spring up, then vanish for twenty years, and then flush up again to the delight of the oldest inhabitant, who is the only man that can spin a yarn about them. It is the land of the delicate scrub, which is as puzzling as the grass and, mostly, as useful; of the mulga the best of all for stock, and one of the prettiest, with its exquisite black tracework of branches against its 'Liberty' grey leaves; of the apple-bush or rosewood or blush-bush, which, when half-dry, is fairly good for stock; of the emu-bush, which droops like the bunch of an emu's tail and is very good fodder; of the gidgea, which is good for fencing, and which drops beans that are good for sheep, and smells so pestilential after rain that they say at Nyngan they can tell you when it is raining at Bourke, because the nearest gidgea is there; of the leopardwood, which is good feed and bad timber, and crops up again as often as it is cut; of the myall, which is good sheep-food; of the whitewood, which is fairly good; and the belar, which is very little good; and the wild fuchsia, whose flowers, full of honey, the sheep at any rate think to be good; and the budda, which is good for nothing except to keep the surface on the ground – to stop the wind from blowing the skin of Australia away and leaving her cheekbones all shiny red and bare and useless.

In certain parts, where men had come out on to that country and cut down the scrub recklessly, the surface of the earth had blown clean away. In some places, where all that exquisite, wonderful plant-life had been gradually developing through all the ages, it took just one bad season to destroy it; and, instead, we found there great patches of 'scalded' clay, as bare as on the day when the last wavelet of some receding ocean lapped over them and left them to evolve a covering for their nakedness.

Scorpions by the Thousand

W.W. Ammon

Hopelessly bogged at Barrabiddy Creek in the north of Western Australia, W.W. Ammon found he had thousands of scorpions for company, along with the usual centipedes, lizards, snakes and mosquitos. He trekked to the nearest homestead through a 'moving mass of vermin'. Later he joined a desperate search through wild country and pitiless heat at Winning Pool Station for a fencer who had been missing from camp for twenty-four hours.

Kangaroos and emus in droves feasted on the rich pastures, while waterfowl of every description foraged the lakes in thousands. Wild turkeys, still free of the scourge of the fox, which did not arrive until many years later, inhabited Minilya in abundance. Of all the stations I ever saw in the north, Minilya would be my choice. But while this beautiful flood country represented almost everything to be desired from a pastoral point of view, to the truck-driver it was the exact opposite. His greatest worry was bog, especially wet bog. And mosquitoes. The Minilya flats were their home; they seemed to be there almost the whole year round and when really bad they even attacked you as you drove along in the truck. Get bogged or break down there and they ate you alive. I shall always remember an Afghan who capsized his wagon-load of wool on those flats. The mosquitoes were so thick at the time that you couldn't walk through them, and in an attempt to work he had lit a circle of cow-dung fires right round his wagon. The smoke suffocated everything but the mosquitoes.

Besides the mosquitoes, the whole area was infested with centipedes, scorpions, lizards, and its quota of snakes. This was normal enough, as these things are found right through the north, but with Minilya there was a difference. When the floodwaters spread, the vermin are forced from their holes. To save themselves from drowning they clasp any piece of floating debris until it becomes loaded to the Plimsoll and rolls continually with the action of those on the underside fighting their way up for air. Let one of these miniature rafts momentarily touch the wheel or running-board of a bogged truck and the scorpions and centipedes evacuate it in a second for the more substantial safety of the truck.

Hopelessly bogged one day at the Barrabiddy, I was sitting in my truck watching the floodwaters swirl by. The rain was pouring down in sheets, but there was nothing I could do about it. It might take days for the flood to pass, and though there was no way of boiling the billy or making a hot meal, I had tinned food in the tucker-box and there was certainly plenty of water, even if it was thick with mud. All of a sudden the first of my visitors arrived – a seven-inch centipede. It raced across the floor of the cab and I squashed it with a boot. Right on its heels came a second one, and I repeated the performance. Then I sat up and started to take notice. Normally the wheels of a truck are the greatest deterrent to all types of crawly things, and I sensed there was something wrong. Seldom can even an ant chasing sugar find its way round dry wheels, along the springs and shackles to the truck floor. There had to be a reason why those centipedes were getting on. Glancing over the side, I saw what was happening. The water had risen over the running-boards and every piece of floating wood that momentarily touched the truck's side was disgorging its struggling, bedraggled load. The running-board was crawling with centipedes and scorpions, and the two I had killed were the only ones unlucky enough to come my way. Others were fast scattering all over the load.

This put an entirely different complexion on my camping on the truck. Soon it would be a moving mass of vermin. And although an occasional scorpion or centipede did not worry the average truck-driver, it would only be asking for trouble to camp on the load with this lot. There was only one thing to do – carry my swag through the flood to Minilya homestead. The distance was four miles and the average depth of water two feet, with an occasional deeper channel. But the bushes that waved and shuddered from the water's force were the unforgettable highlights of that wade. Every bush had suddenly 'blossomed' and borne fruit: fantastic blossoms and fruit of a dozen different colours, red, green, yellow, black, white, and grey, of all sizes and shapes, that wriggled and squirmed amongst the leaves – centipedes, scorpions, snakes, lizards, beetles of a hundred varieties, along with grasshoppers, cockroaches, and countless other creatures, right down to the common old wood-bug, which all clung and fought for dear life to maintain their place of safety. The number and variety would have to be seen to be believed. A big country is the north, and it goes in for things, good and bad, in a big way.

The bungarra, which is to be found throughout most of our arid area, is a common enough sight along the mail-routes and can grow to an astounding size. The largest one I ever saw, the real daddy of the lot, was south of Carnarvon near the hundred-and-twelve-mile catchment shed. Compared to it, the eight-foot whiptails along the coast of Quobba and Gnarloo are mere lizards. Another driver, Tom Allen, and I were returning to Carnarvon after a wheat season at Three Springs when Tom espied it lying beside the road. 'Just have a look at that thing, will you!' he exclaimed. I had a look and its size, even to me who had seen hundreds of them, was incredible. To anyone but a hardened bushman it would have been a frightening sight. At least ten feet long, it had a body as thick as mine, and I weighed twelve stone. Its great bowed legs, as thick as my arms, supported the scaly body a clear foot from the ground, and its little beady eyes watched us balefully as its tongue flicked in and out, registering its dislike of us. When it finally ran away it made as much clatter as a draught-horse. How I wished we had a gun so we could have bagged it for a trophy or to substantiate our story! But it was amongst the big ones that got away, and later when either Tom or I told the story we were generally asked what brand we were drinking at the time, which in my opinion was excusable.

There is a sequel to the story, which goes to prove that a little knowledge doesn't make you an expert – and I was to meet a real expert. There was a shearers' strike on some years later and many of the stations had policemen guarding their sheds and scratch teams. I arrived at Mia Mia shed one night where a policeman, new from the city, had little else to do but gather himself some trophies. I had taken him out on the mail and he always came over for a chat when I put in an appearance. This night he seemed particularly pleased with himself and said, 'You ought to see the big bungarra skin I've got.'

'Let's have a look at it, then.'

He had been so excited that I expected to see something really special; but he brought over a pegged-out skin no more than twelve inches across. 'Oh, hell!' I exclaimed. 'That's only a baby.'

My criticism annoyed the policeman and he said sarcastically, 'Oh, I suppose you've seen bigger?'

'Now wait a minute,' I soothed him. 'As a matter of fact, there are plenty around here twice the size of the one you've got, and I saw one once that could swallow it whole.' I then proceeded to give a description of the gigantic one Tom Allen and I had seen, but I made no mention of where we had seen it. In fact, its habitat was two hundred and fifty miles south of Mia Mia.

An old native stockman, who had been listening quietly by the fire, asked, 'Where you see that fella, Snow?'

'Oh, a long way from here, Bonza.'

'I know where you see him, Snow. Down longa the hundred-and-twelve-mile catchment shed.'

I was astounded. 'Yes, that's right Bonza. How did you know?'

The old fellow chuckled. 'Me know, Snow. Me Shark Bay boy. Plenty big fella down that way – can't carry him. Him not bungarra, Snow, him jillawarra.'

'Jillawarra? What's the difference?'

But the old fellow didn't seem to be able to explain that. He shook his grizzled head in perplexity and repeated, 'Just jillawarra.' So there it was. What the difference is between a bungarra and a jillawarra I never did learn. All I know is that the jillawarra has the appearance and characteristics of a gigantic bungarra and that it is not simply some horrible illusion that crawled from a bottle of grog.

Adjoining both Minilya and Mia Mia on the up-river side is Wandagee, which was originally founded by Gooch and Wheelock some twenty odd years before the turn of the century and is now being carried on by Gordon, the son of old George Gooch. Gordon was crippled as a baby and consequently has never walked without crutches. About this station the book *Lure of the North* has been compiled. I use the word 'compiled' purposely, for to me the book was a disappointment. Being on my mail-run, Wandagee was well known to me, and I perused the book eagerly, but found little more than a compilation of dates and a sketchy outline of business transactions.

Breakdown

Jonathan Green

Travelling around Australia with his family, Jonathan Green experienced a breakdown and stranding at Borroloola in the Gulf Country of the Northern Territory, and then a mechanic of 'imperturbable langour' and a week-long wait for one wheel bearing.

The omnipresent possibility of mechanical failure hangs over the outback traveler like a slowly circling crow; a crow dripping oil but flying on despite some annoyingly persistent clanks and rattles. Some contingencies you prepare for, a flat tyre flapping raggedly round its rim? No problem, we have spares for our spares: one on the back, one on the roof, one under the trailer. A resource that lay untouched until we had all but left the Kimberley, having already negotiated 9000 kilometres, including the rock-strewn length of the Gibb River Road, a piece of track with a reputation for its best practice supply of sharp rocky shards that can shred rubber as soon as look at it. On sections of the road the packed gravel wears thin over long razor ribbons of bedrock, deadly at any speed. In other places, the flints pile in a loose scree that gnaws at the sidewalls, a combination that makes for slow going, white knuckles and bruised rubber. Edging into the north east Kimberley and the five star dude ranch sanctuary of El Questro station, we were almost counting our punctureless blessings when the air fled one of the rear wheels just to the north of Mount Barnett (another station, two star if any, expensive diesel a specialty). Which was no great bother. The next blowout came just south of land locked Cape Crawford on the long straight to Boroloola and the eastern fringe of the Gulf of Carpentaria. It was the trailer this time, its poor wheel caught on the lip of the single lane of gravel-flanked bitumen when we yielded to an oncoming road train. Which seemed like the only sensible course. The road here is a model of resource efficient construction, with the local authorities providing just one thin, sealed lane and enough gravel shoulder either side to accommodate passing manoeuvres. Which only leaves the question of who should yield in the occasional head-on charges between opposing vehicles determined to claim the same slim strip of bitumen. Which is no question at all when one of the vehicles involved is four linked trailers of hurtling death-row beef. A road train writes its own highway code, rules one through ten of which are: get out of the way. And we did, plunging into a vortex of dust and gnawing gravel. Not that busting a trailer tyre was significant of itself. As it turned out that was only the first step in a series of mechanical stumbles. We nutted on the spare and drove on to Boroloola, where, even on a Sunday, the mechanic was at work in the long three-sided workshop set among tall gums in the oil-damped, red-dirt yard to the rear of the mini-mart, busily occupied, as it happened, in changing the odd tyre. These were the first minutes of what turned out to be a week-long occupation, a frustrating vigil that with every lost day threatened the entire premise of the project.

We pulled in, parking in a dusty scatter of semi-complete vehicles. Many of which appeared to be waiting on wheels. Two local men sat on the ruptured front half of a jacked-up bisected grader, nursing a wheel with a flaccid tyre. We rolled in our own ragged little wreath, said our g'days and waited, while the mechanic burst the bead on another tyre in a far corner of the workshop. A corner stacked with new and burst tyres. A theme was developing.

The mechanic emerged in his own good time, and eyeing his new customers, ignored the two black men on the grader and took a look at our wheel. Which spoke for itself. There were tyres to fit in the shipping container across the yard, enough to shoe both sides of the trailer. Work that was soon enough in progress; pretty much a full afternoon's labour as other customers and lunch came and went, and the mechanic worked with the accustomed unperturbable languor of a man who knows the approximate flying time to the next wheel changer. 'I reckon this bearing's no good.' He gave the wheel another muscular tug, a top and bottom wiggle, that seemed to produce a slight looseness, a sly, inner rattle from the bearing that eased the coupling with the axle. Bearing?

'I'd change it.'

Which was easy enough said.

'Couldn't get one before tomorrow.'

This turned out to be an opening bid, but we weren't to know.

'Although I could try this other bloke.'

Which turned out to be an inquiry that involved our man's immediate departure for the far end of town. We waited.

'Nup. Didn't have one.'

No. Of course not. The prospect of setting out across the gulf and up into Cape York with a trailer bearing teetering on the brink of total emotional and physical breakdown seemed, to our admittedly mechanically naïve ears, to be borderline imprudent. We were stuck with what ever remedy we could arrange from Boroloola.

This turned out to be an elaborate logistic choreography that combined aircraft, trucks, phantom mail services and parts warehouse staff in Katherine and Adelaide with the combined IQs of gnats and that sense of urgent energy more commonly associated with week-old wombat road kill.

In the end the guy in Katherine who rang the order to Adelaide, to place the part on the flight to Darwin where it would catch the Katherine truck to meet the weekly Boroloola mining-mail plane, never actually placed the order, even though the guy in Adelaide said, mysteriously, that he had, not that he had managed to place the part on the plane. Which hardly mattered in the end because the mail flights hadn't been running all year. None of which emerged with any great pace.

'We could put it on the bus. Probably take a week.'

In remote Australia there are moments when one's immediate fate is cast into the hands of men and women who, in routine southern city life, one would only encounter as broad character parodies in TV sketch comedy. The woods, as it happens, are full of them. We had already been waiting a day or three in a trailer trash fishing camp peopled by the combined casts of *Kath and Kim*, *My Name's McGooly*, *Kingswood Country*, the *Comedy Company* and *Carry On Camping*, a huddle of caravans and trailers rusted to a halt in dusty car torn scrub about 30 kilometres from town on the crocodile punctuated banks of King Ash Bay. Locals had suggested it as an alternative to the Boroloola van park, back on our first afternoon at the garage.

'Nah, I wouldn't stay in town.'

Town was of course an aboriginally administered settlement, and it seemed that white folk, if they were not proprietors of one of Boroloola's half a dozen businesses and thus emboldened to live on-campus, drifted to the outskirts. Some went as far as the fishing camp, which after all had a clubhouse – composed principally of abutted shipping containers and dongas – a Tuesday curry night, open air darts, boats, beer and the ever-present promise of barramundi. For us it was a place of building anxiety and boredom, a backwater that looked capable of trapping us indefinitely, or forcing the unwelcome possibility of pushing on into the most remote country of our journey on a dicky axle. 'We could put it on the bus' was not therefore, the response we were looking for when we tooled into Boroloola on the appointed day, packed and eager to be on our way, hoping for a fresh bearing in the promised post. 'Probably take a week' was enough to push fainter hearted members of the party to the point of despairing tears.

Polite aquiesance had only taken us so far. Not very far at all in fact. It was time to take charge. After half an hour on the phone it emerged that there was a single bearing of the required type in Katherine, and that Katherine, being the very model of urban convenience, had an airport and several charter operators. Flying time was just over an hour. The emerging proposition was costly but irresistible.

We left the car behind the mini-mart for an oil change and service, booked the charter to arrive at dawn the next morning and did what anyone in their right mind faced with 24 unwanted hours in Boroloola might do, and adjourned to the pub. Which is where we stayed the night, in a one-star donga, that star being earned through the effective connection of mains power.

Sunrise couldn't come soon enough, but wouldn't before its scheduled cue of 6.20 am, at which moment a single engined Cessna blurted out of the red streaked sky, slewed to a halt in the corner of the town airstrip that ran just to the rear of the mini-mart, delivered a small package, and roared away back into the quickly lightening and suddenly bright blue yonder.

A new day, and we had our bearing.

The Waaia Races

Patsy Adam-Smith

*The Waaia country races in northern Victoria were held in Ernie
Brenzing's paddock, two miles out of town, and the young Patsy
Adam-Smith was there to take in all the fun.*

The bookmakers shouted the odds, the horses were lined up at the
barrier, the starters looked to their timepieces, and Waaia races were
off to a flying start.

The racecourse was Ernie Brenzing's paddock two miles out of
town. For days beforehand women had been cooking. Our wood-
fuel copper had bubbled all one day with Christmas puddings and
all the next with hams. The kitchen table was a litter of flour, icing
sugar, eggs, cream, sandwich fillings, sweets to be sold in baskets, and
vegetable salads. There was so much of everything that it spilled over
to the table on the back verandah and the table in the lounge. The
suite in the lounge – we called it the 'front room' in those days – was
out of sight beneath boxes of sponges, brandy snaps, cream puffs and
pastry boats. Mick and I poked our fingers into everything when we
could get away from the everlasting washing-up. We were still on
holidays after Christmas. It was mid-summer and the heat was terrific. The wood stove kept the temperature in the kitchen well above
the century. At midday we took the dishes out to the tank-stand and
went on washing up there away from the enclosed heat, but Mum

must bear with it till the end of the day. She was cooking for the luncheon booth.

Dad had taken the afternoon off from work to help erect the judge's box (a hessian shade over his head) and mend the railings round the course and put up the tents and marquees for the serving of meals, and for the 'refreshment booth' as well as the hessian-encircled lavatories which he called the 'Houses of Parliament'.

That night we children were ordered to bathe in the tin bath out in the wash-house, a thing we normally did only on Saturdays, and told to say our prayers quickly and get into bed. For Mum to tell us to say prayers 'quickly' meant that she was very busy indeed. We were scarcely in bed when she hauled us out again. I was to try on a new dress she was making for me, Mick was to put her 'good' dress on to see if it fitted. Mine satisfied Mum, a few tucks here and there and it would be finished. Then she turned to Mick.

'Oh no! Oh dear God! Kathleen! Pull it down! You couldn't have grown that much!' Mum tugged at the dress. 'When did you have it on last?'

Dad came to the door to see what the hullabaloo was about. Then he saw Mick. He laughed. 'Whacko!' said Dad. 'Roll 'em, girls, roll 'em, and show the boys your knees.'

'Albert!' Mum exclaimed, shocked.

'There's nothing wrong with that song,' Dad said. 'Everyone was singing it when we first met and all the girls were rolling their stockings down and showing as much leg as Mickie . . .'

'That was different.' Mum had the last word. Dad took one final look at Mick's long, coltish legs sticking down from this high-waisted, three-inches-above-the-knee dress and began to laugh again and retreated.

Mum was to be at the course by 10 a.m. to organise an early meal for arrivals who brought horses from places as far away as Seymour.

Before that she had to fill the cakes with cream in the cool of the morning and send them away packed in boxes on the tray of the hotel truck that was picking up the foodstuffs from all the womenfolk of the town. Then she must leave everything in readiness for the guard on the 'Beetle' who had offered to 'do' the train for her and the guard on the goods train who had promised likewise. But before she left our hats and dresses were spread on the bed ready for us; mine, pink cotton with white pique collar and cuffs and my old white hat done up with a new ribbon band. Mick's dress had been let down, let out and titivated till it looked like new to match her new hat.

As soon as Mum and Dad left for the course we got into this finery and went over to the Marvels' place. All morning Mick rode one of the trotters round the paddock and when it was time to leave for the races her dress was wrinkled, concertinaed and dirty.

'What's wrong with it?' she complained when I said it looked awful. Mick's adolescence was passing without the faintest discomfort to her. She was too preoccupied with the fun of living to have time to spare for it. That morning her long legs had hung down eighteen inches past those of her friends the Martin twins, as the three of them rode on the one horse round Marvels' paddock, but she felt no embarrassment. Her new straw hat was nice but she had twirled it round on the end of her forefinger stuck up in the crown and now it had spiralled up to a peak like a witch's hat. She had a small head and couldn't keep the hat on, so put the elastic band under her chin instead of behind her hair.

As for me, the Marvels had helped me achieve – with a new toilette – an elegance of appearance that made me long to know the meaning of the words *dernier cri*, which I'd seen in a book under an illustration that I thought I now resembled. The fullness of the skirt was pulled to the back leaving the front flat and tight. The back was bunched into a sort of bustle and the whole thing cinched in with the belt till I could scarcely breathe. The white panama hat that pulled right down on my head with a brim sticking out for three inches was now unrecognisable. A dent in the crown of the type slashed into men's hats lifted the whole creation up high on my head. The brim was turned up at the back and pulled down in the front over one eye. The pink ribbon was dispensed with entirely. I should have liked to dispense too with the long cotton stockings, but that would have taken more courage than I possessed. Stockings and legs were matters of modesty.

On the way to the races, cars and jinkers passed us on the dirt road. Dust hung like a ribbon along where we walked. We could have moved over closer to the fence and avoided it, but we just didn't want to miss anything. There were horses in boxes behind some of the cars, jockeys rode other horses at a high-legged canter, people we had never seen before went by. A kid in a passing car threw an apple core and it hit Mick and she picked it up with a handful of dust to throw it back, but the hot air of the passing cars tossed the dust back over us. We were hot and perspiration ran in gutters down our dusty cheeks. Mick's perspiration-wet hair hung like rats'-tails, mine looked like a deflated black umbrella.

I knew better than to go near Mum in my 'improved' outfit. I waited at the side of the luncheon booth while Mick went in for orders. I could hear Mum speaking. She said we were not to go near the bookmakers, we were not to speak to strange men, we were not to go to any cars with strange men or women, and to remember that there were men drinking here and *you know what that means*, and do not sit on the seat until you have put paper on it, and here is a shilling each and run along and enjoy yourselves because I'm busy. In the gloom and bustle of the tent she hardly noticed Mick, who came out and repeated the speech to me as, 'Here's a shilling.'

This shilling didn't go far, even in those days. We bought a saveloy and a roll (the roll was the great attraction – I hadn't seen one before).

Then we bought two navel oranges and a bag of lollies and a bottle of raspberry soda which looked like pink froth when you shook it and made you sick when you drank it. Then we heard a loud wail from the whistle of the goods train away off on the track – cock-a-doodle-doo it went as it rolled down the line, partly in good wishes for the celebration and partly a warning that the ice-cream packed in dry ice had been left at the station. Soon it would be brought here to the races and we had no money. This dilemma was solved in (of all places) the lavatory. The 'Ladies' was a can with a wooden seat in the centre of an arena encircled by a six-foot hessian wall. There was a board outside with LADIES written on it.

We were about to leave the convenience when a lady (we'd never seen her before, as we repeated to each other later) entered. We stepped politely aside for her, but she came to us and gave us threepence to stay outside the entrance and make sure no one came in. We couldn't see the necessity for this.

'I think she wants to change her dress or something,' Mick said, but she didn't stay long and she didn't change her dress.

'Thank you,' she said when she left. 'You are good girls.' Mick charged off with the threepence and bought a Dixie, which we shared. We had just finished this when a second lady approached and said the first lady had told her about us and would we stand guard for her too. Again we collected threepence and again we bought a Dixie. Yet another lady came to us. Oh, we were on to a good thing all right!

But this was the end of our windfall. Through no fault of ours this lady's privacy was not complete: a horse skittered away from the starting line and pranced sideways like a crab with the jockey on its back and turned to bolt only a few feet from us. It propped with the jockey hanging on high in the air above the hessian wall of the lavatory. The woman screamed and raced off pulling her skirt down and completely forgetting that she was in our debt.

Some of the jockeys, we thought, looked like men we knew, but surely they couldn't be, not in those magnificent, flamboyant silks. The start was the best part of the race to watch. They were all there together, the glistening, shining horses, the men glittering, dazzling in their scintillating colours. The bookmakers were yelling incomprehensible jargon and the crowd were yelling to jockeys they knew. Then they were off and that was the last we saw of them for a while as trees and a dip in the ground hid them from view. Interest flagged for a time and many now sauntered off for a drink to wash the dust down.

We saw Dad among the crowd under the bookmakers' umbrellas. He had put two shillings on a horse and he told us its name so we could watch it win.

'These are my daughters,' he told the Melbourne bookmaker.

'Half your luck, mate,' the bookmaker said. Dad told us he would buy us another sav and a roll when his horse won. It didn't, and we knew he didn't have another two shillings so we deserted him.

At what we considered to be afternoon teatime by the state of our stomachs we went across to Mum. She was just coming out of the tent with the other women for a breather. In the blinding sunlight she saw us and stopped, staring.

'Dear God help me,' she sighed aloud as she took in our ensembles.

That night the race ball was held in the Waaia hall. This hall was quite familiar to us kids. The school concerts were held there and we'd played the piano and sung and danced there many a time. While the men got the fire going in the open fireplace in the little supper room out at the back and filled the kerosene tins ready for tea and coffee, the big boys scraped slivers from candles and we slid up and down the floor on a stone-filled box bound with an old blanket to make the boards slippery.

Mum had put the flat irons on the stove when we got home from the races and sponged and pressed Mick's dress back to respectability and brushed her hair till it shone like copper. My belt was let out ('Phew!' Dad expelled air as it was levered off), my curls were re-done, stockings washed and dried in the oven. Mum wore a pink ankle-length voile frock, Dad his navy blue suit. We had had six visitors for tea; two were fettlers but the other four were strangers – Mum had heard them say they were staying for the ball so she had asked them home. Their two big cars stood opulently outside our home. I hoped everyone would see them. We didn't ever own a car.

Because it was a pleasant, clear night we all walked to the hall half a mile away. In the cool air the mingling smell of the berries and flowers of the male and female pepper-corn trees was fresh and cleansing after the dust of the day. Curlews cried and keened on the edges of the wheat paddocks. The lantern hanging from the verandah of the Waaia Hotel flickered brightly through the newly cleaned glass. Mrs Beswick, the proprietor of the hotel, whom we called Mrs B, was to come with us. Mum considered it was somehow respectable here to have a publican for a friend, whereas she considered that it wasn't elsewhere. Out came Mrs B, her big bosom gleaming in the moonlight in a white satin dress. Some Sunday nights she would ask Mum and Dad to play euchre and we kids would watch that bosom. As the game began she would lift it onto the table with both hands and it would move slowly across a large area like molten lead and then, as if it had cooled down, would cease flowing and heave to a standstill. Each time Mrs B dealt the cards this mass would move. Our Mum was a neat little person, a tightly corseted contrast to this undisciplined bulk. Now, apart from the bosom, there was something else about Mrs B. She was smoking!

When I read now of the 'flaming twenties' I feel we must have missed them, because this was the only woman I saw smoke. The few I saw wearing lipstick at this time were definitely regarded as being 'bad' in our circle. But Mrs B was 'different' because she was a friend.

Everyone came to the Waaia Race Ball. Mrs Marvel came dressed in the outfit she milked in, the Morans from out Broken Creek way in their outdated finery they'd brought with them when they arrived from Ireland.

When the music struck up for the first dance most of the kids raced round grabbing each other and set off dancing together. The adults avoided them as best they could. Dad took Mum by the arm and began to waltz. Most of the women had partners. Alex Walker, who had ridden a winner today and who could whistle up any bird in the bush so well that he later became famous all over Australia for it, asked Mickie to dance. I thought she would be awful; she looked like a crane with her long, gangly legs. But no, she moved with amazing grace on the floor.

Everything was wonderful, the music, the movement, the dance. And then: 'May I have the pleasure of this dance?' I was being invited to dance! I was eight years old and short and round and didn't get on too well with other kids, but I was being asked to dance!

It was 'old' Bill Leaf, an elderly, small-scale squatter. I wanted to dance. Instead I said, 'I can't dance.' I'd heard about Mr Leaf's dancing. They said he could waltz better than anyone in the district.

'You never thought your sister could move like that till she took the floor, did you?' he said. 'You'll be able to move like that. Come on now.'

Then I was away – 1, 2, 3 – 1, 2, 3 – 1, 2, 3 – balancing on one foot then the other.

'Right now, round we go,' the old man said. 'Long, shortshort, long, shortshort', round and round we went. Once he began circling he didn't stop, round and round and round. He held me in the very old manner, my right arm doubled behind my back, my left hand on his upper arm. I was so secure I didn't falter and when the music stopped I clapped and clapped for it to start again. A sleeper-cutter was playing the gumleaf and a railway fencer had a concertina. They

31

both knew us Smiths and began to play again and off we went once more – 1, 2, 3 – 1, 2, 3 – 1, 2, 3.

'Long, shortshort, long, shortshort, hold your head up, never look at your feet, back straight, heels off the ground. You might have egg-shells pinned under your heels when you're in competitions.' Tight little circles round and round.

When it ended he told me I was good. 'You move as well as your sister.' I raced over to Mickie.

'Did you see me?'

'Old Bill Leaf's got grandchildren.'

'Alex Walker's got his teeth out.'

Kevin was sitting on the edge of the stage learning to play the gumleaf. I said to him, 'Did you see me?'

'Yes,' he said. 'Can you hear this?' He was playing 'I'll string along with you', and I could recognise it.

Later a sleeper-cutter took me up in a three-hop polka. 1, 2, 3 hop, 1, 2, 3 hop, round and round, arms gripping arms. Every now and then my partner would give a high call like a highland dancer, and we'd laugh and go at it harder still. Faster and faster grew the music. The concertina-player was sweating and he wiped his brow on his shirt-sleeve without missing a beat. The axeman playing the gumleaf would 'blow' one and reach in his pocket for another and fix it to his lips and blow the reed-like music again.

See me dance the polka,
Just see me twirling around,
See me dance the polka,
My feet scarce touch the ground,

sang my partner. 'That's the first song Nellie Melba sang in public. She was at a school concert.'

Dancing stopped while supper was handed around, the men carrying big trays with the tea and coffee and the women and children carrying cakes and sandwiches.

'A real blowout', was how Dad described the supper. There were sausage rolls and sandwiches, sponges four inches high filled with cream, sponge rolls, Napoleon cakes, custard slices, chocolate éclairs, meringues, sponge kisses, lamingtons, jelly cakes, and 'wheat stacks' (a name Kevin had given to the big three-deckers of chocolate, vanilla and raspberry-coloured cake joined with whipped cream and iced all over with chocolate icing dusted with coconut, which before serving were cut into manageable slices).

There had been two 'sets' before supper, square dances, four couples to each set. They'd had the Waltz of Cotillons and the Fitzroy Quadrilles. Now Mr Leaf, who was MC, called, 'Ladies and gentlemen. Take your partners for the Lancers!' All the young men shouted, 'Yahoo!' and dived for the liveliest girls. Five sets soon filled, then three couples looked for a fourth. Mr Leaf took my arms and called, 'I'll lead from the floor.' The concertina burst straight into 'Dixie' and we were off.

'Ladies and gentlemen, salute your partner!' We bowed, Mr Leaf to me, me to the old man.

'Oh, I wish I were in the land of cotton, where old friends are not forgotten,' sang the concertina-player.

'Salute the opposite corner, return to your partner and swing!' ordered Mr Leaf.

'Look away, look away, look away, Dixie land.'

'Swing your partner.' This was wonderful. There could be nothing better than this! Round and round we swung, kicking for momentum with one foot while the other pivoted round. Bill Leaf held me as he had when we waltzed with my arm doubled behind my back. All the others swung holding hands, their arms extended to full length. A girl in one of the other sets swung off the floor, her legs hung out behind her as her partner kept swinging her round and round by her hands.

'She's good,' I marvelled to Bill Leaf as we went steadily round and round.

'A good dancer never loses her feet,' he said, and went on round and round, his clenched fist pushed into the small of my back supporting me as I lent on my doubled-back arm. I knew then that we were swinging faster than anyone in the hall and that I could never 'lose my feet' while this old man held me.

Then, 'Ladies to the right, gentlemen to the left. Round you go. Circle twice and lead your partner back to position.'

The music changed. 'There's a track, winding back, to an old-fashioned shack, along the road to, Gundagai.'

'Waaia!' yelled the young men.

'First and third gentlemen promenade your partner.'

'. . . where the blue gums are growing, and the . . . Broken Creek is flowing,' the boys sang on, improvising to fit Waaia's geography into the song.

Dad had a barn-dance with me. He wasn't near so good a dancer as Mum, but what he lacked in skill he made up for with enthusiasm. Holding his partner's arm shoulder-high at right-angles to the body he swept round whacking people left and right with outstretched arms.

'I see you're doing a line with old Bill Leaf,' Dad said. 'You couldn't have got a better bloke to teach you.'

Too soon they called the last dance. It was 2 a.m. and many had long distances to travel home.

A Transcontinental Ramble

G.E. 'Chinese' Morrison

The young G.E. 'Chinese' Morrison, a great walker and later a powerful political figure, wrote for The Age *on his epic 3100 kilometre journey from Darwin to Melbourne, in the steps of the tragic Burke and Wills, who died after they were left stranded at Cooper's Creek.*

It had long been a wish of mine to cross Australia. Lying in bed in Port Mackay with two crippled knees, I first resolved to do the journey on foot. When I heard on all sides of the long stages between stations and the impossibility of travelling without at least two horses, I decided to go alone, and when everyone croaked to me that the blacks would kill me, if the floods did not drown me, I swore I should go unarmed. Fever I had to fear as well as blacks; quinine would be required to combat the former; a telescope might forewarn me of the latter. My telescope was stolen from me in Cooktown: my quinine, by accident, was thrown away at Thursday Island. Of all things none was more likely to be useful than a compass, yet mine was utterly destroyed in New Guinea. What could I argue from these things but that fever would pass me unharming, blacks would never endanger my life nor would I ever be in a situation from which there was no escape but by the use of the compass. At Normanton, when I gave out my intention of strolling over to Melbourne, people professed to think me mad. The rainy season was impending, and many signs, especially the comet, pointed to its being earlier than usual. 'How reckless,' said one; 'so insane,' put in another; 'it's suicide,' added a third. The elderly landlady of the hotel grew eloquent as to the dangers which awaited me. She was no cur, she assured me, but she wouldn't be game to tackle such a walk. Fearing an attack of nervousness, I hurried out of Normanton to a hotel fifteen miles on the road to Cloncurry. Five teams were camped here. It rained with unpromising severity the better part of two days, and as the next house was seventy-five miles away I had just to wait patiently.

On Friday evening, 22 December, the sky was clear for the first time, and starting at once I was thirty miles on my way before it came on to rain again. The teams hesitated, and have been there ever since, I fancy. This long stage is much dreaded by the carriers. It lies through country lightly timbered with the gutta-percha tree, the stunted bastard box, and the cooliebar, a district said to swarm with blacks, and annually subject to inundation. When I was halfway through there came on a violent tempest of wind and rain. The track became a bog and the knapsack got so soddened with water that I groaned under its weight. It was not safe to rest. The accounts I had heard of the track when flooded made me tremble to sit down, so I wearily struggled on through water and mud up to my knees, forgetting the dangers of this dismal, gloomy country in the fatigue of walking. Suddenly the wind died away, the sun shone out through the clouds, the rain stopped, and in a little while I came to where no rain had fallen at all. It had been merely a local storm. The following morning I came to two huts and a stockyard, the cattle station of Veno Park. Two stages of twenty-five miles each through a country whose monotonous flatness is occasionally relieved by richly wooded sandhills, bring you, the first to a cattle station, the second to a public house. Spear Creek, which has been on your left hand, is now lost sight of. The Sanby is crossed, and you are on that immense plain which stretches to the Flinders River. Between the Cockatoo waterhole, three miles beyond the Sanby, and a low hill called Fort Brown, within three miles of the Flinders, there is a dead waterless flat, almost bare of trees, which is buried some feet under water during the rainy season – carriers tell me thirty feet, and I can well believe it, for the high gums on the banks of the Flinders have drift timber in their very topmost branches.

I had a mate when crossing this plain, an old man who sought my company out of nervousness. He was mounted on a poor wretched moke which had a fistula between its shoulders that was sickening to look at. Yet he was very proud of his horse and was quite disgusted because the only bid he could get for horse, saddle and bridle when he put him up for sale was ten shillings. Locomotion was so painful to the horse that hobbles would have been superfluous. His only fault in the eyes of his owner was that he was not a mare. When buying flour for my mate and myself I asked him how much should we require. 'Six pounds,' he replied. 'Surely,' said I, 'six pounds of flour will not be enough for you and me for three days' – we were eighty-one miles from the next house – but he begged of me to trust him for that. Borrowing the loan of the kitchen he baked a damper of the weight and hardness of a stone. We had no knife strong enough to cut it.

I constantly passed teams now till I got into Cloncurry. Water and grass were abundant, and with the thirty pounds a ton for the two hundred and fifty miles from the Norman to Cloncurry, they had made satisfactory profits. I went some miles off the road to see the first sheep station. The country seems ill adapted for the sheep, though horses and cattle thrive wonderfully; but here, over two hundred miles from the coast, the sheep does splendidly on the open downs with gidya ridges, which stretch away to the north-west of Cloncurry. Between the Norman and Cloncurry I saw neither kangaroos, emus nor wild dogs, though the latter abound. There were native turkeys in scores, and every pool of water swarmed with wildfowl. Kites were more plentiful than crows, and you never stopped for a meal but the trees near became grey with kites waiting for you to leave that they might swoop down upon the scraps.

The wretched blacks are shot without mercy. One night I was at a station, whose owner is said to have shot more blacks than any two men in Queensland, when the mailman came in and reported that he had seen a black prowling about the stockyard. Loading his rifle, Mr ———— at once sallied out after him, but came back in an hour quite disappointed that, though he could pick up the tracks by the stockyard, it was too dark to follow them. Alligators are said to swarm in Spear Creek, as the Norman river is called above Normanton; I hesitate to give the dimensions of the largest that has been seen . . .

From Cloncurry my route lay to Winton. A publican in town kindly drew me a diagram by which I was to find my way to a hut on the McKinlay River, 104 miles distant. That map I keep as a curiosity. A distance of nine miles was made to appear twice as long as one of twenty-two miles, a trifling inaccuracy which caused me unnecessary anxiety and torture. The first night I could not sleep from fear that I had taken a wrong turning. In the morning I started to go thirty-five miles without knowing whether there was water on the track, or even water where I was making to. My waterbag holds two quarts and a half, but the day was so hot – the thermometer registered 132 deg. in the shade of the hut I refer to – that by midday, although I had hardly wet my mouth, the water was all evaporated. Still I kept moving, but at half past four I just knocked up. It came upon me most suddenly. Without any warning I was seized with an irresistible desire to throw off all my clothes. I had no wish in the world but to lie down. I camped under a tree. The anxiety of mind, for it was but a chance if water was within thirteen miles of me, added to my thirst, and I suffered torments. All through the night I lay naked on my back, my tongue contracted to a point, my body hot and feverish, my brain reeling. Just as day dawned I staggered to my feet, but which way was I to turn, to the right or the left? In a brief intermission of my confusion I recollected that I had turned off to the tree to the right; but during the night I had got my head where my feet should have been, and I actually tried to pick up the track by walking away from it. But Providence watched over me, and set me on my way.

I was so dazed that the track became more blurred and indistinct every minute. A wide plain now stretched before me, and a belt of timber at its further end gave me hope. I reached the creek and threw down my knapsack, and followed up and down the sandy bed for a weary distance, but it was as dry as the Sahara. On again, and another plain, with another belt of timber was to cheer or disappoint me. The creek was drier looking and sandier than the first one. I was throwing myself down in despair, when my eyes lit on a beautiful pool of water under the shade of a weeping teatree. The reaction quite unnerved me. I rested and drank all day. The mailman came up in the evening and gave me information about the country ahead. The contrast struck me forcibly. There were richly grassed instead of arid plains; creeks no longer dry and sandy, but sparkling with water, and plantations of timber, healthy and vigorous, not a parched and stunted forest. The twin parallel channels of the Williams River meander through a country as beautiful as an English park. Then a vast plain extends to the horizon, where, dancing grotesquely in the sun, is the timber marking the course of the Fullarton River.

Two day's walk from here is the McKinlay River, which drains an immense area of rolling downs. I was tracing up this river, cutting from one point of timber to another, and wondering whether the hut was above or below me, when I saw a man on horseback driving cattle. I drew nearer and nearer to him, and long before I could see his face I recognised the wild war song which had so often inspired me in my voyage to the islands. This was a young Kanaka, a kindly nice lad, from Motualava, beguiled from his home – one of the most beautiful islands of Polynesia – to tend cattle, to do fencing, to mix with gins, amid all the sultry dreariness and cheerlessness of the most utterly wretched district of the Never Never. The manager of this cattle station was in Cloncurry, and the South Sea Islander was in sole charge. I was taken very unwell when with him, and for three days the Kanaka showed me the greatest kindness and attention.

Leaving now the McKinlay River and steering diagonally over to its first sandy billabong, I traced it up till I came to an out-station. In this stage of thirty miles I was two days without eating anything during which I suffered much from thirst. The next stage was twenty-five miles over the ranges in which the Diamantina takes its source. The heat was something fearful, there was an entire absence of animal life, a faintly marked track which turned and twisted to every point of the compass and continually ran out, and no water, though billabongs and sandy creeks were crossed by the hundred. The only excitement that sustained me in my weakness was the fear of blacks – the wild kalkadoons who are so greatly feared in the hills.

At the headwaters of the Diamantina a sheep station was being formed where the countless billabongs resolve themselves into one of the finest rivers in Australia, a river which shall perpetuate the name of Lady Bowen. The Diamantina from its source trends away to the north-east, and then bends round in the shape of a shepherd's crook. I was on it for 113 miles, having it for 56 miles on my left, then crossing it at Dagworth station, and having it on my right for 57 miles, till its junction with the Western at Elderslie, one of Sir Samuel Wilson's properties. Both here and at Dagworth there was immense activity . . . any unskilled man can earn thirty or thirty-five shillings a week; he will be well fed, as a vegetable garden is now an essential part of a large Queensland station. I was out of the country where men are content to exist on salt beef and damper. The money spent by the squatters hereabouts chiefly finds its way into the public houses of Winton, a rising township on the Pelican Waterholes, near the Western River, placed on a high flat, with not a tree near it. The telegraph line is being extended from here to Cloncurry. Vinden station, another magnificent sheep run, is fifteen miles out of Winton. Fifty miles further is Evesham station. Then there is a break in the open downs, and you pass through a lot of gidya scrub country, through Maneroo station to the Thomson River – at this early stage, a trickle of peculiar white water which I stepped across.

The day after crossing the Thomson I was overtaken by an old gentleman on horseback whose companionship I found so agreeable that we travelled on together for seventy-five miles. He was a toothless darkie, a native of the Gold Coast of Africa, a cook by profession, and one of the kindest, most considerate men it has been my lot to meet with. He would ride on ahead and open the gates that I might not break my stride. He would stint himself of water if the day were hot that I might have the more. And this is how we fell out. We had to go one day twenty-five miles carrying water. Though parched with thirst he would not take his share. Not to be outdone I also refused any water, and being annoyed I vowed that we must part. I am glad of an opportunity to record my sense of this darkie's kindness. John Smith was his name, and he was the first black man ever seen in Iceland, having been there when a boy on board a Dutch man-of-war which was taking Prince Henry of the Netherlands round the world.

The Thomson River we left some distance on our right, two stations being situated on creeks running into it. On the Bimerah Creek is Bimerah sheep station, which, like all Fairbairn's stations, is being rapidly improved on a princely scale. Twelve miles further there was a sudden change. The water in the Emu Creek was stinking; the fish were rotting in the mud, and the crows were in hundreds. Up to this creek grass had been in abundance. Not till I was overtaken by rain, 250 miles further on, did I again come to any. Now I had to pass through the downs and gidya scrub, which had been the characteristics of the country for the last six hundred miles, till in three days I walked into the township of Jundah. There is a store here, a saddler and public house, and there will be other houses shortly. I shall chiefly remember it because of the splendid dam of water in the Thomson and because of the interesting fact that every man in the township was more or less drunk. All were lost in drunken amazement at my prodigious walk.

I was now an experienced swagman. My swag was carried New Zealand, or knapsack, fashion. The tucker, spare shoes, socks and shirts, some reading matter and a hammock, the matches, baking powder and canvas basil was rolled up in a single blanket, and the whole then enveloped in a strip of oilcloth and borne on my back, being kept by straps passing over the shoulders. In this way only could I secure the untrammelled use of my arms. The swag was seldom less than twenty pounds; above this its weight varied according to the distance I had to carry tucker. I seldom travelled by night; the heat of the day never troubled me. Indeed, it is my favourite boast that I have yet to see the day that is too hot for me. My own dress was cabbage-tree hat, flannel shirt, and tweed trousers, afterwards replaced by moleskins, and a knife belt and sheath. Boots I wore two sizes too large, and as I always cut the stiffening out of the back before using them, I escaped that soreness of heel which has troubled me on my former walks.

Upon arriving at a station I went straight to the store, bought what rations I required, and camped by the most convenient water. The greatest hospitality was always shown me at stations where I was known, but I made it a rule to be as independent of all help as possible. When I had decided to camp I spread the oilcloth and, having lit a fire, put on my salt beef to boil in the billy. By the time it was done, and the quart of tea made, I had a johnnycake or flatjack ready for cooking on the raked-out coals. The former differ only in size and are distinct from a damper in that they are cooked on the hot embers, whereas a damper is baked in the hot ashes with hot embers outside. No wood that I have seen can equal the gidya for giving the very ash and ember most valuable to us. A johnnycake made with baking powder is a most delicious scone – the very best baking powder is Eno's fruit salt. Of course, I did not restrict myself to these two articles of diet. I would vary them with apples and rice, sago or arrowroot, and occasionally with beef tea and potatoes. Preserved potatoes, when prepared in the water in which you have boiled your meat, are most delicious. Soda is an excellent baking powder; the johnnycake becomes a beautiful yellow, so that you can imagine you are eating bread made with milk, butter and eggs. At the stores – every station has its store – flour was ninepence to one shilling per pound, rice a shilling, apples and potatoes one shilling and sixpence, and meat, though most of the stations do not charge for it, was threepence to sixpence a pound for salt beef.

But to return. No one in Jundah could give me any lucid information where water might be in the next sixty-five miles. It is the uncertainty which predisposes to the fever of the palate. With the river in sight on my left, and never more than five or six miles from me, I knew that I could always get water by turning off to it. This, then, was well enough. But the least intoxicated man in Jundah was most positive that there was one stage absolutely without water for eighteen miles. He had offered to fight anyone who contradicted him, yet his statement passed unchallenged. I therefore inferred that he was speaking the truth. If, then, I had been thirsty, had turned off five miles to water and found none this eighteen miles, it would have gone hard with me. As it happened, my anxiety was uncalled for. At several places in the sixty-five miles cattle tracks crossed the path, and by following them I was always brought to water, but so stale and filthy that it gave me severe griping pains in the stomach, which interfered much with my walking. For a greater part of this distance my way lay through a corner of a vast cattle run owned by two men, and in extent larger than Yorkshire and Durham.

On 15 February I came to the most interesting river in Australia. Fifteen miles above this, the Thomson had joined the Barcoo. Wading waist-deep through the combined stream, I paused halfway to admire the glorious reaches of the river opened up above and below me, and the high banks crowned with magnificent timber. Every description of wildfowl floated idly on the unruffled surface of the current, and it was idleness which reigned supreme over the encampment of blacks in the timber on the opposite bank. I was so delighted with seeing Coopers Creek at last that, despite an empty tuckerbag, I must need camp for the night on its margin.

Seven miles from the crossing I reached a cattle station, and twenty-eight miles further another. The sky now became overcast, the sun was rarely visible, and everything foreboded rain. I rested a day or two and went on. A slight drizzle fell persistently. Not heavy enough to keep me awake, it made all my things sodden. There was no sun to dry them, nor had I sufficient patience to steam them before a fire. Once I lost my box of matches, and calling at a house to replenish them was given as a favour nineteen lucifers. These had to last me two days, sleeping out in the meantime. I cannot imagine any severer trial for one's nerves than when hungry, with no food cooked, nor any house within a day's walk, to have to light a fire in wind or rain with your last match.

On 23 February the Thargomindah and Windorah mailman served me a dirty trick. While I was camped for lunch he and another man came up to me, both well mounted, and driving packhorses. It was a hot, sultry, thirsty day, and I had a larger stock of water than usual, having filled my two-quart billy as well as my waterbag. These men asked me for a drink, and before I could stop them, they had emptied my billy of all but a cupful, though they were within two miles of water on horseback, while I was over twenty-eight from it on foot. I made it a rule of my walk never to ask or accept a drink from any traveller, whether on foot or horseback. It gave me satisfaction to be independent even in this.

The same evening of my meeting with the mailman a foot traveller overtook me and we camped together. We made an excellent break-wind, lit a roaring fire, for we were once more in gidya country with abundance of firewood, and calmly settled ourselves for the night. But we were not long asleep before the slight drizzle which had fore-warned us was succeeded by a heavy pelting rain that knew no ceasing. One could hardly believe the effect of that rain. In the morning our camp was on the only dry ground within sight. For fifteen miles we did not see land. The track was a clearly defined channel between the bushes. The creeks were running into a very strong current, and we were so often in water up to our armpits that I travelled with nothing on but my shirt. We reached shelter, there to be detained for three days. It rained for seventy-six hours at one stretch. In five days nine inches and thirty points fell. Dams were burst everywhere. The whole country into Thargomindah was become a vast series of swamps and flooded creeks.

Buckling to it, every danger vanished at my approach. Wading through swamps and swimming creeks with long distances to carry food, I yet experienced no fatigue; the dash of excitement kept it away. Where the swamp extended for miles it was but natural that in threading my way among the trees, with no guide but the sun, and water often to my breast, I should wander from the track, but a wide cast on the dry ground would as surely discover it to me. When the water was in motion, centipedes in hundreds and an occasional snake constantly floated across the path in unpleasant proximity.

The snakes I saw in my walk were more varied than numerous. On the red mulga ridges I killed several mulga snakes – a finely marked brown snake nearly six feet in length. When I was at the headwaters of the Diamantina, a black passed me, trailing after him a snake nine feet six inches long and as thick as a cable. It is a kind of rock python, which often attains a length of twelve or fifteen feet. The black would have me to believe that it was not deadly. It is a man's duty to kill every snake he can. I have killed the brown snake, the tiger snake, the poor harmless carpet snake, and a black snake with a blue belly. There were many I had no means of identifying, not the least interesting being an active little fellow which was disturbed by my coming and commenced to wriggle about in a most fantastic way. Just as I turned for a stick it made one spring off the track and vanished down a hole not large enough to introduce your two smallest fingers. Many anecdotes of snakes were told me. People so unkindly take advantage of one's credulous inexperience.

The Bulloo I crossed in a boat; a deep wade then put me on the track to Hungerford. At Thargomindah I had laid in such a large supply of flour and beef that for seventy-five miles I was absolutely independent of everyone. Timber and water were abundant. By this time I had trained myself to do with very little water. I could walk twenty-five miles without wetting my lips. The corellas flock to water at sundown; the thirsty traveller need but be guided by them, and he will infallibly be brought to water. The Paroo was greatly swollen. I had been told to be careful, as the bed of the river is thickly timbered with the Ypunyah. The stream was not less than half a mile wide, and you cannot see the opposite bank till quite close to it. But caution was unnecessary. I walked slap in, and crossed without difficulty. Hungerford is across the river. The boundary between New South

Wales and Queensland passes through the centre of the town. The hotel is in Queensland, where the licence is less; the store is in New South Wales, where there is free trade. I had done with Queensland. Drinks were now sixpence, and mutton was to take the place of beef.

In crossing the Paroo, twenty miles below Hungerford, I waded in a careless way into the stream, with my heavy swag on my back. Gradually it got deeper; it came over my waist; it reached my breast, my chin then was in the water; the next moment I went out of my depth altogether. The current in among the lignum bushes was very strong, and being impeded with my swag and boots I was a long time floundering about before I could get into my depth again. The experience was of use to me. I stripped and found a passage among the trees; then, returning for my things, I swam over with them in comfort.

Not till I was a hundred miles below Hungerford did I overtake the floodwaters of the Paroo and wade through the last of the swamps. There were public houses now every ten or twenty miles into Wilcannia. Away out in that wretched country of claypans and sand ridges, with its uninteresting scrub, its vast flats of saltbush and occasional stretches of barren hills, I suddenly came on a beautiful lake which wandered away to the east till its outer margin was hidden. For a little while I felt enthusiastic about the country I was in, but having to toil for some hours through heavy sand my misplaced enthusiasm was turned into ridicule. The scene constantly opening before me seemed the very incarnation of dreary desolation . . . Weak and fagged, and badly in need of a spell, I could not rest till I was in Wilcannia.

I got in an hour after the telegraph had closed on Easter Monday; it was Wednesday before I had the means of buying any food. With no money in my pocket, and camped on the flat below the hospital, where those vagrants who have knocked down their cheques in the hells of this town rest till recuperated enough to start away with their swag, my experience of Wilcannia was not a cheerful one. Another young fellow was in a similar predicament to myself, but he knew a Chinese cook at one of the hotels, and twice sponged a supper. On the second evening another of us camped there was put in the lockup and got a fortnight. Another had been living on this flat for months; no one knew how he lived; he hadn't a sixpence.

On the Wednesday I got money and gave a farewell *al fresco* feed to all the tramps and vagabonds, after which I left on the seventy mile track. At the end of the seventy miles is Mount Manaro station, situated in the hollow of the enclosing hills. The way lies through vast clay flats of saltbush and mallee, interspersed with sedges of mulga, boree, leopardwood and sandalwood. The walking is heavy, and there is one stage of twenty-three miles without water. Above Ivanhoe the country is comparatively picturesque. Immediately after leaving it I got into the endless saltbush plains, the few clumps of box and pine on which can be seen such an incredible distance. The large box which gives its name to the One Tree Plain can be seen twenty miles off. There are public houses every ten or twelve miles. The landlady of one of them poses in Melbourne society as a squatter's wife. Up here she is known as the Scrub Turkey.

I travelled now very rapidly. From Hay I passed through Deniliquin, Echuca, Rochester, Elmore, Heathcote and Kilmore, reaching Melbourne on 21 April. While in my own colony it was a perfect picnic. Instead of immense tracts of country owned by one man, and given up to sheep, there were a succession of beautiful little farms, each with its haystack, its neat little cottage, its substantial fence, and its scene of vigorous activity. Ploughing was in full swing, clearing and grubbing. The beautiful hilly country, seemingly so fertile, and supporting so excellent a class of people, pleased me beyond measure. Certainly, I thought, my colony may be the smallest, but it is the healthiest and most beautiful of them all. This fact I have left to the last. I came seventeen hundred miles through the interior of Australia without seeing a kangaroo. My only objection to writing this account of my walk was a natural one. If it had never been written many people might think that I had done something wonderful. They will read this and see that anyone who cared to take the trouble and give up four months of his time could have done the walk more quickly than I did, more easily, and with less discomfort to himself.

Bush Pubs – Oases on the Plains

Jock Marshall

Jock Marshall runs across the cheque busters, hatters and death-adder men who would turn up at remote country pubs and find themselves overnight inhabitants of the drunks' room.

There used to be a pub on a track to nowhere in which nobody seemed to live. The owner had a large spread of sheep country that went with it, and he kept the pub as a service to the termites and the few men who lived scattered about the area. It contained some cases of bottled beer, a kerosene refrigerator and nothing else. On a small bench stood an open meat tin that held assorted change, and there hung above it a bottle opener attached by a piece of string to the wall. Beside the opener was a notice that requested the rare customer to replace in the refrigerator fresh bottles from the cases for any cold ones that he cared to use, to leave his payment in the meat tin, and above all not to 'for Christ's sake, shake [steal] the bloody opener'. The owner only visited the place to refill the refrigerator with beer and kerosene. History has it that nobody did shake that opener.

Not many pubs today keep a drunks' room. This was a room exclusively reserved for the habituals who hit 'town' once every eighteen months or so with a cheque to cut out. It was used also to house the young sparks from the stations out on a spree after the local bush race meeting. But the old cheque busters usually laid claim to it. They were mostly men who led unbelievably lonely lives maintaining a remote bore pump far out on some station run, or an equally solitary existence such as dogging. The dogger, or dingo hunter, is an almost incredibly skilled bushman who prefers a life of solitude and independence to that of a station hand working for regular wages. The state governments pay a bounty on the scalps that he takes, and if he is unable to cash in his scalps at a police station, he will do so at the store or the pub, counting them out over the bar. These solitary men are usually known as *hatters*. Some of them go under the name of death adder men, for it is reckoned they will bite your head off if spoken to before noon. Men who seldom have the chance to talk they become garrulous with their kind and argue endlessly and with great contentment during their rare meetings. On arrival at the pub they would usually go straight to the drunks' room, select a bed from the half dozen stretchers, and throw their swag on it. Then they would enter the bar and hand over their cheque to the publican. Thus they would 'blue' their cheques. The pub-keeper would usually hold back a proportion so as to be able to taper them off the grog and dry them out and get rid of their shakes.

There was never much noise from the drunks' room at night, for the bibulous activities of the day brought exhaustion, and the room would rock instead with the stertorous snoring of the occupants. Accustomed as these men were to waking at daybreak, the pub-keeper would often leave some rum available with which they could warm themselves in the chilly dawn. This was a wise precaution, for if he did not, he was likely to be roused out of bed for a pipe-opener. There was a kind of tacit understanding between publicans and regular cheque busters – a sort of code of tolerance which ensured a surprising minimum of disturbance. Tough and leathery, they would finish their spree, roll their swags, take back

their odd left-over cash, load up with tobacco, tea and other neces-
sities, and disappear for another long year or two into the wide
landscape whence they had come.

A strange band of characters, they seem to be dying out.

Bugger Australia Altogether

E.M. 'Mick' Kelsall

River-town boy and itinerant worker E.M. 'Mick' Kelsall takes his life of strife and adventure into an Italian farmer's tomato fields, with hilarious consequences.

The Italians had departed from the scene around Moama because many of them had failed to pay for the land they leased, and the farmers realised that the tomato-growing area would take years to be brought back to productivity. The Italians also had a problem because there was no regular irrigation, and they would often be forced to try and water by hand to save their young plants.

The next area they invaded was about three miles out of Echuca at a place called Boileau, on the Goulburn road. The Boileau township's main building was a pub, and its main customers were the farmers who had properties out along the Goulburn, and the log bargemen, for the pub was only a few hundred yards from the Murray. When the bargemen had made a good drift they whiled away many an hour making the publican's life a misery.

I got a job tomato picking with an Italian nicknamed 'Gentleman Joe' who was married to an English girl and had two little kids. Thanks to his wife's tutoring Joe's employees had no problem understanding his English.

After a few days riding my bike to be at work by seven o'clock,

I decided it would be much easier to camp on the job, so Joe shifted the blood and bone and chemical sprays out of his shed and I moved in. It was a very crude billet, but didn't worry me, for I spent so little time there.

I soon grew fond of Joe and his family, even though he paid only six shillings a day for the ten hours we spent plucking tomatoes with our backs bent out in the red-hot sun. I was the only one to be given any relief from this grind, and that was when his wife's sisters came out to visit them.

As a gesture of goodwill to the girls Joe would say to me, 'You go put on your swimsuit and take the girls to get wet.' This was probably the only time I was ever paid for such a pleasurable job, and it also built up my ego to be seen with such beautiful girls. Usually when work finished that night I would be asked to eat with the family and the two girls – an Italian meal of spaghetti cooked by Joe. The girls refused to eat the sauce that went with it and would just sprinkle it with sugar, much to Joe's disgust.

Joe employed only good, experienced pickers, for new chums did too much damage by not covering exposed fruit with the branches of the plant, thereby letting the sun burn the tomatoes. They would also leave the stems on the fruit, which meant that Joe would have to knock off grading to pull stems off. They did many other things like putting their feet on the top between the plants to rest their aching backs, which hardened the earth so that moisture could not penetrate through to the roots of the plant.

Many and varied were the types of men who took on tomato picking – out-of-work carpenters, woodcutters, grocer's assistants, and many of the town's young bucks, who were just putting in a day to get enough money to go to a dance. The latter resented the green paste that adhered to their hands from the tomato plants, for it was extremely hard to wash off, and the girls resented it when a green stain showed up on their evening frocks.

Aboriginals who lived in or near the town would also pick toma-toes, and one young Aboriginal was working to keep the pot boiling while he trained for a career in boxing. Because he could use his fists he was given the greatest respect by the whites who bent their backs with him in the tomato plantation, but one passing white man was not so smart.

When flocks of sheep were driven along the road Joe would send some of us down to be sure that sheep didn't get through the fence and damage his plants. As a flock was being driven toward Echuca we lined up along the fence and kept shoving the woolly pests back as they tried to get to the green plants. The drover, a big, sullen-looking man, kept looking our way but said nothing.

One of his kelpie bitches came along the fence to keep the sheep away from it. She was on heat, and a little nondescript dog that had been hanging around us for the few scraps that we would throw his way, slipped through the wires and, without any preliminary, got joined to the bitch. The drover was mad about this and came over and brought his whip handle down with tremendous force between the two animals, almost severing the little mongrel's instrument of enjoyment. As the little dog hobbled away maimed, the drover leered at us and said, ''E won't be doin' any more rootin'.' Not wanting to become involved in fisticuffs with anyone so physically superior, we all kept quiet, but the Aboriginal who slipped through the fence, faced up to the drover and told him through clenched teeth, 'I think you're an overgrown, cowardly, useless, white bastard'.

The drover grinned and replied, 'The one little nigger boy must think it's his lucky day, but it ain't see'. Then he made a wild rush with fists flailing. If one of the blows had landed the young man would have been asleep for a long time, but he was far too fast as he dodged and weaved, then let go a straight left to the face. As the drover tired the Aboriginal boy beat a tattoo of blows to his opponent's face. It was not too handsome when the fight began, but as the big chap sank to the ground his face was a pulpy mess. Looking down at him the coloured lad said, 'Now I ought to do to you what you did to the little dog!' But Joe interrupted any more action and the drover got up and staggered across to the pub.

All the market gardens were watered from the irrigation channels that had been extended out to the farms at the Echuca Village Settlement, and there wasn't a man working for Joe who didn't welcome the break from picking tomatoes to watering them.

One had to be experienced at this job too, for if the gate from the main channel was opened too wide the man doing the irrigating found it almost impossible to control the amount of water that went into the small channels between the tomato beds. One day, when the main channel gate had been opened too wide, a whole block of tomato plants was partially flooded. Joe sent us into the water to try and rescue what fruit we could.

Reluctantly we took off boots and socks and were lugging heavy kerosene tins of tomatoes through the muddy water, when one chap let out a loud yell and we all saw a tiger snake glide away under the plants ahead. We all vacated the water as one, and gingerly picked our way down to the packing shed, and told Joe there was no way we were going back into the water to keep a tiger snake company.

Joe became very angry at the thought of poverty-stricken tomato pickers going on strike, so he shouted and gesticulated and when he saw we were unmoved he decided to get us back into the water by shaming us. 'Come with me,' he shouted. 'Show me where this snike is.' We showed him approximately where the snake disappeared, so he whipped off his boots and socks, rolled up his trouser legs and prepared to enter the water.

'Don't go in there, you silly bugger. If that thing bites yer, yer got less than twenty minutes to live', advised our spokesman.

'Aah!' yelled Joe with rage. 'I know you not fright of the blooda snike, you no lika the blooda water.' With that he stepped into the channel, grabbed a plant, lifted it and yelled, 'Look no blooda snike'. He moved further on, lifted another plant and again said contemptuously, 'Look no blooda snike', but on the next attempt he just got to the 'blooda' in the sentence when the 'snike' reared his ugly head a foot above the water. 'Jeeza Christi', Joe whispered as he threw himself backward to be half-buried in the mud.

He only stayed there for a fraction of a second and was out and running. I don't think his feet touched the ground from when he left the water until he arrived at the packing shed. It was said, 'The Lord walked on water, but Joe ran on air'.

We all traipsed back to the shed, where Joe was sitting on an up-ended tomato case. He looked up listlessly, gave a wave of the hand and told us to, 'Go home boys, and bugger the water, bugger the tomart, bugger the snike, bugger Ostrilya and bugger me.'

The Big Forest of Wang Wauk

Les Murray

Poet Les Murray walks through the deep forests of Wang Wauk in northern New South Wales and relives his long family connection with the country, participates in a 'soundless visual symphony' and recalls the hardships and dangers of the timbergetting days.

The newly luxuriant woodland my great grandparents John and Isabella Murray encountered when they took up their land at Bunyah in 1870 is now pretty well confined to State Forest No. 295, Wang Wauk, and to the high ridges of the Kyle range that run down into it from the northwest. This is the forest I have known all my life, the one I walked in first and the one I'm likely to walk in most often in the future. Together with Bulahdelah State Forest, No. 296, it forms a gigantic prone figure of a deep-sea diver or a hooded man straddling Boolambayte Lake and the Pacific Highway with two long legs. This map-figure lies on the landscape with its big head at Bunyah and an arm crooked down behind Coolongolook Mountain cradling a detached forestry block that was once the site of the abortive Telararee goldrush. Embracing 8,651 hectares, State Forest 295 comprises all the government forest preserve that drains by way of the Wang Wauk and Coolongolook rivers into Wallis Lake and thence the ocean. Bulahdelah State Forest, No. 296, the two legs, hips and one shoulder of the map-giant, taking in 10,166 hectares, drains by way of Boolambayte

Creek and the Myall River into the Myall Lakes. High on the more northerly thigh of the giant, shared by both state forests, is the superb O'Sullivans Gap Flora Reserve with its cabbage tree palms growing between the beige to milk-blue boles of tall flooded gum trees, and its rainforest patches; when returning by road from the south, I always regard this twisting arcade of luxuriant bush as the gateway to the north coast. Further south in the same leg, just inside SF 296, is the Grandis, the tallest tree in New South Wales, a flooded gum some 76 metres or 250 feet in height and as big round the base as the average second bedroom. Pinned on to the south leg roughly behind the knee is Bulahdelah Mountain Forest Park, a protected habitat of the rare subterranean orchid *Cryptanthemis slateri*, an endangered species. The small rocky mountain there was once the world's chief source of the chemical alum, formerly used as an astringent in medicine and as a mordant in dyes; now its main use is as an absorbent in catbox litter. My mother's father Fred Arnall started work up there, in drives that opened on near-vertical skips and blue sky, when he was a sixteen-year-old Cornish orphan, and he stayed in the district long enough to marry Emily Worth, daughter of a Coolongolook family whose name has been represented in local timber-getting since the beginnings of settlement.

The first time I entered Wang Wauk State Forest lies well before conscious memory, but it was almost certainly on Black Saturday in February 1939, when I was five months old. I was taken to a swimming hole in the already burnt-out forest to stay with the women and the other small children of the district, while the men and big boys fought to save as much as they could from the terrifying, irresistible bushfires that were now sweeping through the farms. Since then I've gone there for picnics, for solitary rambles, to cut poles and fenceposts, to help my father search unsuccessfully for a lost gold claim in a gully overgrown since the claim was filed in the 1930s, to botanise, to be quiet among the trees and birds. Sometimes when driving about the roads in there, Smedleys Cutting road or Horses Creek road, Worths road or the steep pinch up Possum Pie, or the exhilarating Koolonock road that hangs cornice-like on one side and then the other of the high steep spinal ridge dividing Wang Wauk from Bulahdelah forest, I indulge a kind of soundless visual symphony, watching the tree species change in response to the different soils. High up there will be forest oaks, whose non-deciduous needle leaves turn bronze in autumn and used to be taken by the black people as their signal to move away from the coast to winter in the sheltering hills. With these will be greyish-mauve spotted gums, then white mahogany and grey ironbark and seasonally orange-streaked grey gum, telling of stony ground; a brush box or two will indicate moister shaded soil, and then perhaps the warm chestnut trunks of soaring tallowwoods will take over, with black ironbarks and maybe a shift to blackbutt on drier soils, then these will give way to dizzying bluegums, flooded gum and turpentine far down on the creek levels. Often the symphony will be faster and more complex than this, and a flowering vine, say wild hops or native clematis or beige-belled wonga, will bring me to an admiring stop, or I will slow down to drink in the warming scent of bloodwood trees in bloom. Always, too, I pay heed to the grassy tunnels of abandoned roads, and the many ancient stumps, fluted with decay, that still show the neat slots cut into them with three or four skilful swings of the axe sixty or eighty or a hundred years ago to take the often-round improvised 'boards' on which men ascended to fell or even to top soaring trees, working five or ten or a hundred feet up with no thought of safety harness. And I find myself thinking of an age I saw the very tail end of, the era of bullock teams and trundling iron-shod jinkers, always called 'trucks' by the men who used them. The very last team working in our bush ceased operations only a little over twenty years ago; it belonged to Eric Bennett, of Coolongolook, a quiet, gentle man who was for a while my uncle by marriage.

Men who cut and drew timber in the 1930s and through the boom time of World War II, when vast tonnages of timber went to build wharves all over the Pacific for the forces that were driving back Japan, all agree that the logs they felled, or 'fell' as they say, were the second generation, sticks that their fathers and predecessors would have disdained, though they were still mighty logs, often three or four feet in diameter at the butt. The truly great trees, giants surviving from away back in Aboriginal times, and often having a girth greater than that of a thousand-gallon iron water tank, were cut down and drawn to the mills by men whose names still, but only for a little while longer, ring in local tales. Ned Toms was admitted by all to be the finest judge of timber in his generation, as well as one of the hardest workers: his bullocks were worn out in a couple of years, and had to be replaced continually. Albert Worth was his pupil and successor, a man said to be able to smell white ants in the crown of a tree when standing at its base. Other mighty men were the Holdens, Herb and Albert, Bill and Stan, whose trucks had 'cotton reel' wheels, not spoked but solid timber cut in the round from a log, Frank, Percy and Bailey Bunt, whose name endures in Bunts Creek, Archie, Jim and George Carter, John Griffis, Jack, George and Billy Mitchell, and Harry and Dargan Mitchell too, Tom and Jim Batchelor, sardonic jesters who also cut and drew in the state forest to the east of Coolongolook that now bears their family name, Don and Frank Worth, Jake and Billy Newton, Bucca Wauka Bob Paterson, Jack Tull, Albert McDean, Billy Newman who has a road named after him in the forest, Mick Ronan, the Burnses, Arthur, Billy and George, the Aboriginal family of French, Harry and Morgan in the older generation and then their sons Clarrie and Bill, the latter of whom was always known as Plugger. And then there were Gomer Woodward and his brother Jack, whose head was crushed by a loop of bridle chain as a log slipped off the skid up which it was being snigged on to his bullock trucks. This tragedy occurred in the teens of the century, and an identical accident almost killed my father Cecil Murray in the 1930s; if the log and the skid had fallen to the ground, rather than lodging on the nave of the truck's wheel, I would never have existed. Many of the men I have named began work in the bush well before the turn of the century, and often they shifted over to fulltime farming after a decade or two in the timber. Very many of the early settlers in fact used the sale of timber off their selections to set up in dairy farming, and that was after they had used some of the timber to build their original dwellings. A typical case was Henry Tagg, whose son George was a bullock driver for many years; Mr Tagg senior was a punt captain in the Myall River timber trade, until he bought a block at Willina that had taken his eye. He was nicknamed Peter Positive for his assured demeanour, and the quality was probably a godsend in the hard scrabble of a selector's life.

When Allan Murray and his sons entered the timber business in the late 1920s, most private cutters and teamsters were concentrated in the northern half of Wang Wauk forest. The southern end and much of Bulahdelah forest was the preserve of Allen Taylor's logging tramway, which ran from Horses Creek over the steep little Mayers Range where the Wang Wauk Forest Way now runs, and thence down to the now-dying village of Wootton and on to Mayers Point on the main Myall Lake. From there, steam punts carrying huge layers of logs would chug down the deep Myall River to Winda Woppa, on Port Stephens, whence the timber would be transferred into deepwater ships to go to Sydney, Newcastle, New Zealand or California. The tramway was first powered by horses, which crossed the many bridges on close-fitted decking; later they were replaced by narrow-gauge steam locos. The tramway ran from 1900 to 1944, employing hosts of men from Wootton, Bulahdelah and all the districts round about, and it died only when the riverboats and the coastal steamers they served were killed off by the war. Now, only a few relics of the tramway remain. On Horses Creek, a bridge still carrying its rusted steel rails has survived bushfires by virtue of the shady moist creek bush around it. To city eyes, it probably looks like a smallish mouldering sister of the Bridge on the River Kwai. There is now a small cleared picnic area at one end, with barbecues and labelled trees, and large yellow-flecked black goannas there competing with the currawongs and noisy mynahs for tourists' scraps, often coming out to demand them even before the sausages are cooked. The leeches, for their part don't have to wait; for them, the tourists themselves are the picnic.

The teams drawing out of the north end of Wang Wauk State Forest used to haul their logs in to Bunyah and down to Coolongolook, at first to the mills there, later mainly to the wharf, or else they would follow a now-disused road down the Wang Wauk to just past where it becomes a tidal saltwater river. In either case, much of their timber went to Wrights' mill and shipyard at Tuncurry. Hundreds of sailing ships were built from native hardwoods on our rivers, and the timber construction lasted well into the era of steam. In early times, millions of super feet of ironbark went to make paving blocks in the cities; turpentine went to construct wharves and the cabbage tree palm had its role in providing stakes for oyster leases, as it still does. Another unlikely-seeming timber consumed by the bullockies themselves was grass tree (*Xanthorrhoea*), from which they cut the brake shoes for their trucks; no other timber had so little slippage. In that age and before, rainforest trees weren't protected as they are nowadays, and from private and Crown lands alike went coachwood, rosewood, the rare brown pine (*Podocarpus elatus*) and many more, lumped in with the hardwoods. At the same period, of course, rainforest was still being routinely cut and burnt to clear it. Nowadays, the only native softwood in commerce from our part of the state is the coastal callitris (*Callitris macleayana*) or coast cypress pine, not present, so far as I know, in either of the two forests I am discussing.

When the teams were using it, the Bunyah Road, never a show-piece thoroughfare, degenerated into a morass of deep trenches and liquescent or sun-dried clay scarps; no other wheeled vehicle, whether car, sulky or bike, could negotiate it, and most traffic went round by other roads. Ironically, the beginning of the end for the teams, and the victory of mechanisation, began with something as simple as gravel. When Stroud Shire first gravelled the roads in the mid-1930s, bullocks that used them began to go lame. The going was too hard and sharp for their feet, while at the same time the thick loose surface absorbed the inertia of the trucks' wheels and meant that the bullocks had to pull harder and more constantly to move their great tonnages of load. Soon the teamsters began to bring their loads only to the edge of the forest, establishing dumps with huge permanent loading skids over which to slide the logs on to the first motor lorry jinkers. Arthur Fenning and Jack Saxby were among the first lorry drivers to cart logs, though tabletop lorries had long been going into the bush to haul sleepers, girders and suchlike small timber. The log dumps, a few still used but mainly derelict now, are still a striking feature of the bush, squat cliffs and bunkers of grey timber and dirt. In their heyday, the dumps were apt to look like brontosaurian paving, or a vast corduroy laid on the ripped, deliciously raw-smelling bush soil. I can still remember them like that, back when what are now called sawlogs, American style, were still known universally by their Austral-ian term of mill logs. 'Mill logs today?' snort the old men. 'They're bloody telephone poles! We wouldn't have looked at anything that small.'

Those who walk the forest in the memory and reverie of my region include many who made, very late in Western terms, the momentous step across from the age of muscle power to the age of the machine. Men still alive remember riding into the bush in the mists of dawn and hobbling their horses to browse all day on the rich kangaroo grass between the trees, while they swung their axes and drove their wedges with scarcely a break till sundown. Often their bullocks would be nearby, located by their bells' iron music as they grazed together. It was the work of only half an hour or so to round them up, put on their yokes and bows and link up the snig chains to draw a hundred-foot barked spar to the trucks for loading. The bullocks moved slowly between the trees, avoiding obstacles, and the log following behind made little more than a groove in the soil, because it was narrower than the team and so couldn't smash much that they had avoided. When bulldozers arrived at the end of the Second World War, they crashed straight through, up slopes and down gorges, destroying twenty future trees and three or four present ones to extract a single log. But they were much faster, and so earned more money for their operators. Most timber-getters have always been contractors, rather than employees on wages, and they tend to come from families with a fierce love of personal independence. The ancient steam traction engines had been as slow as the bullocks, and a fire risk to boot, so they worked mostly outside the forest and were never serious competition. When the bulldozers came, and the last bullock teams disappeared, as usual a host of subtleties vanished. There was, for example, no more need for men who could judge the strength and potential of a bullock, or select which should be leaders, no more call for training animals to respond to voice and tone, and no more use for the tricks of psychology that overcame the animals' fears and occasional jibbings. To cite just one such, it used to be well known that if a load became stuck, bringing the team to a halt, their first pull when re-starting would be the most powerful. Their next would lack heart, though it would still be energetic; the third would be despairing and weak, and there probably wouldn't be a fourth. The way to get a further powerful effort, after a short spell, was to lengthen the slack of the chains considerably, then gee the team into motion; they would move tentatively, register the joyous lightening of their load, and be in full, confident motion when the chains tightened. This was particularly effective when, as often happened, the second of two linked loads became stuck in a creek or a mudhole. Putting the first into motion established a heartening inertia, and the management of inertial forces was as much at the heart of bullock drivers' skills as it is central to those of dozer drivers. Sometimes inertia would do most of the work, by accident or design. Two men hauling a bloodwood log up Pappinbarra Mountain north of Taree, well into the caterpillar age, saw their load slip out of its bark smoothly as a leg out of a stocking and begin a sizzling end-on descent, splitting some trees, riding up through the high foliage of others in momentary arcs, till it plunged down through the tangled vines at the mountain's foot and buried its entire length almost parallel with the surface of the soil. And there it stayed. In the bullock era, logs were regularly drawn by block and tackle to the top of a steep hill and 'speared' down, or else drawn down festooned with knotted chains, often called ruffle chains, that 'grabbed' in the earth and prevented their racing down past, or over, the bullocks. One log that got away from my father and his brother Eric on Martins Mount, just northwest of the state forest, skied down with such impetus that it leaped over the cleared flat at the bottom, cleared Darlings Creek and plunged fifteen feet deep into the soft soil on the other side. It took both their teams together to joggle it free.

Minor injuries were, and remain, commonplace in the bush, to be borne with stoicism and humour. One fatal accident per year is the industry average on the coast between Newcastle and the Queensland border. As I was writing this, a man was cut in half by a circular saw at a mill near Sawtell. Relatively few of the old generations of cutters and bullockies seem to have been killed or maimed in the course of their work, and the Horses Creek tramway in its forty-four years of

operations had just one fatal accident. A deflected axe, wedges pop-
ping out of a log, a tree kicking back past the stump as it fell, all
these were menaces to watch for, but really the men's skills became so
profound and instantaneous that before a bad accident could happen
they had usually stepped away from it to watch the play of forces,
perhaps with a curse of a laugh. 'Go it, you bastard!' 'By jabers but
that was close!' Death and maiming were originally more likely in
the sawmills than the bush. To name just two cases out of many, my
grandmother's brother George Payne lost his arm in an instant in a
mill at Moto. And a man named Hector Newton was feeding a log
past the guide rollers of a mill at Nabiac when, as can happen if a
log develops even an imperceptible skew as it rides into the saw, the
outer scantling ran out, flew up and was flung by the screaming blade
end-on like a shovelnose spear; Newton was impaled through the
heart and died instantly, and he was not the only victim of this exact
pattern of accident. The coming of the chainsaw, so much swifter
than the old man-powered axe and crosscut saw, brought an increase
in horrendous injuries to the bush itself, as well as a new source of
close-shave stories. The man who trod on a black snake on a steep
pinch and slid down its entire length while desperately holding a revving chainsaw away from his body survived unbitten by either, to be
laughed at as a liar by all except the timber men, though their belief
also didn't prevent them from laughing. A nearer thing happened the
day the same man put his saw into a thick branch that had a 'bind'
on it, that is, one which was under tension; it's often impossible to
detect the presence of tension in a tangle of branches or a lodged tree.
When the branch was severed, the strain it had been under released,
tossing man and saw a dozen feet. Its trigger jammed, so that the
blade was still chewing furiously at the air, the saw fell on its handle
end between the man's sprawled legs and stood upright for a long
millisecond. If it fell backwards, he would be split in two, or at the

least torn open in hideous death. If he raised a hand, he would lose it and the arm too. And then the blade fell away from him, and gnawed at the soil between his feet. Another man, working alone as no one should ever do in the forest, was noticed by a Masonite Corporation supervisor named Clarrie Dawson to be sitting oddly hunched on the ground near his camp. It turned out the man had somehow dropped his whizzing chainsaw in his lap, and was proceeding to bleed to death. Rushed to hospital, he was saved, and even his genitals were eventually restored to full working order. At the Masonite factory's offices in Raymond Terrace, though, none of the men who had rushed to help Dawson with the injured man really wanted to dictate the contents of the accident report to the pretty young typist. Dawson had to do that himself. 'Er . . . extensive lacerations,' he paused, 'to the penis . . .' 'Poor man,' said the typist, never missing a beat in her rapid typing. Nowadays, the various Forestry district offices have chainsaw examiner-instructors on staff, who check and brush up the skills of all workers wishing for a licence to cut timber in the various state forests.

Men working in the bush are also nowadays required to wear yellow plastic safety helmets. No such protection existed in September 1939 when my father's brother Archie, an experienced sleeper cutter and just three months married, was killed by the falling top of a dead tree. My father had refused to fell a certain tallowwood, just before retiring from the bush to start working a dairy farm of his father's, on the grounds that it was too difficult to haul out and anyway dozy, that is, afflicted with subsurface rotting, at one or more spots high up. His father, who supervised operations from horseback, was stubbornly convinced the log was good and could be secured. As he rode off after breakfast, my grandmother, afflicted all her life with flashes of the bad gift of prescience, rushed out, calling and calling to him to warn him of a terrible foreboding she had. He failed to hear, and at three that afternoon, as the disputed tree fell, it brushed against a tall dead one beside it and set up a whipping vibration in it. Hearing a cry of 'Look out!' Archie made his only mistake and ran without looking up. The long snapped-off top section of the dead bole hit him squarely in the head and burst his brains out. Handsome, waltzing Archie was so well liked and bitterly missed that over a thousand crowded Krambach cemetery for his funeral.

The Long Drought

Geoffrey Blainey

Australia has been prone to drought throughout history to the present day, and the effects of a drought are examined by Geoffrey Blainey here in a study of the drought of 1895–1903, from A Land Half Won.

The first year of the drought was probably 1895. It was not yet called a drought – one year does not make a drought. By 1897 the long period of dry weather was being labelled as 'drought' in many districts where that word was not used lightly. The Great Drought had barely begun. Tens of thousands of small farmers suffered. In Victoria for three years the wheat belt produced virtually no wheat for export; and many Victorian bakehouses and confectioners were selling bread and cakes baked from Californian flour. Farmers slid deeply into debt. Blacksmiths and farriers, storekeepers and cordial makers in the small towns totted up with slate and pencil the increasing sums owed them, and they in turn owed increasing sums to banks, traders and agents in the city.

In the interior the price of fodder soared. If a traveller decided in 1900 to drive his buggy five hundred miles across the plains on any track between Hughenden in north Queensland and the New Mallee in South Australia, he would have paid a small fortune along the way for chaff and hay for his horses. He would also have met, along the track, scores of people who told – if they were not too proud to tell – of the jobs, livestock, and savings they had lost in the drought.

Many old pastoralists, household names in their district, were fighting to survive. In the tropical ranges near Hughenden, Robert Christison watched the blue sky each day for a sign of a cloud. Even a cloud as large as a man's hand would have been welcome, offering the hope that more clouds would appear and that finally rain would fall.

Christison was in his sixties, an age when he hoped his pioneering ventures in Queensland would have been rewarded, but instead his livestock were dying in the warm mud of the waterholes or on hard, bare paddocks. As the grass disappeared, men were sent to cut the mulga scrub so that the leaves could be eaten by sheep and cattle: and Christison noticed how, at the sudden sound of an axe, the skinny sheep would break into a run in the hope that green leaves were awaiting them. In the whirlwinds of dust that sometimes brushed across the bare ground, the cattle became invisible from only five steps away. The dams were silted, and the mechanical pumps which lifted water from artesian bores were halted by the clogged dust. Many of the cattle and sheep were so weak they could no longer safely cover the long distances to the remaining points of water and fodder. Even when stock were sent in railway trucks to the meatworks near the coast, their price was pitiful because sellers were many and buyers were few.

Like many pastoralists Christison thought incessantly of rain – mostly the rainstorms and cloudbursts of long ago. Turning to the diaries he had kept for thirty-five years, he re-read them in the hope of finding patterns that might indicate when the drought would end. On humid nights he would sit inside his house, listening and listening for the sound of drops of rain on the iron roof, and almost jumping with nervousness when the iron chanced to 'ping'. On some evenings the sky was black with clouds, and lightning was flickering on the horizon, and the air was so full of moisture that even the sugar and salt in the house were soggy; but in the morning he would arise and look outside to find not one puff of cloud floating in the blue sky.

Robert D. Barton, living out towards the Barwon River in north-west New South Wales, experienced drought from 1897 to 1902. He had brief relief when heavy rain fell on April Fool's Day 1899. As the drought ran on he skinned dead sheep until the bare plain 'was carpeted with skins spread on the ground'. In the long heat the ground cracked open, and several cracks were so deep that the horse wagon carrying the sheepskins sank to the axles. Five thousand of his sheep remained, and in the end he drove them east to the uplands of New England where rains were more regular. There he put up a tent, lived on bread and salt beef, and, with his dog for company, waited for news that the rains had fallen at home.

In many southern districts the roadways were congested with travelling stock, eating the grass on the wide fringes as they travelled slowly from nowhere to nowhere. But to reach those safer districts required risky expeditions. In 1899 drovers set out with 14,000 sheep on a short journey from Evesham station to Rockhampton, and 11,000 sheep died on the way. In the same year, 2500 fat sheep were driven only 45 miles in the Gilgandra district in New South Wales, and on the road 800 died of thirst. On dry stock routes many parched sheep refused to drink when they reached a dam, and pannikins of water had to be poured down their throats. Others drank too much and died.

The older pastoralists had spent a lifetime on the land and perhaps more than any other group of new Australians they had come to terms with it, but even they did not know the full range of its moods. In the 1880s they had spent huge sums in boring for water and in scooping out dams in the dry rim of the pastoral country. Their own experience suggested that they should prepare more for scarcity of water than for scarcity of grass. In this drought, however, millions of sheep died from starvation rather than thirst. The carcasses lay on hard earth, within sight of the gushing artesian bores which had been drilled with borrowed money. As many of the loans could not be repaid, scores of sheep stations passed into the hands of banks, pastoral companies and other mortgage-holders.

Overstocking was another sign of unfamiliarity with the new land. Too many cattle and sheep grazed in the years of expansion, and they imposed strain on the vegetation and topsoil. In the south-eastern quarter of Australia the food eaten annually by imported sheep, cattle, horses, rabbits and other herbaceous animals on the eve of the drought must have been many times the amount consumed by the native animals a century earlier. The country therefore would be slower in recovering from the drought. The drenching rains, when they came, would be less fruitful than if the land had been stocked cautiously.

In a large country no drought is universal. In every year between 1895 and 1903 a few districts had lush or passable seasons. There were even regions which, especially vulnerable to drought, escaped lightly. Between 1895 and 1903 the Gulf country of Queensland experienced only one miserable year. Most of the Gulf runs did not lose livestock, but they could rarely send cattle along the parched stock routes to the markets of the south. They were marooned, not crippled, by drought.

It is surprising to discover that the great drought was marked as much by cold weather as by hot. In Melbourne the drought years tended to be colder than average, though the Decembers tended to be hotter than normal. In many districts freak snaps of cold weather came during the drought. On 7 August 1899 the snow fell heavily in Melbourne, and at lunchtime schoolboys were throwing snowballs in the Fitzroy Gardens. In the first week of July 1900 many railway lines in New South Wales were blocked by falls of snow heavier than any previously recorded. A white blanket was spread westwards from the Upper Hunter to Condobolin. Telegraph lines collapsed, trains were halted by snow and slowly buried, and in the town of Bathurst many verandas and roofs collapsed under the weight of snow. A year later a heavy fall whitened virtually the length of a straight line drawn between Melbourne and Brisbane.

Dust storms preceded or followed snow storms. In south-eastern Australia the area of ground ploughed for wheat in 1900 was almost six times as large as that ploughed in 1866, and a vast extent of that tilled soil was no longer compacted by moisture and so it crumbled into powder and was blown away by the winds. Many fences were submerged by the drifting soil and stretches of railway were buried. On 21 November 1902 so much soil was blown from the interior that Melbourne was drenched with dust, and in the afternoon the sun was almost hidden by the dust in the air. In inland towns that afternoon the darkness of the dust storms was almost as intense as the blackest of nights, according to the Bureau of Meteorology. Lamps were lit in the houses, and along country roads on both sides of the Murray the falling fireballs emitted a strange light.

The grave year of the Federation Drought was probably 1902. Already the casualties were heavy. The number of sheep estimated to live in Australia had been almost halved in one decade, falling from 106 million in 1891 to 54 million in 1902. The cattle too had almost halved since 1894, declining from twelve to seven million, so that most working men virtually ceased to eat good beef. The rabbits too were decimated.

The losses of a long drought are not all recorded in statistics. Much of the loss is worry, disillusionment and humiliation. Even when a drought is almost over, graziers have no sure way of knowing whether it has finally ended. A drought can die slowly, its dying watched almost disbelievingly by tens of thousands of families who are close to insolvency. Their tension is heightened by the knowledge that if a creditor presses them they can overnight be forced to leave a property, which, though now a liability, could blossom into an asset after one day of rain.

On the northern plains of Victoria – now replacing South Australia as the main wheat fields – Farmer Coote kept a diary. His neat ink entries show that the end of a long drought can be identified only in retrospect. On 5 March 1903 he noted that the overnight rain had been so heavy that his dam overflowed and sheets of water covered his paddocks, but a week later he was surprised to see – at eight in the morning – a fierce dust storm. Towards the end of that month he recorded another two dust storms driven from the outer lands by the northerly winds, and as he pickled the wheat seed in preparation for the next season's sowing the sky became black with dust. In April, while his draught horses were discing the paddocks, dust storms rolled past and stung his face and half-blinded him. In the first fortnight of April the dust blew on four different days, but sometimes the dust was milder and was prelude to a little rain. Later in the month heavy rains fell, and the big horse Bess was even bogged while pulling the plough and soon the new grass was sprouting everywhere.

That was not his diary's last reference to the red dust. On 1 July, with a high wind blowing, he rode a horse into the town of Quambatook. 'Dust flying for the greater part of the day', he wrote. He was worried, knowing that in winter a sand storm would endanger the green shoots of wheat and grass and sometimes smother them. But his drought in fact was over.

The drought which ran from 1895 to 1903 vividly marked a new phase in the climate of the south-eastern part of Australia. A climatic map of that vast block of land embracing Birdsville, Longreach, Rockhampton, Sydney, Melbourne and Adelaide shows the arid zone moving slowly towards the coast long after that drought was over. The arid zone encroached on the semi-arid zone, and the semi-arid zone invaded the sub-humid zone. From the late 1880s or the 1890s through to the end of the Second World War this most productive rural area of Australia was to experience, on average, relatively dry seasons. The evidence suggests that the fluctuations in climate were one of the vital causes of the long prosperity of the forty years to 1890 and of the leaner decades which followed.

Many times the mood and motivations in Australian history had been strongly influenced by climate. The first English settlement in Australia had been based on an unreal optimism about the climatic paradise at Botany Bay. Even after that paradise had vanished and the early estimates of climate had been falsified, a similar optimism began to illuminate the interior of the continent. A great inland sea was sought, and the lands near that imagined sea were assumed to be fertile. No sooner had the inland sea been replaced by parched land on the maps than a new optimism glazed attitudes to climate in the settled districts. That optimism, still strong in 1890, fostered the faith that Australia – in resources and population and economic power – could be a second United States. The fall of the banks and the unexpected drought in the 1890s ended that faith. The movement to federate the colonies into the Commonwealth of Australia was in part the result of that humbling. A people who had often floated in the blue sky of fantasy had come down to earth.

The Sugar Lands

Alan Frost

The North Queensland coast, with its hinterland mountains, lush rainforests, fast rivers and sugar-coated plains, is the background for Alan Frost's writing about the activities of canecutters, rail networks, mighty mills and the many immigrant families of sugar growers.

As the rainforest scrubs were cleared from the Herbert, Tully and Johnstone River flats, paddock after paddock of sugar-cane was planted, and central mills built to extract the sweet juice and refine it into sugar. Sown progressively, the cane matured from the middle until towards the end of the year, when all work in the fields must cease with the onset of the monsoon.

The industry had its setbacks. In the mid-1870s, it nearly succumbed to rust, until resistant strains of cane were found and propagated. Rapid expansion on the one hand, and on the other the ban on the employment of Melanesians, implemented slowly between 1890 and 1904, led to labour shortages. In Europe, aided by government subsidies, growers at times produced sugar from beet more cheaply, and always there was competition from the West Indies, Fiji and other areas.

Yet sugar was to be a mainstay of the nation's economy for one hundred years. And by the 1920s a quite distinctive way of life had developed on the Queensland sugar lands. Using such machines as the steam plough, hundreds of small landholders planted and tended cane. Gangs of cutters harvested it; miniature steam engines hauled it in trucks (cages) along rickety 'tram-tracks' to the central mills, where it was processed.

Viewed from a distance, there is a certain romantic aura to harvesting sugar-cane. Imagine lines of men wielding razor-sharp machetes moving progressively through the fields, bringing down the towering stalks. In reality, though, it was terrible work. Accommodated in primitive barracks, the men worked from dawn to dusk in increasingly hot and humid conditions. The labour involved constantly bending to cut and trim the stalks, and lifting them into the trucks, so that it was back-breaking. There was the danger of the knife glancing off the cane, and slicing a limb. The creatures of the fields added to the hazards. It was found in the 1930s that one of the principal hazards, Weil's disease, was spread in the urine of rats which infiltrated the inevitable scratches on the canecutters' hands and feet. This led to the habit of firing the canefields immediately before cutting, to clear them of animals and snakes and incidentally to permit a cleaner cut, by getting rid of grass and weeds. It is an awesome sight to see the dense tropical night lit for kilometres by the deep red flames of burning cane.

Cutting cane was pre-eminently work for young, fit, single men. Arduous and grimy as it was, it might have its reward, for with rates of pay up to four or five times the national average, a good cutter might earn in three months what another labourer earned in a year. The seasonality of the work and the monetary return gave rise to that way of life so powerfully evoked by Ray Lawler in his play, *Summer of the Seventeenth Doll* (1955), set at the moment when the ageing cutters' bodies are failing them, and the women with whom they have co-habited in the off-seasons are looking for a more stable domesticity.

Canecutters were unionised at the beginning of the twentieth century; but in the 1960s and 1970s ever-increasing mechanization left them redundant. In the 1980s, the occupation of canecutting was deleted from industrial awards.

It was once my privilege to spend a week in and around Innisfail with someone who had, fifty years earlier, helped to clear and plant the South Johnstone canefields, and then to harvest them.

Ray Jordana was born in Mataró, a manufacturing town in Catalonia, in 1909. Early, he lived with his family in France, where his father went to find work in an iron foundry. Then his father migrated to Australia in 1916, going first to Melbourne, where he learned that there was already a handful of Spanish at Innisfail, so that he travelled north and began to cultivate sugar-cane in partnership with another Catalan at Mena Creek. Meanwhile, his wife and son lived with her family in Spain, where he sent them letters describing how in Australia people might ride horses and keep chickens freely – facts which gave the young Ray, accustomed to the confines of industrial towns, potent images of plenty and freedom – 'the idea of things running wild and your having them was beautiful'.

In 1919, Jordana sent for his family. They took a ship from Spain, going east through the Mediterranean, down the Suez Canal to Columbo, on to Perth, then up the east coast via Adelaide, Melbourne, Sydney and Brisbane, with young Ray marvelling at the broadness of Australian streets after the narrow ways of Spanish towns. It was a strange journey for them. The food on board ship was good; there was the excitement as each new port came into view, but his mother, who suffered chronic ill health, was sick most of the way. Jordana met his family at Townsville, took them up to Mourilyan by a smaller boat, then out to Mena Creek by train and trolley car.

And there, lacking the commonplaces of shops in the street (food was delivered by carriers once a week) and a shared language, the Jordanas began their family life again. It had been his intention to return to Spain after a time; but with the arrival of his wife and son, and the birth of another son, Jordana decided to stay. He was helped to this decision by the experience of some neighbours who did return to Spain, only to be disappointed. As Ray later commented, 'it wasn't that the place had changed over there, they had changed'. He used an example from food to explain this observation. In Spain, steak was what his family had had on odd visits to Barcelona; at Innisfail it was available all the time: 'there was nothing else eaten but meat in North Queensland in those days'.

Ray's major immediate task was to learn English, which neither his parents nor their Spanish neighbours spoke. He went to school until he was fifteen, at first tramping along the tramlines for five kilometres, later riding a pony. He joined about twenty other children, including Spanish, German and Yugoslav, as well as Australian. He continued to educate himself after he left school, borrowing books from the local School of Arts, and taking correspondence subjects. He did so quite deliberately, for experience had already shown him that civil servants, bank managers and shop assistants were much more respectful to those who 'spoke the King's English and spoke it well'.

There was a pipsqueak of a bureaucrat of some kind, I think it was . . . it was an official office anyway, I don't remember what it was. We had to go up a set of stairs, and a little verandah and then you went into a queue there, and you passed by. And there were two or three . . . they might have been an Italian, a Greek, Maltese, who knows, a Yugoslav; they came in from all types, and all parts of Europe . . . there in front of me.

And this pipsqueak was being rude to them. Because they couldn't express themselves, sometimes they could not make themselves understood, and so on. I'm waiting in the queue, and we're advancing. And he was rude to every single one of them.

When it came to my turn, I produced the papers I had to produce there, and I asked him in very perfect English, would he mind perusing these. I forget the language I used for the purpose of conveying that, but it was absolutely academic English, you know. The bloke nearly stood up on his head. And brother did he treat me with courtesy from then on!

In 1924, Ray went to work for his father. Five years later, after the death of his mother, he left home, and went canecutting. The members of his gang cut an average of five to six tons per day, and were paid six to eight shillings per ton, for a daily income of about £2, which was about £12 per week, or £250 per season. The cane was usually not burnt, so that it was heavier, and cutting it was slower. They began work at five o'clock in the morning, and continued through the day for eight or nine hours, until exhausted. They worked in the rain. They competed with each other to see who would be the 'gun' cutter. Ray said later that no slave should ever have been asked to do that work: 'you could only do it for the slavery of self-interest – the accumulation of wealth'.

Jordana's point was that the money canecutters earned gave them the capital to become growers. As his father had done earlier, in 1934 he bought a farm near the Goondi mill; but he soon came to see that he was not experienced enough to succeed. In any case, he was restless. Earlier, he had spent off-seasons in Melbourne, where he knew Vance and Nettie Palmer and the radical lawyer Maurice Blackburn. In 1936 he sold his farm and moved south, living with the Blackburns. The group's outlook reinforced his own inclinations, and he went to Spain where he served in the Republican Army. When this was defeated in 1933, he escaped to France, was interned, then made his way back to Australia.

After a period of working for his father again, Jordana enlisted in the RAAF, training as an engineer. He married after the war, and took up a sugar farm at Silkwood. In 1953, he sold this, buying two banana plantations at Mission Beach, where he again laboured intensely. Then, in 1957, the family moved to Brisbane so that the children might continue their education, with Ray buying a newsagency. In later life, Ray revisited Spain several times. Interesting as he found these returns to be, they never caused him to doubt his identity as Australian – not necessarily in relationship to a particular place, such as Innisfail or Brisbane, but in relation to the country as a whole. He much preferred the openness of society here to the rigidities he experienced in Europe.

First Time in the Bush

Louisa Clifton

Louisa Clifton, daughter of a new settler at the model Western Australian town of Australind, spent her first night in Australia in a tent in the bush in 1841.

I must attempt before I lie down for the first time in the bush, to give you some description of the picturesque romantic scenes in which we are now engaged. We have just made our beds on the ground, arranged our tent for the night, and with the moon shining brightly through the canvas over head, solemn stillness reigning around, except when broken by the merry laugh of gentlemen encamped round a log fire, the chirping of the grasshoppers and now and then the breaking of a wave upon the distant shore. You may fancy Mary and myself kneeling at a table we have rigged up in the centre of our abode, alternately writing and talking over this strange page in our history.

Papa with a party of young men came hither this morning and left Mary and me to follow with a boat load of goods &c later in the day. Mr Eliot and Mr Stirling went on board the *Parkfield* just as we were going and insisted upon taking us up in their boat, a proposition we readily agreed to rather than commit ourselves to the care of Dr Carpenter. We sailed almost all the way up this beautiful estuary, under a sky of surpassing beauty, the heat intense and scarcely a breath of wind. On arriving, we found our tent erected and two or 3 others scattered about, on the slope of a deep declivity a few hundred yards from the waterside, commanding a lovely view, surrounded by beautiful trees, but in a state of charming confusion, the sand, ankle deep, almost the only floor.

Our kind friends Mr E. and S. insisted upon getting everything to rights. We all went to work under a scorching sun to cut rushes for the carpet, turned everything out; they then spread them, arranged this table which with a nice English cover gives an air of comfort to the apartment; put up books; in fact, in the course of an hour or two we found ourselves in order. Mrs Austen then kindly came from her settlement with a loaf of bread and cold meat, a most acceptable present after the labours of the day.

An immense fire of branches was soon lighted on the level ground a little distance below our tent, water boiled, and tea made, and having fortunately got up our plate chest containing knives and forks, teacups &c, we sat down to a welcome repast, and with more comfort than we could have imagined possible. I wish you could have seen the interior of our new abode, some sitting on the ground, others on our mattresses rolled up; I making tea upon a gun case seated on a hassock in the midst. By degrees all the young men collected to this centre of comfort and sociability. I forgot to describe in due order a scene which amused us vastly. While we were engaged within, we found the Government Resident, the magistrate of the district, Mr Eliot and Mr Gibson, hard at work without, kneading dough to make damper, in other words, unleavened bread, which has since been baked in wood ashes, and promises to do justice to the skill of the manufacturers.

I cannot describe half of the amusing and curious incidents of the day nor convey to your mind an adequate idea of the picturesque appearance of a bush encampment in such a climate and with such scenery on all sides. Papa and Mr Plowes have a tent; Mr Eliot and Stirling and many others are by this time reposing on the bare ground, wrapped in blankets by the side of a large fire. We have just made our beds and are so completely tired that we are longing to lie down in them. The nights are extremely cold and we are beginning to feel very chilly, and the sand underneath strikes damp and cold. Mama, Ellen and all the party are to come up on Wednesday.

I find myself involuntarily providing against the motion of the sea, altho' we have been almost entirely at rest for the last fortnight. The delight of feeling still, relieved of the burden of preparation against pitching and rolling and a thousand other charms in being on terra firma again compensates most fully for the personal exertions which will be required for some months to come; and then the indescribable blessing of not going to Port Grey. I feel a sensation of 'home' in this place; civilization is partly known. There are only 3 or 4 settlers, but there is the truest hospitality and kindness, and instead of being out of the reach of any human beings, we here at once meet with a hearty welcome and with ready assistance and co-operation. I cannot tell you how truly kind Mr E. and S. have been. The former is a very agreeable gentlemanly man, and the latter is most pleasing, and tho' a colonist not less the gentleman. All is hushed and still and I must to my rest as we are to be up at 5 in the morning.

An Old, Old Country

Douglas Stewart

The weight of the centuries pressing on an old, old country is felt by Douglas Stewart on a fishing trip at Brindabella in the southern highlands of New South Wales.

All was quiet, and rustic, and as civilized as a farm may be. But there was really no subduing the wildness of Brindabella.

The lean stockman brought down a mob of cattle from the snow leases, and all night long they roared and bellowed and groaned around the homestead, speaking of snow and darkness, the granite peaks and the high bush and tussocky uplands where the dogger set his traps for the dingoes. I suppose the cattle were being branded, or the calves were being separated from the cows. They made the most fearful uproar.

In the dining room at night, thunderstorms came in and rang the telephone. Even in the shack – sorry, the 'chalet' – even in the chalet on those sunny mornings when silver light came streaming through the chinks in the ceiling and we lay luxuriously in bed drinking Mr Bluett's tea, there used to be, regularly, a display of singular – and oddly beautiful – ferocity. It was given by a little grey bird that flew in and hunted around the undersides of the shingles for moths that had settled there during the night. It would seize on one of these great furry insects, half as big as itself, and, furiously struggling to devour it, batter it to pieces on the dressing table. Specks of moth-fur, moth-dust, moth-motes, floated up glinting in the silver light.

It was from the shack, too, through the big window that opened onto the great bald slab of granite across the river, that I watched one morning the magpies taking toboggan rides down a gum-tree. It was a day of flying storms and sun-showers. The gum-tree hung great bunches of shining wet leaves in the light. And down these bunches of leaves, from the tree-top almost to the ground, the magpies glissaded one after another in turn, like skiers on a snow-slope or boys on a muddy hillside. Four or five of them, glossy black and glittering white, were rollicking in the game. They filled the whole morning with their delight.

Beyond them towered the mountains. I have never, elsewhere in Australia, felt that impression of the extreme antiquity of the land which so many people have recorded; but here at Brindabella, and particularly when looking at that grey granite bluff across the river from the shack, I did indeed feel the weight of the centuries. It was something to do with the bulk of that great bluff, like the back of an elephant, a mammoth more likely, curving above the tree-tops; and its greyness; its stoniness; its smoothness. It intruded among the trees like a living creature; but a creature of stone, patient, immobile, worn smooth. It was old, old, worn-down country . . . and, thinking of the rabbitter and old Bob, the lair of old, worn-down people.

Wee-loo, wee-loo, wailed the black cockatoos, crying out their ancient aboriginal name as they flew overhead down the river. They were that exotic bird the funereal cockatoo, rare and shy; very big, quite startlingly so; very black, with yellow feathers under their wings and tails; and that long-drawn, wailing cry, forlorn and frightening . . .

The stream itself was a wild little creature, the loveliest and wildest of them all; crystal and silver in the sunlight, dark under the granite in the gorges, green and yellow in the pools with the reflections of the wattles and the ribbony-gums; fierce as a snake in its sharp and frequent floods. In the valley it ran sparkling under willows. Bubbling over rocks and shingle, moving in that ever-enticing progression of rapid and run and pool, rapid and run and pool, sinuous, lithe and musical as it hurried down out of the mountains, it was the very model of a trout-stream . . .

The small, just undersized fish we caught had often had a curiously weazened appearance; dark, shrivelled, *old*-looking. They were, very likely, fully matured fish; old men of Brindabella who, in that clear swift rocky-bottomed stream, had never had enough tadpoles and yabbies and all the teeming life of quieter waters to fatten them. Just once, away downstream from Bluett's near where the old quince-trees grew in the clear paddock, I saw a big fellow. Far across a wide pool and under the screen of a weeping willow, quite out of reach of a cast, he floated in liquid sunlight, showing his rosy side as he swam lazily into the green depths. He was the most superb three-pounder. Two- pounder? Four-pounder? He was the lord of the mountains, the one big fish of Brindabella; and, so well was he protected by the width of the pool and the tangle of willow and tea-tree on the bank under which he cruised, I suppose he is there to this day.

A Bishop's View of
Bullock Driving

E.H. Burgmann

E.H. Burgmann came from a German immigrant background and was the son of a timbergetter, bullock driver and dairy farmer in the Taree district of New South Wales. In his country churchman's garb, he gave some advice on a bogged cart to some unbelieving bullockies.

Among other things my father at times drove a bullock team. I must resist the temptation to tell of the excitement of breaking-in young bullocks, but in that also my father and I worked together with complete understanding and efficient co-operation. His standards were high and to win his praise gave me great satisfaction.

As soon as I was tall enough to lean over one bullock's neck and reach the bullock on the other side with a bow, I learned how to yoke up a team. I never really graduated as a bullock-driver, although I did much work with them and occasionally took over the team for a while. Bullock-driving is a difficult art and very few men make really good drivers. A team knows when it is being handled by a new-chum, and few things are more terrifying than a team of sixteen bullocks that is getting out of hand.

On the other hand, to see the artist stretch out the team for a stiff pull is a great sight. Every bullock is brought firmly into the yoke; he stands at the 'ready', and the pressure is increased till every bullock in the team is set for the pull. The whip plays lightly beside any beast that hasn't fully got his mind on the matter, but no bullock is really hit. Then, when all is set, the signal is given in the driver's own way. Every ounce of strength in the team is exerted to the uttermost at the same moment. It is a stubborn load which doesn't move, and the good driver seldom asks his team to do the impossible.

The driver who can handle his team in this way has attained a degree as difficult of achievement as any ever conferred by the world's great universities. Supreme artists are rare among bullock-drivers and elsewhere. Most are just pedestrians who carry on. But I have seen a great artist who drove bullocks superbly – and didn't swear . . .

I remember, years after, when I became a parson, falling in with two bullock teams hopelessly bogged. I saw at once that they were asking their teams to do an impossible thing. It was an up-hill pull and the wheels were sinking deeper every time they moved at all. I got off my horse and asked if I could help. I was not made to feel particularly welcome and I knew very well how the presence of a parson could cramp a bullock-driver's style; but I quietly got a stick and kept the polers and pin bullocks up to their job.

Then I ventured to suggest some different methods. I knew I had to work tactfully. The fellows tried to be civil, but I knew they wished me far away. However, I was on my own ground, even if they didn't know it. As their efforts proved more and more hopeless, they showed signs of being ready to listen. By this time I had worked out a solution. I told them to pull the load back down the hill, leaving enough bullocks in front to keep the pole of the front truck straight. Once this was done and hard ground regained, the holes they were in could be avoided. My plan was at length accepted and I directed the doings.

In a very short time all was well and I rode off quickly to make up for lost time.

A day or two later the drivers turned up at church. They remarked to a friend, 'That b—— parson knows more about bullock-driving than we know ourselves.' I had probably been trained in a much rougher school.

In a Wet Season

Henry Lawson

*Henry Lawson takes a train journey from Bourke to Sydney,
through the 'long, long agony of scrub and wire fence'.*

It was raining – 'general rain'.

The train left Bourke, and then there began the long, long agony
of scrub and wire fence, with here and there a natural clearing, which
seemed even more dismal than the funereal 'timber' itself. The only
thing which might seem in keeping with one of these soddened flats
would be the ghost of a funeral – a city funeral with plain hearse and
string of cabs – going very slowly across from the scrub on one side to
the scrub on the other. Sky like a wet, grey blanket; plains like dead
seas, save for the tufts of coarse grass sticking up out of the water; scrub
indescribably dismal – everything damp, dark, and unspeakably dreary.

Somewhere along here we saw a swagman's camp – a square of
calico stretched across a horizontal stick, some rags steaming on
another stick in front of a fire, and two billies to the leeward of the
blaze. We knew by instinct that there was a piece of beef in the larger
one. Small, hopeless-looking man standing with his back to the fire,
with his hands behind him, watching the train; also, a damp, sorry-
looking dingo warming itself and shivering by the fire. The rain had
held up for a while. We saw two or three similar camps further on,
forming a temporary suburb of Byrock.

The population was on the platform in old overcoats and damp, soft felt hats; one trooper in a waterproof. The population looked cheerfully and patiently dismal. The local push had evidently turned up to see off some fair enslavers from the city, who had been up-country for the cheque season, now over. They got into another carriage. We were glad when the bell rang.

The rain recommenced. We saw another swagman about a mile on struggling away from the town, through mud and water. He did not seem to have heart enough to bother about trying to avoid the worst mud-holes. There was a low-spirited dingo at his heels, whose sole object in life was seemingly to keep his front paws in his master's last footprint. The traveller's body was bent well forward from the hips up; his long arms – about six inches through his coat sleeves – hung by his sides like the arms of a dummy, with a billy at the end of one and a bag at the end of the other; but his head was thrown back against the top end of the swag, his hat-brim rolled up in front, and we saw a ghastly, beardless face which turned neither to the right nor the left as the train passed him.

After a long while we closed our book, and, looking through the window, saw a hawker's turn-out which was too sorrowful for description.

We looked out again while the train was going slowly, and saw a teamster's camp: three or four waggons covered with tarpaulins which hung down in the mud all round and suggested death. A long, narrow man, in a long, narrow, shoddy overcoat and a damp felt hat, was walking quickly along the road past the camp. A sort of cattle-dog glided silently and swiftly out from under a waggon, 'heeled' the man, and slithered back without explaining. Here the scene vanished.

We remember stopping – for an age it seemed – at half-a-dozen straggling shanties on a flat of mud and water. There was a rotten weatherboard pub, with a low, dripping verandah, and three wretchedly forlorn horses hanging, in the rain, to a post outside. We saw no more, but we knew that there were several apologies for men hanging about the rickety bar inside – or round the parlour fire. Streams of cold, clay-coloured water ran in all directions, cutting fresh gutters, and raising a yeasty froth whenever the water fell a few inches. As we left, we saw a big man in an overcoat riding across a culvert; the tails of the coat spread over the horse's rump, and almost hid it. In fancy still we saw him – hanging up his weary, hungry, little horse in the rain, and swaggering into the bar; and we almost heard someone say, in a drawling tone: ''ello, Tom! 'Ow are yer poppin' up?'

The train stopped (for about a year) within a mile of the next station. Trucking-yards in the foreground, like any other trucking-yards along the line; they looked drearier than usual, because the rain had darkened the posts and rails. Small plain beyond, covered with water and tufts of grass. The inevitable, God-forgotten 'timber', black in the distance; dull, grey sky and misty rain over all. A small, dark-looking flock of sheep was crawling slowly in across the flat from the unknown, with three men on horseback zig-zagging patiently behind. The horses just moved – that was all. One man wore an oilskin, one an old tweed overcoat, and the third had a three-bushel bag over his head and shoulders.

Had we returned an hour later, we should have seen the sheep huddled together in a corner of the yards, and the three horses hanging up outside the local shanty.

We stayed at Nyngan – which place we refrain from sketching – for a few hours, because the five trucks of cattle of which we were in charge were shunted there, to be taken on by a very subsequent goods train. The Government allows one man to every five trucks in a cattle-train. We shall pay our fare next time, even if we have not a shilling left over and above. We had haunted local influence at Comanavadrink, for two long, anxious, heart-breaking weeks ere we got the pass; and we had put up with all the indignities, the humilia-tion – in short, had suffered all that poor devils suffer whilst besieging Local Influence. We only thought of escaping from the bush.

The pass said that we were John Smith, drover, and that we were available for return by ordinary passenger-train within two days, we think – or words in that direction. Which didn't interest us. We might have given the pass away to an unemployed in Orange, who wanted to go Out Back, and who begged for it with tears in his eyes; but we didn't like to injure a poor fool who never injured us – who was an entire stranger to us. He didn't know what Out Back meant.

Local Influence had given us a kind of note of introduction to be delivered to the cattle-agent at the yards that morning; but the agent was not there – only two of his satellites, a cockney colonial-experience man, and a scrub-town clerk, both of whom we kindly ignore. We got on without the note, and at Orange we amused ourself by reading it. It said:

'Dear Old Man, – Please send this beggar on; and I hope he'll be landed safely at Orange – or – or wherever the cattle go. – Yours, – .

We had been led to believe that the bullocks were going to Syd-ney. We took no further interest in those cattle.

After Nyngan the bush grew darker and drearier, and the plains more like ghastly oceans; and here and there the 'dominant note of Australian scenery' was accentuated, as it were, by naked, white, ringbarked trees standing in the water and haunting the ghostly surroundings.

We spent that night in a passenger compartment of a van which had been originally attached to old No. 1 engine. There was only one damp cushion in the whole concern. We lent that to a lady who travelled for a few hours in the other half of the next compartment. The seats were about nine inches wide and sloped in at a sharp angle to the bare matchboard wall, with a bead on the outer edge; and as the cracks had become well caulked with the grease and dirt of generations, they held several gallons of water each. We scuttled one, rolled ourself in a rug, and tried to sleep; but all night long overcoated and comfortered bushmen would get in, let down all the windows, and then get out again at the next station. Then we would wake up frozen and shut the windows.

We dozed off again, and woke at daylight, and recognised the ridgy gum-country between Dubbo and Orange. It didn't look any drearier than the country further west – because it couldn't. There is scarcely a part of the country out west which looks less inviting or more horrible than any other part.

The weather cleared, and we had sunlight for Orange, Bathurst, the Blue Mountains, and Sydney. They deserve it; also as much rain as they need.

The Rising of the Fish

Eric Rolls

The phenomenon of the rising of fish from the depths of the Namoi River, New South Wales, was described by Eric Rolls in his book The River.

I was astonished to find that the river had risen a foot or so. Perhaps I was already too late for good fishing. The water was very muddy. There were several cars on the other bank and people walking along looking expectantly at the water. I saw someone I knew.

'What's going on ?'

'The fish are coming up.'

'Where did the water come from?'

'There were storms on the Mooki. It's running a banker. Cox's Creek is pretty high. Your road is cut.'

The Mooki was a river which joined the Namoi at Gunnedah, about forty miles upstream. Cox's Creek joined the Namoi much nearer. It was the first time that the river had surprised us without warning. We usually knew for days when the road would go under water. The storms had been heavy and not reported because it had not rained in the towns. All the cultivation land in the watershed had been ploughed for winter crops and run-off had been fast.

Cars continued to arrive. Newcomers called out to those already on the river.

'Any up yet?'

'Not yet. Be an hour or so yet.'

'River's coming fast.'

'You ought to see it a few miles up. Water's like soup and there's a line of people on each bank pulling out fish as hard as they can.'

'They reckon they took away utility-loads at Gunnedah.'

'Did'ya hear about the cod old Jack Stripes and his missus had a go at. His missus saw it first. It was swimmin' along in shallow water. She gives a hoy to Jack and goes in after it. Wraps her arms around it and it just keeps swimmin'. So old Jack goes in too. He grabs it on the other side and the cod just pulls 'em both along. Then it kicks out into deep water and just dives outa their arms.'

The rumours were coming ahead of the fish. I ran to the Land-Rover and drove home for gaffs, bags and the family. 'Come on! Come on! The fish are coming up.' A neighbour's son had called in so he came running too.

The river had risen another foot in the half-hour or so since I left it. The water looked as thick as cream. It slid along rather than flowed. The colour was light sandy, not the usual dark red of flood water. And something was happening.

Along the edge of the water there was a crust of shrimps. Some were dead; most were alive. They were massed together a foot wide and several inches deep. It gave the impression that the water was folded back like a blanket. Then up through the mass of shrimps the more powerful yabbies began to force themselves. There were all sizes: small brown ones no bigger than the shrimps, bigger ones blue-backed and blue-clawed; and here and there huge ones, bigger than we knew existed, with foot long whiskers and black claws six inches long. The biggest all came up the same way. First the pincers poked up out of the shrimps. They opened and shut as though the yabbies were grasping the air. Then there was an upheaval among the shrimps and the black heads lifted clear with whiskers trailing. Pincers came down and pressed against the shrimps to keep the yabbies propped clear. Sometimes a claw picked up a shrimp, crushed it in halves and dropped the halves. There seemed to be no purpose in the movement. The claws were made to seize and crush and they seemed to act without direction – automatic pincers which opened and closed when they were touched. The yabbies' eyes looked crueller than their claws. They were as pitiless as shiny black beads.

It took longer for the fish to come up. We walked along slowly watching. Then we saw the occasional nose of a fish break the surface behind the shrimps, gulp air and withdraw.

Men on the other side patrolled too. They carried a strange assortment of tools – rakes, shovels, pick-handles, an occasional gaff, wire hooks, nets. One man with a rake saw the nose of a fish. His rake splashed into the water; there was a flurry of water and shrimps as he raked. No fish came up. He raked again. No fish. A few yards farther on he tried again. He lifted the rake so high in his excitement the fish was gone before the rake hit the water. A boy made a grab with his hands, missed, and nearly fell into the river. Then someone hooked a big catfish through the gills. He held it up to show us.

There was no one but ourselves on our side of the river, since the road to town was under water. Water rats sat out on the bank untroubled by us as we moved quietly. Turtles pushed ashore through the shrimps. Then the water grew suddenly muddier and all together the fish came up, thousands of them, and lined up behind the shrimps. Their mouths poked out of the water gasping and that was all we could see. We knew which species and what size they were by the shape of their mouths. In places big catfish rested shoulder to shoulder. We had never believed that there were so many fish in the river.

Bushman Junior

Edward S. Sorenson

In his observant and witty Life in the Australian Backblocks, *Edward S. Sorenson turned his gaze on a 'ragtag' phenomenon of pioneering life – Bushman Junior.*

About the first thing that impresses itself upon the stranger when he makes a casual call at a far-back bush home is the animal-like habits of the younger children. They cling to the skirts of the rough-shod, sunburnt woman, stealing timid glances from behind her, and nudging and whispering to one another between whiles. The bigger ones are inside, peeping through the cracks or round the doorpost; and, looking round suddenly, the stranger might notice a smudgy face pop down behind a bush some twenty yards away, and another withdraw hurriedly behind the trunk of a tree. These are a couple who had been too far away when the alarm was given that 'Somebody's coming', and hadn't time to come in. They are often scattered about the bush along the creeks and water-holes, and particularly in scrubs, ever hunting like Aborigines; but when the mother bangs a tin dish with a stick, or coo-ees for dinner, or the moment the alarm of 'Somebody's coming!' is raised, they rush for the house as fowls run in for protection when menaced by hawks. This class is almost as wild as kangaroos; but others treat strangers and everything else with a stolid indifference.

Their clothing is of the scantiest, mostly ornamented with a host of patches, and ragged at that. 'Anything does for the bush', the mother tells you. When you see them playing possum in the trees, and sliding down the straight poles, you quite agree with her that anything does. Hats, which have no longer any definite division between crown and brim, are worn till the head wears right through, and what remains drops round the neck; they are then patched with calico, bagging, or wallaby skin, and made 'as good as new'. Clothes last a long time in the bush. And boots? Look at the hard, blackened, prehensile-toed feet, scored with hundreds of lines and cracks that only the scrubbing brush can clean, and you will know they are strangers to boots. Indeed, some of them are twelve or fourteen years old before their feet are encased in their first leather coverings. You will notice one with a roll of dirty rag round the toe, tied on with a piece of twine or a wisp of kurrajong bark; another has a thorn in his foot, and limps on his heel; while a third has a daub of tar on his instep where there is a cracked sore. The soles of their feet are seldom pierced or bruised; they can race unflinchingly over rocks, and even walk over a bed of bindy-eyes. The sun never affects them, even though they are running about bareheaded in the heat of a midsummer's day; it only browns them. When naked, these children present a comical appearance, their bodies being white, while their legs, arms, necks and faces are severely tanned.

Their food is plain, even rough, and very little varied. They augment it with much that grows around them; fruit they get occasionally in the scrubs and, like the wild birds, they have a fine, discriminating sense of what is edible and what is poisonous. They hunt for birds' eggs, and they root turtle-eggs out of the sand and roast them in hot ashes. They climb to enormous heights after young birds and possums, and are skilled in all the native methods of catching fish. They bathe at all hours of the day; the dwellers along the rivers are almost amphibious.

In the great humming gum bush that is veined by coastal rivers, childhood is spent under the most pleasant and favourable conditions.

Winter is the hardest time for these little folk. At night they gather round the big fireplace, squatting in the ashes, and squabbling for choice places, while keeping a begrudging eye on the scanty wood pile. Their own little arms have to carry the sticks during the day; at best they have a horse and slide to draw it, or a box-cart drawn by a couple of goats. This, of course, is a boy's delight no matter where he is situated. Where goat races are held annually, their joy in training Billy and riding him in the Overland Cup is supreme. Here is a country paper's description of a billy-goat race which happened out Mackay (Queensland) way in July 1903:

> There were six entries – Barton, Kingston, Lyne, Deakin, Bamford and Glassey. There was some trouble in getting a fair start. Barton, a fine, fat goat of the angora type, appeared to require all the track. This Lyne resented, horns being freely used. Bamford, a jet-black animal, was hopelessly outclassed. Kingston, a fine grey goat, should have made the pace warmer, but he got at the clothes-line the night previous and gorged himself with a baby's flannelette night-dress. Glassey made a hard fight, but his horns appeared to be always in the way. A protest was lodged against Barton for wilful jostling, but after an exhaustive inquiry the committee disallowed it.

Hard-worked, horny-handed little mites they are, most of them, whose knowledge is of cattle and horses, of reptiles, beetles, birds and animals, and their home and playground the trackless bush. They master the secrets and mysteries of life at an early age through constant association with the native fauna, flock and herd, and hearing the talk of their elders. Their most admirable traits are their homeliness, courage, self-reliance and mateship.

They can ride almost as soon as they can walk. You will see a little mite throw the bridle-rein over the neck of a big horse, and lead him thus to a log or stump, and there put on the bridle and mount; and presently you will see him cantering bareback across the hills. I noticed a little fellow one day trying to mount a rogue. Time after time he brought him side-on to a log, and each time as he prepared to cross his back the old horse sidled away so that he stood at right angles to the log. At last the boy led him into a fork where he couldn't sidle away, and triumphantly mounted.

It is surprising how soon these children learn the bush, what clever little heads they have for working out the problems of their timbered world. I have met them, boys and girls, riding along mountain spurs, miles away from home, looking for cattle. And if you ask them at any time in what direction home lies, no matter how they have turned and twisted during the day, they will at once point to it like a compass. Fences do not stop them from going as straight as the crow flies either; they strap down the wires, with a stick across for the horse to see, and lead or ride him over. Rail fences give a little trouble; but when a loose top rail is found, they jump their cuddies over the bottom one. They can describe a beast minutely, even to a single white spot at the tip of its tail, or a tiny black streak on its off-side horn. They can recognise a beast or a horse at sight, though they may not have seen it for a couple of years or more; and they have a wonderful memory for brands and earmarks. Though they may be otherwise illiterate, they will squat on the road, and with a stick faultlessly portray the brands and earmarks of every station and selection for miles around them.

I was one day travelling towards Bourke with a mob of Queensland cattle when a boy rode up and asked me where they were from. I named a squattage south of the border. He grinned.

'You can't stuff me with that', he said. 'Them's Queensland brands.'

'How do you know a Queensland brand from a New South Wales brand?' I asked him.

'Why', he said, 'a Queensland brand has letters an' a number; New South Wales brands ain't got no number.'

Another day I was trying to catch up to a man who was riding a day in front of me, and asked a boy at a wayside hut if he had seen him pass. He didn't remember him according to my descriptions; but he had seen a person go by wearing a straw hat and riding a brown horse branded H.P., with a star on its forehead, off-white fetlock, and carrying its tail a little aside as though it had been broken, and it had cast its near fore-shoe. This was correct in every particular; yet that boy had never seen the horse before in his life, and had just leaned lazily on a rail as it was ridden past him.

In regard to ordinary school tasks they are poor scholars, principally through lack of opportunity. The bush school is often a small, isolated building standing among the trees, with no fence around it and no house in sight of it. But little tracks, winding through the bush in many directions, show where the children come from. Some of them walk four or five miles to school, starting away at daylight on winter mornings, and returning in the twilight or after dark. When the grass is white with frost or wet with dew, or when rains have left pools and sheets of surface water along the track and set the creeks and gullies running, the bush kiddies carry their boots in their hands or over their shoulders to keep them dry, putting them on when they reach the school. In the dry interior regions, besides the usual dinner-bags and books, they carry bottles and water-bags. They get over rivers in flat-bottomed punts, and any creek that is too deep to ford is crossed on the trunk of a tree that has been felled across from bank to bank; they pass through mobs of half-wild cattle, and at times through miles of burnt and burning grass; but they very seldom come to any harm. Some drive to and fro in light traps; others ride – at times three and four on a horse – and have races, jumping contests over logs, humiliating busters, and all sorts of adventures along the road. Many a coat is peeled off on the school track, too, and many a punched nose goes bleeding to the water-hole. Frequently half a dozen are seen running through the bush, the big ones in front, the little ones, flushed and panting, in the rear. They have been playing on the road, or have started late, and are making up for it. Some have to run part of the way home, so as to be in time to put the calves up or to change their clothes and carry an armful of wood or a bucket of water for the morning; and if they live on a farm they have to join the parents after tea in the barn, husking corn. Preparing for examination under these circumstances is pretty stiff work for Bushman Junior.

Like his elders, the budding bushman shows commendable grit and extraordinary endurance under trying circumstances. Out west of Broken Hill in October 1902, a boy named Barraclough, aged twelve, while riding alone in the bush, was thrown from his horse and broke his leg. He dragged himself along the ground until he obtained a forked stick and, using that as a crutch, he recovered his horse, which he mounted by pulling himself on by the mane. Then he rode twelve miles home, and was subsequently driven to White Cliffs, a long, rough journey, for medical treatment. Very young children sometimes wander away and get bushed, and these, too, show remarkable endurance. A little girl, named Evelyn Harris, two and a half years old, was lost in August 1902, near Bollon (Queensland), and was found the following day walking along Mitchell Road, having covered a distance of twenty miles. A two-and-a-half-year-old son of Chris Connors, of Packsaddle Bore, between Broken Hill and Milparinka, wandered among the mulga and sandhills from Thursday afternoon till Sunday afternoon in the bitter cold weather of June 1904. When discovered he was still trudging along, though pretty well done up from starvation and exposure. In August 1901, Linden Culnane, aged nine, and

Alfred Collins, aged seven, lost their way while rabbiting at Reno, near Gundagai, and wandered about the bush for thirty-six hours in bitterly cold and rainy weather. Eventually they reached a settler's hut on Cooba Creek, having travelled thirty miles. On the other hand, a little girl named Edith Liddle, aged two and a half years, was lost at Mulya, near Louth, some time in 1902, and no trace of her was ever found. Such a happening is among the most bitter experiences in bush life.

Perhaps the most remarkable thing about bush children is that they are very rarely bitten by snakes. They roam the day long about creeks and billabongs with bare feet and bare legs, playing in scrubs, wading through long grass and ferns, turning over bark and logs, thrusting their hands into hollows and burrows, and almost invariably come off unscathed. When I was going to school we used to think it fun to kill a snake by jumping on it. If it was a green or whip snake, one of us would pick it up quickly by the tail and, keeping it swinging around, chase the other children with it, finally cracking its head off with a sudden jerk. It is only in districts where snakes are rare that they are dreaded by children; where they are plentiful they are generally treated with contempt – except at night. The average bush youngster has a horror of darkness, and talks in awe-struck whispers of hairy men, ghosts and bunyips. This fear is inculcated from babyhood. The mother can't always be watching in a playground that is boundless, and she knows the horrors that wait the bushed youngster. So she tells them there is a bunyip in the lagoon, and gigantic eels in the creek; and beyond that hill there, and in yonder scrub, there is a 'bogey-man'. Those fairy tales keep the children within bounds – until they are old enough to know better. Then they can take care of themselves.

Storm over Ayers Rock

Richard Piesse

Uluru, previously known as Ayers Rock and one of the world's best known landmarks, is usually seen as a great red monolith, rising majestically from the plain and displaying its colours under the passage of the sun. Richard Piesse saw it in a dramatically different mood, underneath a rainstorm.

If you have not felt or smelled the soothing deliverance of solid rain for four years and, on top of that, another three years previous to those four, two tremendous deluges inside a few hours and within your region are more than enough news to fill the radio waves to you and to every anxious settler for 100 miles and more around.

So ran the tidings from Ayers Rock late in November, 1964: 'It's come!' Out of a cloudless sky, hundreds of miles over the limitless plain to the south, out of nowhere and almost in a flash, two whirling dust-storms-cum-rainstorms, several hours apart, gathered up the Rock in their midst and left it glistening and gurgling with the sound of falling waters.

Such an experience, unusual at any time, is even more strange for anyone who has seen the desert only under open skies in its accustomed mood of transcending silence. It left our small party, on whom the blessing descended, refreshed in body, elated in spirit and riding excitedly on the higher planes to which the experience of a traumatic natural event can rapidly lift the human mind.

First you are aware only that a vast swirling, mauve-and-yellow cloud of dust is bowling across the desert in your direction. Then, from the lee of the Rock and lulled into a false sense of security by the shelter of a car, you are aware that the sky above and around has been completely blotted out. As the gloom gathers, its purples and mauves and orange-browns grow more intense, and the wind begins to shriek; there comes to everyone an eerie feeling, a sensation of being about to witness the end of the world.

Then are vouchsafed the deliverance, the soothing wetness, the huge drops streaming down – the rainstorm itself. The airstrip is quickly a murky no-man's-land.

The road is a ditch of puddles, a flowing drain, a Venetian canal (with our car a stationary, stalled gondola), and then a river fed by a delta of creeks surging out from the Rock. They in turn are fed by a hundred waterfalls, cascading solid plumes of foam and spray thundering down several hundred feet from the lower bastions of this lonely fort. What a sight to gladden an explorer's heart!

An hour afterwards, with the car again able to move forward two miles or so out in the desert, you still ask the question 'Where's all this water coming from?' You cannot hear the waterfalls from this distance, but they continue to flow almost unabated. The wonder of it all is that the desert sands and the sunny skies would pretend no storm had passed this way at all.

From another angle, Ayers Rock, after the storm and bathed in sunlight, appears like a shimmering, silver-grey blanc mange that could easily wobble over.

Bathurst

D'Arcy Niland

Here is a marvellous evocation by novelist D'Arcy Niland of Australia's first inland city, Bathurst; of the characters, the incidents and the style it developed through its evolution from outpost, to boom town, to regional centre.

Bathurst itself was little more than a military outpost to start with, a government town of convicts and officials. The earliest settlers lived on the outskirts, because Macquarie's orders were that no private houses were to be built until the town site was properly surveyed. That's why you've got the wide streets to-day – space enough for a bullock wagon to turn with ease, as Macquarie wanted it. James Byrne Richards, a man with an eye for parks, gardens and squares, laid out Bathurst like a gridiron, finishing the work in 1833. He designed Melbourne after that. I've never seen Melbourne. They say it's not bad.

In the middle 'twenties some jokers organised the Bathurst Hunt. They decked themselves out in a scarlet frockcoat with black velvet facings, a buff waistcoat and white breeches and top boots and galloped after kangaroos and native dogs. Five quid a year it cost to join. Stupid cows, I don't know where they thought they were. Didn't last long, though, I'm glad to say. No place for that kind of pommy antics here.

All the time important expeditions based on Bathurst were going out in all directions – boots, and wheels, and boats charting the country and finding millions of acres of fertile land. The landtakers, driving their flocks and herds, followed. Wagons and drays piled with their worldly goods, that creeping civilisation trickled out into the interior in the wake of the explorers, squatted and built and did their own exploring. It wasn't easy, and the blacks and the bushrangers didn't help. There was a pitched battle between settlers and bushrangers at Bathurst, and they strung up ten or eleven outlaws in 1830 just near where the Tech is now in William Street. But there was no going back. We had this country by the throat then and nothing could stop its development. By 1851, Australia had 405,000 people and seventeen million sheep. The amount of wool exported had risen from 245 lb. in 1807 to something like thirty-six million lb. The wool industry was number one. But there was a labour shortage, and immigration was down to nothing, and the heads everywhere didn't seem to know what to do to help the one or the other. Then one single man, in that year, solved it all just with the shake of a tin dish.

Edward Hargraves, Mister Gold-dust himself – he found it right here at Ophir, and in they came in their hundreds of thousands from all over the world, swarming back even from California where they'd gone in '49. Hargraves had been one of them. At the Californian diggings, he noticed country that resembled areas around the Bathurst district, where he used to have a sheep station; and that's what brought him hurrying back to start prospecting. From Sydney to Bathurst, along the western highway – over the old trail blazed by Blaxland and Evans – they went to the diggings. All kinds, travelling every which way: walking, riding, in carts, in wagons, with wheelbarrows, without provisions and implements, some of them. Ship after crammed ship spewed them out on the quays. The Sydney shops were bursting with gear and equipment – blankets, tents, picks, pans, Wellington boots, moleskin trousers, Californian hats. Ships were without crews, office desks empty, farms left to the crows. It was the first of the great rushes. Victoria was losing its population; so they offered rewards and gold was discovered there, in place after place, that led to a fortune and the twenty-five-minute war at Eureka.

By 1861 our population had jumped to over a million. Victoria alone produced in those ten years gold worth £100 million. But, apart from bringing about a tremendous increase in the wealth and population of the country, the discovery of gold at Bathurst led to something else. Men made fortunes just washing dirt. But it was hard on others who saw nothing for their pains. Some among them became farmers, and some, the skilled workers looking for city jobs, were grabbed up by smart businessmen who started factories; so you can say the 'fifties saw the beginning of our secondary industries.

Bathurst became a municipality in 1862, the same year Cobb and Co. came there to set up headquarters that were to last for fifty years. Cobb and Co. was one of the greatest transport outfits the world has ever seen. They made their entrance to Bathurst like a royal circus troupe – a cavalcade of American coaches with leather springs, drawn by scores of mettlesome horses, with bearded and moustached whips driving. You could set your watch by Cobb and Co. They were fast and regular, with marvellous drivers. They not only coached gold from the fields; they tied the towns together all over inland Australia and put a network of red lines on the map. Night and day they ran. From Victoria to Queensland they harnessed 6000 horses a day, and covered 28,000 miles a week. Using relays of horses, they could make the 600-mile journey from Sydney to Melbourne in five days. Railways pushed them finally out to the backblocks and motor transport delivered the death blow. The last coach finished up in Queensland in 1924.

Ben Hall, the bushranger, was going strong in the 'sixties. I heard it said Hall wasn't a bad type at all, until his flirty wife ran out on him.

Then he took to the game. He made a daring raid on Bathurst in '63, that turned the town upside down with excitement. Not long after he captured Gold Commissioner Keightley and held him to ransom after Keightley had shot dead one of his men named Burke. Mrs Keightley had to drive like the wind of heaven to her father, twenty-five miles away, in Bathurst, to get the money and be back by a certain time. Five hundred pounds, it was. They made a great stageplay out of the affair. In 1865 Hall was betrayed by a Judas friend, and plugged with bullets. Thirty or more. He was twenty-eight years old. The friend got half of the £1000 reward money, and the police that did the killing the rest.

In 1885 Bathurst became a city, and just as if to mark the occasion Ben Chifley was born. He was reared in Bathurst, too, on his grandfather's farm at Limekilns, and he lived in Bathurst all his life. At twenty-four he was the youngest first-class engine driver in N.S.W. Chif was always mad about politics, and nobody around these parts was surprised when he ended up as Prime Minister of Australia in 1945. We lost a good 'un when he died six years later. In this town of memorials there are several to Ben Chifley, including the big dam and the humble home he lived in.

We've turned out other famous men, too. And we've had some notable visitors. Charles Darwin was one. And Lord Kitchener. He came to Bathurst in 1910 to unveil the South African war memorial. I saw that. Only a young fellow then. The memorial is at one end of King's Parade opposite that of Evans at the other. Kitchener denounced Breaker Morant for shooting Boer prisoners. There was another man who did the same thing. Lieutenant Handcock. He was accused of disgracing his city and his country by acts of criminal violence, and his name is the only one missing from the scroll of those who went from Bathurst and served in that war. It was deliberately left off. Both Morant and Handcock were executed after court martials, and are buried in Pretoria. You could get an argument in a pub any day about the rights and wrongs of it.

To-day there are 17,000 people in Bathurst, and it's full of business, commerce and prosperity. The State Government is the biggest boss. Wool and cattle are the backbone of the district. It's full of the old and the new, last century grafted on to this. You can see old Government House, built in 1817; or the modern carillon tower, red brick and 100 feet high, with its bells weighing from eighteen lb. to thirty-one cwt., the only one of its kind in Australia.

Yet I don't know. The trains come in, buses, planes, with their loads of people. I'm not sure whether they realise they're in Australia's first inland city and the third oldest settlement in the country. Or, if they do, whether they care. Tradition and history don't mean much to some people. They want to go to the pictures, have a cup of tea in a café, or snore off under the great elms in Machattie Park. Doesn't interest them to know it's on the site of the old jail – all those beautiful lawns and gardens, the begonia house and the swans' lake, where hate and brutality and suffering used to be.

A man's got it as modern as he wants it in Bathurst. He can go for a swim in the Olympic pool, to the night trots, to the greyhound track, to the motor races at Mount Panorama. He can get a job in a shoe factory, a flour mill, a vegetable cannery, a cordial factory or the railway workshops. He can even sing at the annual eisteddfod in October, if he's good enough! But he's got more than that. He's got a bit of early Australia to himself here. Does that matter? Well, I think it does, if you've got a feeling for history, which is only people, anyway, tumbling around each other like pebbles in a mixer. I stand at that door sometimes of an evening and look out and I think: Where have they all gone? I can see where I came from, born and bred in their tracks, and I'm real proud of them for what they were and what they did. Every time I go into town I go along and have a look at old

George Evans, and we have a bit of a think together. You know what happened to him, don't you? He became a bookseller in Sydney. He pioneered the business. I often wonder what made him take it up and become the kingpin of the trade.

Borroloola

Keith Willey

Veteran journalist Keith Willey had a lifelong love of movement which took him to far-flung places all around Australia, including a return to the outback gulf settlement of Borroloola, which he found 'still did not amount to much'.

The quaint gulf country township Borroloola may soon be swamped by mining developments, following discovery of a vast field of silver-lead and zinc on the McArthur River, about fifty miles away. Exploitation of the deposits, which have been assessed as 'richer than Mount Isa', could add a city of 20,000 people to the string of new towns springing up along Australia's northern coastline.

Borroloola is still about as quiet as you can get, with only three permanent residents, not counting welfare officers and Aborigines; but obviously great changes lie ahead. Development is expected to really 'go' by about 1970. Already more vehicles have passed over the couple of hundred miles of dirt track from Daly Waters in the past twelve months than in the previous fifty years. The mining boom will destroy Borroloola's isolation, ending its charm for the old-timers and bagmen, who have made it their camping-place since the Overland Telegraph Line went through to Darwin a century ago. In a way, it is the end of an era.

Most Australians have heard of the Borroloola Library. Many years ago a bushman, in Melbourne for a spree, met a V.I.P., who asked him what residents of the outpost needed most. 'Books,' he replied. In due course an entire Carnegie Grant library, hundreds of volumes, arrived by sea and was stored in the police station. Prisoners became omnivorous readers, and books circulated as far east as Charters Towers and west to Kimberley. The library has long since succumbed to white ants, but even to-day you are likely to be startled around lonely campfires in north Australia by erudite questions on Shakespeare or Marcus Aurelius. The late Bill Harney, incomparable raconteur and poet, boasted that he received his education in the Borroloola Library. He read every volume while serving a sentence in the police lock-up for duffing cattle.

'The Loo' consolidated its reputation between the wars, when it claimed the highest average age and the lowest birthrate of any town in the world – over seventy years, and 'not a damned white woman for 100 miles'. The residents were a colourful band, the most famous being Charles Scrutton, who had been second-in-charge of the Jardine expedition to Cape York with cattle in 1865. He died about 1928, aged near the century mark. While far on into the nineties, Scrutton still could chase a chicken for dinner, and draw a picture of himself which would have won a prize in a contemporary art show.

Then there was Tom Lynott and his brother, famous teamsters who pioneered the sites of many towns in north-west Queensland. One of these was Winton, where they made their camps during the 1870s, before F. C. Urquhart, balladist and 'black police' commander, took the first wheeled vehicle over the Selwyn Ranges and founded the fort at Urandangie. Stock-riding on McArthur River station in 1889, Tom turned up what may have been a link with the vanished explorer, Ludwig Leichhardt. He met a 'wild white man' wandering with Aborigines between the McArthur and the Roper. The man had long, fair hair and a beard. He was sick and partly crippled, and two old women were carrying him about. He replied to questions in a foreign language which Tom recognised as German, though he could not understand the words. Ever afterward he maintained that this was Classen, deputy leader of Ludwig Leichhardt's last expedition, which had disappeared more than forty years earlier while trying to cross Australia from east to west. Before any official move could be made to confirm the man's identity, stockmen intent on vengeance for a cattle-spearing foray raided the native camp. Among their scores of victims was the 'white blackfellow'.

Another famous Borroloola resident of years ago was Freddie Blitner, who fought many victorious duels with the Aborigines, using their own weapons of spear and waddy. Freddie was christened the 'Freshwater Admiral' when he attempted to launch an eighteen-foot crocodile one night in mistake for his dugout.

Roger Jose, a bearded patriarch who passed on a few years ago, was the last of the pre-war vintage. Roger married two Aboriginal sisters and lived with them for forty years in an upturned tank. Though he worked from time to time, mending fences, or repairing roads under government contract, he would take only minimum payments, as he refused to be bothered with income tax. He was a deep thinker, whose philosophy was: 'Man's riches are the fewness of his wants'. Roger claimed to be a nephew of Arthur Jose, the *Times* correspondent and Australian historian, and the son of a noted Dean of Adelaide, who had come to Australia as a surveyor, gone to China as a lay missionary, and ended up high in the church hierarchy of South Australia.

Of course, not all the characters were white. Outsiders might have dismissed Billy Hooker, who died recently, as just another old bush blackfellow, but in Aboriginal eyes he was Borroloola's Number One citizen. Billy was the celebrated rainmaker. About ten years ago he began a downpour which continued for weeks, flooding wurlies and gardens. Dripping Yanyula tribesmen berated Billy, who promised to stop the rain, but could not. Finally the infuriated natives hurled Billy, together with his sacred rain-stones, into the McArthur River. For four years after that Billy sulked alone in the bush, but he returned in triumph for the great rain-making war with Yellow Fred, which was to restore him to his pedestal. Billy had announced his retirement, and was in the process of selling his magic gear to Yellow Fred. But after getting hold of half the rain-making equipment, Fred refused to pay. Vowing to 'drown-im Borroloola' if necessary, Billy called on such a series of storms that Fred, shamed before his followers, left the district.

With many memories and stories of Borroloola in mind, I set out from Darwin recently to see what had happened to the old place during the three years I had been away from the Northern Territory. We drove south to Daly Waters, then cast for more than 200 miles over a rough dirt road. Ten years ago this was a track used, maybe, once or twice a month; but this time, in a five-hour journey, we saw three other vehicles, and the surface was broken and rutted by heavy transport.

As we drove along, plain turkeys, heavy birds with long necks and huge, staring eyes, ran into the brush, and then rose awkwardly to flap slowly away among the treetops. Once we disturbed a pack of dingoes trying to cut out a calf from a group of four cows. The dogs, big, rangy animals, had circled the little herd. The cows stood round the calf, facing outward. Now and then a dingo would dash in, trying to get under the lowered horns to nip at the cows' heels. If only they could break the circle and get the bigger beasts on the move, several of the dingoes would keep them going while the rest drove the calf off in another direction, where he could be killed at leisure. Whether they would have succeeded I do not know, but we broke up their little game with no damage done.

Borroloola, on the McArthur River, still did not amount to

much – a store; the abandoned pub crumbling to ruins in a grove of tamarinds and giant mango trees; an Aborigines' welfare station further up the McArthur, where an earnest schoolteacher is trying to teach the three R's to a few score happy-go-lucky Yanyula children; the Aborigines' camp on the far bank of the river, where Billy Hooker once held sway.

I asked at the store for Jack Mulholland, who generally 'sits down' at the old hotel site as a sort of unofficial caretaker. Jack is not so very old, but he retired from the world long ago. During the war he went bush from Tennant Creek in an ancient vehicle and stayed out in the desert for years, living on bush tucker and calling at stations rarely, when he felt like a yarn or needed something. He had taken with him every book he could find on radio, and ever afterward he has been an expert on the subject, able to fix any battered old wireless brought to him. Jack went up to Borroloola years ago and married an Aboriginal woman. Once he invited a visitor to dinner, adding: 'Of course, I'll have to ask the wife first.' The visitor, thinking Jack might be worried about how a stranger would react to sitting down with a lubra, assured him: 'I don't mind.'

'No,' Jack replied severely, 'but she might!'

I was disappointed to find that Jack was away, along with almost every other man in the district, including even the Johnson family, the hermits of Vanderlin Island, out in the Gulf. They were all working for Mount Isa Mines, the storekeeper informed me, 'on the silver-lead field'. That was the first I'd heard of the mining boom-to-be. The resident welfare officer, Tas Festing, had more to say about it, and I filled in the details at Mount Isa some time later. The company has a survey crew of sixty men on a mineral lease near the McArthur River, about fifty miles from Borroloola. Though assessed among the richest in the world, the ore body of zinc and silver-lead is complex, posing treatment problems. Samples have been sent to experts overseas for advice. If the problems are solved, Mount Isa Mines will spend up to $200 million on building a deepwater harbour on Port McArthur Island, at the mouth of the river: a railway running eighty miles from the mine to the coast, and causeways to the island. Detailed plans for these works exist already; dams to divert the river from the proposed open-cut; thus creating an artificial lake for boating and water ski-ing; a town which will spread over several islands in the Gulf of Carpentaria. The population will increase by about 1000 a year to an ultimate figure of more than 20,000. This should bring a market and some mild prosperity to surrounding cattle stations, which at present are among the most run-down in the north.

The Department of Works has earmarked large sums for improving the road from Daly Waters, and may build a more direct access route from the Barkly Highway. Tourism is a long way off, but as driving conditions improve, more visitors can be expected to trickle through, for Borroloola is widely famous as 'the end of the line'.

All this activity worries Harry Blumantels, the forty-one-year-old bearded Latvian crocodile shooter, who has assumed Roger Jose's old role as Borroloola's self-appointed welcomer and 'mayor'. 'Too many peoples,' he told me, shaking his head. 'Soon I must go far, f-a-a-a-r away, and find quieter place.' Harry fought with the Germans against Russia during World War II and came to Australia to find peace. After years as a crocodile shooter in Cape York Peninsula and remote parts of the Gulf of Carpentaria, he settled at Borroloola. When Roger Jose died, his sorrowing widow, Biddy, sold their strange residence, an upturned 25,000 gallon tank with holes cut in it for doors and windows, to Harry Blumantels for precisely £21/16/1½.

Why such an odd price? Harry shrugged. 'I want to include every kind of your funny Australian money,' he said, 'even the halfpenny.'

Cross-Country Caravan

Alan Marshall

In 1942, after writing humorous articles for AIF News, *Alan Marshall hit on the idea of taking a horse-drawn caravan around Victoria, collecting messages from country people for the men and boys at the war front. His evocation of the eventful life on the road with his wife, Olive, is interspersed with drama, such as the bogging of Millie, one of the horses.*

The road ran through flat country cracked into jigsaw puzzle designs. The surface crumbled when you walked on it. But the rain continued and the soft surface turned to a paste that clung to your boots and formed curved pads that weighted your feet like the lead soles of a diver.

Each morning the caravan left two parallel scars from its resting place to the road. The horses' hooves were caked with clay so that when they reached the metal they trotted in silence as if on a carpet.

Grey swamps lapped an horizon of ti-tree and scrub. Passing squalls of rain stung shadowed patches of water into an agitated leaping. The spiked reeds quivered and bent to wet gusts, gusts that drove upon our faces and made the horses tuck their heads low on their chests.

The days were ragged with flying clouds, gapped with sunshine that burst from patches of blue and shattered into a million raindrops that transformed the sombre droop of every branch.

The flat road was skirted by shallow pools and muddy flats. In the late afternoon we plodded on searching for one firm piece of ground on which to camp. Brimming drains fenced us to the road. The tired horses dropped to a walk. The treeless plain offered no shelter. At last, in desperation, we urged the horses through mud and water and came to rest on a stretch of gleamy clay as slippery and soft as grease.

With a nose-bag hanging from the head piece of each crutch and the end of a halter in each hand, I looked round for a place to tie the horses for the night. It had to be so situated that they could turn their backs to the wind.

Sometimes it meant a long walk to some low clump of dillon bush submerging a panel of a fence, or to a solitary she-oak singing in the wind. If it were early I hobbled them out for an hour or two, but it had been a bad season and there was very little grass for them to pick.

Before we retired for the night I refilled their nose-bags. With the light of my torch piercing a tunnel in the darkness I left the warm caravan and set off with a butt of chaff to where they were tethered.

They heard me coming and whinnied a welcome. I stayed with them a little while, feeling troubled that they should have to stand out there alone in the cold dark.

This feeling of responsibility for their comfort troubled Olive, also. Sometimes in the night when we were warm in bed and the caravan rocked to a gust of rain, she would say, 'I wonder how the horses are?' and I would grunt and wonder, too. Then we would lie in silence, listening to the wind and rain and experiencing, in every shudder of our caravan, the buffet sweeping on Jim and Millie in darkness. It was menacing to us and we imagined they felt this, too.

I had a spare pair of crutches with spikes instead of the usual rubber tips. They enabled me to walk on slippery ground without fear of falling. I often regretted the years I had been without them – a friend had made them specially for this trip – and I found a new delight in climbing slippery banks and traversing greasy stretches of clay, the feeling of safety in such places being new to me.

With the horses unharnessed and tossing heavy nose-bags in a search for oats, Kim and I wandered away on our evening walk. The rain driving parallel with the earth didn't worry us. These bleak places broken by swamps, these long stretches of lignum dappled with large, wind-swept areas across which the roley-poleys, born of summer, bounded like live things, fascinated me.

I brushed through dripping tussocks and pushed my way through the ti-tree skirting the flat water. Harsh cries of water-birds blended with the wind and rain. There was a constant flapping, the gurgle of feathered bodies skidding to a landing. Screeching plovers swept up from clumps of rushes and fought the wind that tossed them from gust to gust before they dived for the sheltering tussocks.

Black duck, circling in an evening flight, rocketed by, then banked, swooped and raced low over the water, going down wind in a speeding calm of their own making.

Kim plunged into thickets, scaring the water-hens into frenzied dashes for safer clumps. Their trailing legs furrowed the water of narrow leads and inspired him into desperate leaps to grab them.

We circled home and near the caravan a burst of wet sunlight broke through the clear band of sky resting on the horizon. I looked up at the marching clouds pitted with shadow. Flickering against the luminous bulge of their eastern fringe, a flock of birds moved into silhouette.

I yelled to Olive. She appeared at the caravan door.

'Look,' I cried, pointing.

She joined me and we watched a fleet of pelicans winging up wind like bombers on a mission. They sank lower to miss the unopposed wind of the sky and passed over the caravan in V formation. Their heads were tucked back to their shoulders, their heavy bills thrust forward like pikes. They flapped a little, then soared a little. When their wings stopped beating they dropped like parachutes; then a few strokes and they would rise again. Their progress was a synchronised rising and falling, a victorious advance to the triumphant music of their wings.

Their passing saddened me. I was bound to the earth while they winged down a highway in a land of clouds.

I sent a wild, wind-borne 'Hoo-oo-oo' after them, then followed Olive in to dinner – Irish stew on blue plates, coffee in yellow cups standing on red saucers, a green tablecloth and a golden light from the pressure lamp that warmed the caravan and made the wind and rain an emphasis of the comfort we were enjoying.

Since our experience in being blown over we were apprehensive of wind that rocked the caravan.

'Is it safe, do you think?' asked Olive that night when the caravan rocked to a gust.

'Yes,' I murmured sleepily. 'It's blowing head-on,' but later I woke to a violent jerking as if the caravan had hiccups.

'What's that?' asked Olive, still not quite awake, but sitting upright in bed.

I got my torch and went out to investigate. Two wandering cows plunged away in the darkness. Our bag of chaff, stacked behind the driving seat, was pulled over and the chaff was trickling to the ground.

'Soolem!' I cried to Kim.

He tore away and I could hear the indignant cows galloping ahead of his furious barking. They troubled us no more that night.

One afternoon we drew in beneath a clump of tobacco bush growing on the edge of a wide irrigation channel not far from where the channel entered a lake.

It was cold and showery. I hobbled the horses and walked to the edge of the lake to see the birds. Swans rocked on the waves like anchored buoys. Further out dabchicks and teal appeared on crests then disappeared in the troughs so that the surface of the lake flickered with black dots as the birds rose and fell.

I wanted Olive to see them so I went back to get her. I glanced round for the horses when I approached the caravan. Jim was grazing quietly on the high bank of the channel, but Millie had disappeared. I walked on to the road and looked to right and left – no Millie.

I was astounded. She always grazed quite close to Jim. I climbed the bank and looked down at the water. There she was. The hobbles were strange to her and she had fallen head-first into the channel.

She was standing in water up to her shoulders, and was shivering violently. There was mud on her head, and her mane dripped water. She pricked her ears and looked at me as if I were the answer to a maiden's prayer. Her pendulous underlip was trembling as if she were about to cry.

I called Olive to see this latest 'last straw,' and we stood together on the bank and discussed what we should do, while Millie regarded us hopefully.

'There's only one way,' I said with despair. 'I'll have to strip off and dive down to unfasten those hobbles.'

I took off my coat and unbuttoned my shirt. A cold rain began to fall. I began to shiver like Millie.

'Let's try something else first,' said Olive hurriedly. 'Could we pull her out?'

'We could try,' I said. Anything was better than diving into that icy channel.

Olive got the halter and I looped it on to the end of one of my crutches. I reached out over the water and juggled the head piece over her ears and round her nose. She never moved. I drew it tight and we both took up a stand like a tug-of-war team on the mark. I thrust the ends of my crutches into the ground so they would not slip, then we began to pull.

Millie plunged and floundered. She fell sideways and we heaved so that she landed with her shoulder on the bank. She struggled with us as we continued our pull. Her hobbled legs came over the bank and she bounded out with such violence that she knocked my crutches from beneath me and I almost took her place in the channel.

Her other shoulder caught Olive, who was thrown to her hands and knees. But Millie was out and she stood very quietly till we got our feet again.

We made hurried enquiries after each other's condition, then turned our attention to Millie, who was almost rattling with the violence of her shivering.

'I'll run her up and down the road to warm her,' said Olive. 'We don't want her to get pneumonia.'

She ran to and fro past the caravan with Millie jogging behind her while I filled a nose-bag with chaff and got a water-proof rug from beneath the driving seat.

When Olive brought her back we covered her with bags then threw the rug across her back as an outer covering. We watched her eating, wondering whether her ducking would give her a cold.

'A horse,' I said learnedly, 'is more delicate than a cow.'

This profound statement didn't impress Olive and certainly didn't contribute anything to our treatment of Millie, but in some way it satisfied me.

A fortnight later we were fifty miles away, camped beneath a clump of belah trees, those trees that are never silent but sigh even when the air is still. They grew slowly and with difficulty from mallee sands that, in the summer time, are drained of all moisture by the hot sun.

In open spaces where the trees had been cut down the north winds had carried away the surface soil in the red dust-storms that darkened towns further south. The underlying sand, free to wander, moved across paddocks in rippled hills leaving scooped hollows and barren clay-pans behind them.

We often climbed these hills and looked down the steep lee side to where the vivid green barley grass was slowly being smothered. We trailed our fingers along the ridge and the whole steep surface of the hill flowed like water, spilling out between the grass stems and moving a tiny space further on its journey.

Trees in their path were buried till only the top limbs showed above the sand; fences disappeared; abandoned houses pressed back the flood that divided and moved round to meet again in allotments that once were gardens. Then the sand, banked up by the wind, climbed over the back roof and the house and hill were one.

Yet, stare at them as you might, the hills were always still. They moved without motion like clouds on a still day, though their day was a year and their movement a creep – earth clouds that obscured, not the sun, but things born of the sun.

One evening I walked from hill to hill reading stories from the tracks of the creatures that had passed that way. Here a fox had crept toward a clump of spinifex, here he had leapt into a run, but, now a rabbit's tracks stretched beside or merged with his own. Over the ridge they were lost in a patch of trampled sand from which the fox tracks continued alone.

I climbed a pine ridge and looked down into the wind-scooped hollow behind it. The uncovered skeletons of three Aborigines lay on the sand beneath me.

It was very still. I could not hear a bird. The day was empty of life, yet a breathing, a waiting, a listening was here.

I stood without movement, faced with countless eyes that watched me and waited.

I moved down the steep incline, my crutches sinking deep in the sand. There was only the sun and the sand and a belah tree and a guard of Murray pines.

The skeletons were of two adults and a child. They lay side by side, the child in the centre. Their heads faced the east, their arms were outflung as if they were tired and were resting there. I sat down beside them and lifted the skull of the child in my hands.

No barrier is as great as that between the living and the dead. All that I wanted to know I would never know – its name, why it had died so young, whether it had been happy.

Some Major Mitchell cockatoos flew by. They called as they passed, a sound the child must have known, too. I placed the skull back on the sand and went away, but after that I felt like an intruder in the country around their grave.

Birds and Snakes

Gordon Wentworth Broughton

In his Men of the Murray, *Gordon Wentworth Broughton gave an entrancing account of drama and sudden death among the birds along the Murray. The abundance of snakes led to some close shaves for his surveying party, and some macabre humour and the daily despatch of browns, kings and tigers.*

As we worked along our new river length the slowly rising flood waters broke out here and there through gaps in the banks and spread far out into the lignum swamps. Magically the wild fowl began to gather in thousands, coming in from the far Darling lakes as their waters slowly dried up. Squadrons of pelicans sailed majestically about, contending with dense flocks of ibis and spoonbills for frogs, lizards, centipedes, and all the ground life disturbed by the advancing flood waters. Black swans abounded, and we counted ten species of wild duck, including the awkward, lonely musk duck and the rare bluebill or 'spiney tail'. Black and white geese gathered in small flocks, their numbers vastly diminished from the time of the early settlers to whom they were familiar.

Busy among this concourse of larger birds were hundreds of whimbrels, avocets, stilts, plovers, sandpipers, and their kin, and in the reed beds, water hens, red legs, and bald coots scurried about. Very occasionally, too, if we crept quietly we would catch a glimpse of a shy landrail or spotted crake.

Round the fringes of the yellow waters herons and egrets stood in motionless dignity or suddenly struck downwards, impaling a frog or a small lizard.

Perched on logs or on the lower limbs of dead trees were the black shags and the black and white divers, enemies of the fishermen because of their vast appetite for small fish. High over all sailed dozens of swamp and duck hawks, sparrow hawks, and falcons, swooping, according to their size and kind, on tiger snakes, frogs, insects, ducks, shags, water rats or stranded fish. In these quiet waters there was silent but ferocious warfare between the birds of prey, the snakes, the rats, and stray goannas, all contending for the teeming life in and around the lignum swamps. In this battle the kookaburras played a bold part, with their brethren, the blue kingfishers fighting for insects and small fish.

On large patches of green swamp grass, beyond the flood water edges, snipe could be found. Tramping in leggings and sodden boots, I hunted these birds on occasional week-ends. Lack of a retrieving dog was a big handicap, causing much needless mileage in mud and slush. The birds would rise suddenly, whirr away in swift zigzag flight, then just as suddenly drop vertically into the dense swamp grass. It was good sport and great training for keenness of eye, most particularly in finding shot birds.

The black swans soon began nesting in the lignum-dotted waters, and frequently, when we were traversing a low bank where flood waters had spread far out among the lignum, I would turn the telescope of the theodolite across the swamp and pick out a swan's nest, with one bird sitting quietly on it, and the other feeding near by.

All this bird, reptile, and insect life, with its drama of hunting and sudden death, was a fascinating study to us who lived so intimately among it. As the men and I worked along the traverse lines we would sometimes hear a sudden frantic rush of wings overhead, and then, seconds later, a dozen or more terrified black shags, wings closely folded, would plummet into the river like stones and disappear. A duck hawk, high above, had hurtled down on the flying shags. If the hawk made a strike in mid-air he would sweep away clutching his victim, but sometimes the shags hit the water just in time. It was then that the hawk, suddenly braking with outspread wings at the very surface of the water, twisted his tail fan-like, and with an incredible exhibition of aerial acrobatics skimmed away with dry wings. After missing his strike, the hawk would sometimes land on a dry tree near by and sit there with head lowered and feathers ruffled, seemingly disgusted with his abortive effort.

On odd Sundays the men and I would go snake hunting, armed with slender green pliable sticks, or four-foot lengths of doubled fencing wire. The tiger snakes, which swarmed on the little flood 'islands' in the swamps, never came forward and attacked us, but lay still, watching our movements. It was unwise to approach them from behind, for they could throw themselves back and strike, so we walked up to them head-on, then suddenly broke their backs with the wire or willowy stick. One day we met a really savage – and frightened – tiger snake bailed up in the hollow butt of a big river gum, where he had been resting when we walked round the tree. He lashed about in fury but would not come out, and we left him master of the situation.

At one of my future camps near Pental Island, above Swan Hill, two of my men, left camp-caretaking while I was on leave, killed ninety tiger snakes in a little over two weeks. At that time there was a temporary revival in the snake skin fashion for women's shoes, and the men sold their skins to a Swan Hill buyer for a good price. Pental Island, about sixteen miles long by one to two miles wide, lies between the Murray and the Marraboor billabong in Victoria, and in those days was notorious for its snake life.

As we worked along the river bank among the coarse dry grass, the men sometimes played a trick on me which never failed. Intent on field notes or on sighting behind and ahead, measuring angles, I would hear a sudden hissing rustle in the grass at my feet. Bounding in the air, by reflex action, I returned to earth fervently hoping that the snake beneath me had wriggled far enough away not to strike me as I landed. Then I would become aware of the stony face of the man nearest me, and the complete absence of snakes. Beside my feet lay the three hundred-foot steel tape, one man at its rear end and the other leading, a few yards ahead of me. At a signal from him his mate had given the tape a sudden jerk, and its friction on the dry grass produced a sound exactly like the quick movement of a snake – a sound acutely familiar to us all. Tensions relieved, there would follow a flow of abuse from me, grins from the men, and we would proceed with the job.

No one was ever bitten, even though we killed both black and tiger snakes daily, but however intent on our work, there was constantly in our minds a keen sub-conscious awareness of the danger round us, for the tiger snakes lay quiet until they were either trodden on, or disturbed by the dragging steel tap.

The only member of the party who really deserved to have been bitten was the cook, for old George, with a confidence born of colossal ignorance of the things of the bush, treated all snakes with contempt. Frank Turner and I, out shooting one Sunday among the lagoons, came on George cheerfully attempting to drag a black snake out of a log by the tail, while he banged away at it with a short dead stick about a foot long. Frank strode up, pulled George violently away, and in a tone of utter disgust remarked, 'Georgie, Georgie, you chuckle-headed old Pommy bastard, for Christ's sake remember we need you to cook our scran!' George had no conception of the fact that a snake, held as he had it, will often either double back on itself and strike, or suddenly shoot out of a hole or split in the log and bite the man on the hand. We lit a fire of dry sticks and green leaves at the mouth of the log and, waiting at the other end, killed the snake as it retreated from the choking black smoke.

Speaking of men lost in the mallee, Andrew Ross told of dull days when the sun was hidden and the endless sea of low scrub gave no sign of where north and south might be; no sign, that is, to those without bushcraft who had lost all sense of direction. Opening a large single-bladed pocket knife and holding it upright with the point of the bright steel blade on his thumb nail, the old man explained to me that even on the dullest day the blade would cast a faint shadow across the nail. From this shadow, a man, unless he was a new-chum, could roughly gauge the north point by his judgement of the time of day. If he had a watch and the sun was out, his task was simple, for he held it flat in the palm of his hand and turned until the sun shone on the figure 12 of the dial, noted where the hour hand was pointing, and knew that north lay half-way between.

There were signs in the mallee wilderness, said Andrew, that would give lost men guidance if they knew how to read them. The porcupine grass, which frequently grows in semi-circular clumps, almost always has the arc of the curve bent towards the north, so that, taking an average of several clumps, one could get a good idea of direction. Also, on the south side of needlewood trees the bark has a paler tinge, and the tops of cypress pines protruding above the mallee incline slightly to the north-east away from the prevailing wind, the foliage on that side being warped in towards the trunk. To the Aborigines, who read the signs of the bush as a whiteman reads a newspaper, there are many other directional signs discernible only to them.

Out on the wide saltbush plains, where, far back from the river, station owners had excavated small 'tanks' in hollows or in the bed of dry watercourses, a lost man in danger of perishing for lack of a drink could find one of these lonely and widely scattered tanks if he knew how to go about it. The sheep, so Andrew reminded me, walked into a tank along tracks of their own making which converged from all points of the compass like the spokes of a wheel. Standing on one of these tracks, a man would not know (unless he was bushman enough to relate the direction of the freshest hoof marks to the time of day) whether the track led right or left to the tank.

The solution to this problem was for him to turn a rough right angle off the track and count his paces until he struck another. Then he followed this new track for two or three hundred yards, turned off it at a right angle and counted his paces until he cut the first track again. If this distance was shorter than the first, the tracks were converging towards the tank, if not he turned right about and followed in the opposite direction.

Armed with an axe or a tomahawk, anyone lost in the mallee, who knew the water-bearing type of tree, could get a drink by draining short lengths of the roots into the dented crown of his hat – provided, as Andrew remarked grimly, that he was not yet on the edge of delirium and had the mental stamina to endure the slow process.

Crossing the Dead Heart

C. T. Madigan

In 1939 the geologist C.T. Madigan led the first ground crossing of the Simpson Desert, a hot and waterless series of sand ridges extending for 200 miles. As he relates in Crossing the Dead Heart, *there were some grim moments.*

The new start was most propitious. The camels were rested, the party in high spirits. As we progressed, a clump of trees – probably mulga – was seen to the south between sandridges, and we passed three little pools of surface water. This must have been where the water beetles came from. Two small mobs of budgerigars were noted, and some finches and wrens. A flight of twenty crows seemed interested in us.

The sandridges were big but seemed less formidable to the refreshed cavalcade. Andy, as usual, was running here and there, continually snatching up plants for Crocker or lizards for Fletcher. He had a remarkable memory for what had been already collected, but was rather given to pressing on them what he considered better specimens of the same thing. Towards the end of the day his enthusiasm would often outlast their receptiveness. He was both an example and a task master. It was in the larger field of biology where his contributions were most valuable and most needed. He could always tell at a glance, by its last tracks, whether a reptile or a mouse was in its hole, whether at home or gone visiting, as he said, thus saving a lot of useless digging.

A big lizard of the frill-necked variety was caught that day.

Early in the afternoon Andy found the hole of a marsupial rat which he said was at home, so he and Fletcher and others began to dig it out. They thought they would not be long, so elected to stay behind to avoid delay, expecting to catch us up later. I knew the exasperation of trying to overtake a camel string on foot – you gain about half a mile an hour on them, although they seem to be going so slowly. Their long, slow strides are covering a lot more ground than they appear to be. It is when they are in sight, and then only half a mile away and even within hailing distance, that it becomes so irritating, when you are struggling to close the last short gap and your pride forbids you to call them to halt. It is bad enough on a road, but stumbling through the tufts of spinifex was going to make it much worse. However, we meant to camp early, so I left them to gain their experience.

In good country, on tracks, the Australian camel covers about three miles an hour. In hilly country in the MacDonnells I had found two and three-quarter miles an hour a reliable average. In these sandridges I was reckoning on two and a half to two and a quarter, but had so far been unable to check it as there had been no clear nights for longitude observations. The hourly rate of the camel is extraordinarily constant; in fact it is most difficult to vary it. The pack camel cannot be hurried up to any extent, nor does he slow down, but swings along hour after hour at his own fixed gait. This makes route traversing on camels very simple and accurate. It is only necessary to keep a note of the direction and the time of every halt and start. The times are liable to be overlooked at first but it soon becomes a habit to jot them down, like winding on the camera film. At the end of the day the time of marching is added up to the nearest five minutes, and this multiplied by the rate gives the day's run. It is usually possible to check the rate at the beginning of a journey by the time taken between two known points, but we could not check the sandridge rate on our easterly course till I could take a longitude.

We had been told that the first national broadcast had not been a success, and I was to repeat it to-night. The reception had been weak, due probably to the dampness of our equipment. We were also to try a little earlier, soon after sunset, instead of 7.30 p.m. That was the reason for an earlier camp. We had seen nothing of the digging party trailing us up, and had made camp before they appeared. In the valley between sandridges the view ahead or behind was always limited by the next sandridge a few hundred yards away. Even from the crest of a sandridge only two valleys could be seen, each with a series of crests beyond it, so that to see anyone at a distance it was necessary for both to be on a crest at the same time.

At last the diggers came in, tired and disgruntled, with a quaint story to tell. Before we moved on, a big excavation had been made, Andy working like one possessed. Work apparently went on at the same rate in relays till they had dug themselves out of sight, with shafts and tunnels and regular underground works. The sand was easy to work in, but the amount moved was terrific; and still the hole went on. At last the party began to despair of ever coming to the end of the hole, and questioned Andy more closely on the habits of this subterranean creature. Andy calmly replied, 'Him bin dig on fast as you dig after him'! Whether Andy himself ever expected to succeed, perhaps by physical exhaustion of his quarry, or whether he was letting our ignorance overcome his better judgment, was not clear, but the others at once gave up what seemed a hopeless task, picked up their tools and began the weary chase after the camels. When they came into camp even Andy's spirits were damped. It was too bad having the long walk after the failure of the mining operations. Marshall got a good picture of the later stages of the work.

That day I reckoned we had progressed thirteen miles in six hours. We crossed forty-four sandridges, as big as any we had seen. They were rather more irregular and wider on top, without such well-defined crests. The feed had not improved, but was rather worse. There were some green acacia bushes at the camp, of which I had hopes, but Jack said the camels would not eat them. Firewood was very scarce.

It was a miserable camp, with a cold damp wind. Conditions in the open, with poor light, were about as wretched as they could be for a national broadcast, but this time reception had improved, and the broadcast was successfully recorded. Perhaps the conditions were reflected in the reproduction and helped to give it realism and local colour. There was some comfort in the thought.

While we were trying to warm ourselves round the fire something suddenly hit Albert in the back and fell to the ground. It was found to be a bird, attracted by the light of the fire. It had been hard to get specimens of these little birds, but when this one recovered we let it go.

The rain had raised the humidity, and extraordinarily heavy dew became a nightly experience. It was as much trouble as rain. Every night everything became covered with water, the drops all running together to form a veritable layer. We could have used it to augment our water supply, had it not been obvious by this time that water was not going to be our problem, but feed for the camels.

The cheerfulness of the new start scarcely survived the day. The going had been heavy and the feed showed no signs of improving.

Next day we were still in giant sandridges, the biggest yet. They must have reached a hundred feet. They were more symmetrical, with the approach side steeper, and there were sometimes short transverse dunes on the top of them. We made rather a late start owing to the dew, but got in our six hours of travel, and it was quite enough. The going was very heavy. The wider crests with more loose sand greatly increased the camels' tasks. We passed a few little patches of munyeroo during the day, but otherwise it was very barren. In the afternoon some of the camels began to stumble and fall. We pushed on, hoping to find some feed and firewood to camp on, but it became worse. At last I had to stop. There was some dead needlebush for the fire but no feed at all. Again Jack criticised me for not stopping earlier where there was a little feed, but it was my way to hope for something better ahead and to put the miles behind. The only satisfaction I had that day was to travel hopefully. I reckoned we had made eleven miles, in which we had climbed over forty great masses of sand. They were the highest sandridges we had seen. There was nothing but sand and spinifex between the ridges, no feed, no signs of claypans. A few finches were noticed, a hawk, and a flock of nineteen crows. I wondered if they were the same crows as we had seen the day before, following us. Something sinister about these carrion birds.

It was a quiet and sober camp that night. Things were beginning to look serious. The day's march had definitely given cause for some misgiving. We were not yet half way across the desert, and the camels were beginning to fail. One was developing mange and seemed almost done. There was still over a hundred miles to go to reach the Mulligan, but there could be no question of turning back, for returning was now no easier than go o'er, but on the contrary would be much more difficult if one's expectations about the country ahead proved correct. Jack Bejah was depressed. He spoke of leaving one or two camels behind to follow us if they could, but this would have been against all the principles of exploration. Once you begin to abandon your gear it is a sign of approaching collapse. You should not have any gear you can do without. I told him to redistribute the loads but to keep the string together. It was no good spreading ourselves over the desert. We must come into that Queensland feed any day now.

We were sending a press message almost every night, with a longer one at week-ends, but I had promised Mr. Simpson a special personal one from the middle of the desert. It was hard to decide just where this was. We were now half way to the Queensland border, where we would be in known country, so that this was about the middle of the unknown part and we seemed likely to be near the climax of our difficulties, so I decided to send the message from this camp. It read: 'Mr. A. Simpson, Ru Rua Hospital, North Adelaide. Camp 10, June 18. This is promised message of greetings from the middle of Simpson Desert. All going well. Natural history collections mounting. Beautiful coloured desert wrens and finches, some probably new. Physiographical observations very interesting. No rock so far since leaving River Hale Tablelands. Camels feeling heavy work just now in giant sandridges. Little feed. None to-night but conditions will improve in next few days. All party well. Regards. Best wishes. Madigan'. The message was endorsed. 'Sent to V.H.U.9., 7.20 p.m., Sunday, June 18, R.A.S'.

Mr. Simpson had been in very poor health for some time, and had gone into hospital in a serious condition before we left Adelaide. There was an unhappy possibility that he might not live to hear of the end of the expedition he had financed. Birds were mentioned as he was particularly interested in them.

It was a clear night again at last, and I was able to take star observations. This careful navigation was not really essential, as there had been no features worth fixing since we left the Hale, but there was satisfaction in it. We could go east and strike the Mulligan without even the aid of compasses, but we would not know which side of the old Kaliduwarry Station we were on, and might have difficulty in finding it and waste time in locating ourselves before setting a course for Birdsville. Also I expected to find the course of the Hay River, if nothing else, where no one had seen it before, and this was worth fixing. If disaster should befall us and aeroplanes had to be sent out, we should be able to say exactly where we were; so I took my observations as opportunity offered. This was the first clear night since leaving the Hale, and our first opportunity to fix our position since then. The night was cold, the light poor. Papers, books, maps and instruments were soon wet with dew. Sitting out in the open among the spinifex under these conditions, not to mention considerable physical fatigue, did not help the accuracy of the calculations. I kept making mistakes and finding myself in the Pacific Ocean, which was no place to go to bed in. At last I got it right and was able to pin-point our position on the map. It was 24°44' south and 136°59' east. We had come seventy-eight miles from the Hale in thirty-five and three-quarter hours, giving an average rate of just over two miles an hour. My daily dead reckoning had made it seventy-nine miles, one mile out in seventy-eight. This was the reward for a late night, an aching back and a shivering frame. We might be in considerable difficulty in the worst place in the world, but we knew just where it was. My companions had long ago turned in, quiet and somewhat worried, and were now all fast asleep. I got into my pyjamas as usual, distributed all my clothing along the side of the sleeping bag on the ground sheet, not forgetting boots and socks and hat, else they would be soaking wet in the morning, covered and tucked everything in with the other half of the sheet, and crawled under. I was pleased with the results of my calculations. That feed couldn't be far away now! It was a little bit fuggy shut up in this waterproof and almost air-tight groundsheet, but very warm and comfortable. The camels couldn't stand many more days like to-day, but we could take easier stages. The chronometer was wound and put away in the bottom of Jack's big box – must get a better fastening for that, the piece of stick came out to-day. Nice the way the wireless was working – we must all send more messages home – been neglecting that. We'd be in that feed any day now . . .

Next morning there was some readjustment of loads, but soon the damp packages were heaved up and the wet cordage knotted, the camels jerked themselves on to their feet, and the long string began to wind slowly over the first sandridge. How were we going to fare today? Across the valley and on to the top of the next sandridge – and there before us lay a small claypan covered with water. Down into the valley, to find the clayey soil was carpeted with munyeroo! No waiting for something better this time. There were a few low mulga bushes at the end of the claypan, a suitable place to camp. Round to these, and down went the camels, and off came the loads laboriously put on a quarter of an hour before. We would let the camels graze here all day. If we had only come on another half mile last night it would have saved us a lot of work and some anxiety! This water and the green munyeroo must mean the edge of the rain country. Anyway, we would give the camels all the feed they wanted and a spell before tackling the sandridges again. They were soon chewing at great mats of munyeroo pulled up from the ground and dangling from their mouths.

It was a beautiful sunny day. We opened up the baggage and spread everything out to dry, then took a walk round the camp. Two sandridges away to the north-east there was a group of five claypans with gidgee trees, the first gidgee we had seen since leaving the Hale. This certainly looked like the edge of the rain belt. There was more clay here in the soil between the sandridges, and a thinner cover over the underlying rock. Nodules of ironstone lay around, and pieces of chalcedony. Crocker discovered a small rock outcrop of chalcedonized sandstone. More interesting still was the discovery of signs of the former presence of aboriginals, the only such indications seen in the whole desert crossing. These were chips of chalcedony, typical of aboriginal workshop sites where knives, scrapers and spearheads have been made, and also parts of grinding stones, one a piece of schist that must have come from the MacDonnells. This disproved my theory and Winnecke's that aboriginals never entered any part of the desert. It was obvious that in wet seasons they had followed streams down from the ranges to the north, probably only on short visits. We were then not far south of a group of claypans I had mapped during the 1929 aerial reconnaissance. Several claypans had been noted in the northern part of the desert, suggesting that they represented the ends of unnamed streams that come down from the MacDonnells and flood out in the desert. In wet seasons the blacks could obviously follow these streams down from the north, just as Fred Rogers went down the Hay. It was the natives of the east, west and south who had denied all knowledge of the desert, but it was now obviously no more than the southern parts that could be quite unknown to any aboriginal.

The largest of the claypans was only fifty yards across and they held at most a few inches of water. It was too shallow to dip up so some of the party dug a sump in our camp claypan to draw from. When the water in it settled it was still a nice yellow colour, but proved quite good for drinking water. Buckets were filled and put on the fire, and everyone had a hot bath – the first all-over wash for a fortnight. Out of our gallon a day there was enough water for everyone to wash face and hands once a day, but that was as far as it would go.

The sandridges here were more wavy and broader on top, and the crests of live sand were steep on both sides. There were lower saddles at intervals along the crests giving a jagged profile to the summits. Most of the bigger sandridges showed this saw-tooth effect more or less; the live sand along the crests slopes gently up northwards for a hundred yards or so to a summit and then falls rapidly away to start another rise, thus making serrations along the top of the sandridge. The serrations were more regular and marked in the centre and eastern desert than they were round Andado. Here at this camp they were strongly developed and the saddles between them so pronounced as to make better crossing places. This had not been so for the first sixty miles, when the ridges were practically level along the top and one place was as good as another to cross.

The tension of the last few days was now relieved, and Camp 11 was a very cheerful one. Albert made a pair of beautiful jam tarts. The pastry could not have been bettered. Marshall took some colour films of camp life, in which the tarts showed up to great advantage in a monotonous setting, for the desert colours were practically confined to the red of the sandridges and the grey of the spinifex. There was still very little herbage or green plants, but the munyeroo, now dying off, made brown mats on the lower ground. It is a low, spreading and succulent plant of the portulacca or pig-face family. Again it would have been better to have gone on for another couple of sandridges and camped among the rather poor and scattered gidgee at the next claypans, but this camp was quite good enough. I had ridden on to the crest of the next sandridge before deciding to off-load, but still another sandridge denied us the view of the group of claypans and trees that lay beyond.

Andy was in great form this night. He loved a good camp. Now everything was rosy for him. He said, 'This life good, walkabout, homestead no good, live longer this way', a very profound truth as applied to him and all his people. I don't think he had ever seen the sea, but when something lead the conversation to it he said he didn't like the sea – 'too wet, no tracks, land more better'. I was sitting aside writing notes while the rest of the party talked, and I took the opportunity of recording some of Andy's remarks, which were a constant entertainment to us. His conversation was always jerky, consisting of short statements without elaboration and often with little connection, like a series of wise-cracks. It was often interesting to try and fill in the gaps that he left blank in his train of thought. Andy went on: 'Can't sleep during day. Night long enough. Last night too long, make my jaw ache. First one side then the other. This fellow clever more top (God). Bring down water, ducks, plenty. (Ly-Ly did not know of God. He expressed his pleasure at a good camp more crudely, with his bloody widgetty, bloody yam, bloody mobs.) At Marree they think I not come – too many people – country too dry. At Warrina my people say not go – Frank say not go. I say I chance myself – never mind perish'. Andy was boasting now. For the past two days he had obviously been wishing he had not come. It was interesting to hear that his people had warned him not to come, at Marree and again at Warrina. It was Jack who had turned the scale. At Andado he was still undecided.

As I had missed the time signals for a couple of nights I made sure of getting them that night, and as it was clear I took further observations to check our position. The results agreed sufficiently well. We were about seven miles south-west of the claypans I had mapped from the air, so I decided to go north-east next day to locate them. Those we were at seemed too small to be the same. I also wanted to check the position of the claypans, which had been plotted only from dead reckoning in the middle of a five-hour flight.

We left Camp 11 next day, June 20, and started on the north-east course. We were now travelling obliquely to the sandridges and thus crossing fewer. They were becoming smaller, too, so that the going was much easier. We passed the first group of claypans, and then another pair of small ones beyond the next sandridge, one surrounded by munyeroo, the other in quite a grove of gidgee. After a few more sandridges we came to the south end of a broad valley of gidgee, with trees visible to the horizon. A sandridge came to an end here, and we rounded its northern extremity. This was the only end of a sandridge we saw in the whole desert journey, the only one we did not have to cross. There was probably a claypan up in the gidgee.

We did not investigate, but continued on our course and were soon crossing sandridges again.

Later in the morning I saw a big brown snake that disappeared down a hole. We halted to dig it out. The hole was a long one, probably a mouse hole, and followed a log buried in the sand. Andy as usual dug with the excitement of a terrier. At last we came to the snake at the end of the hole and pinned it with a forked stick and eventually killed it. It was a venomous species nearly six feet long.

The country was improving and green herbage began to appear. We crossed another valley, or inter-ridge space, with gidgee trees in it, then one with a stony patch in the middle, and in the next we came on a wide claypan a couple of hundred yards across covered with about two inches of water. We tried the camels at it but only a few of them wanted to drink. After another wooded valley, at the end of seven miles on the north-east course, we turned east again. In the next two miles we passed four claypans, the last surrounded on all sides by sandhills, a regular hole in the sand like those we were to see later near Lake Eyre. This one was about three hundred yards by a hundred and fifty, and had about an inch of water on it. We went on for another couple of miles without seeing any more claypans, and camped. This was obviously the group of claypans I had seen from the air, and gratifyingly close to where I had placed them; in fact as accurately placed as such an area could be, without plotting each individual claypan.

The sandridges were now only about thirty feet high, and closer together. There was green sandhill wattle about, and green spinifex and canegrass, with plenty of camel feed. There had been several halts on this day. We had covered about twelve miles and crossed thirty-nine sandridges. It had been a very interesting day, with more variety than we had known so far in the desert. At every mile the vegetation was improving and there was already abundance of feed. The day's march had put it beyond doubt that we had entered the Queensland rain belt and there was nothing further to worry about. It was only a matter of time and the other side of the desert would be reached. For a few days we had been haunted by the possibility of failure, but those days were behind and the crisis was passed. The rest should be easy.

It was more obvious than ever that the journey would be impossible except after exceptionally good seasons, and even then the desert would present some difficult patches. The distance is short, but the going so heavy that progress must be slow, and good feed for camels is thus essential. The journey cannot be hurried by day-and-night travel, as the camels must be given frequent rests, and six hours' march a day is enough in the heavier parts. That night we knew that success was sure. A message was sent to the University of Adelaide.

Lost in Friendly Territory

Roger McDonald

Novelist Roger McDonald, working as a shearer's cook, goes for an afternoon walk in Darling River country and gets himself lost, to be guided back by the sound of the compressor engine at the woolshed.

Most of the shearers I was cooking for were Maoris, a travelling people. The new arrivals – shearers and rouseabouts – stepped from the bus at Broken Hill after the long haul Auckland–Sydney–Adelaide. Trans-Tasman air fares left them broke. With sheds organised Rewi bundled them into his car and they hurtled through the night at a thousand clicks an hour. Headlights revealed ghostly boomers drifting up to the side windows and if they were lucky, flicking away. Sometimes they hit. Crammed in the back seat were eighteen-year-old girls from Napier, forty-six-year-old men from Timaru, mid-twenties married couples from Whanganui. They'd studied maps but couldn't believe it was a two- or three-day drive to Sydney or the Gold Coast. They woke up in strange places: couldn't believe those places. The doors of the rooms opened on flatness. Earth was red, sky pale, then molten. Grass had never been invented. It was a furnace in the middle of the night. The birdcalls were weird. Insects crawled on the skin. Snakes were a nightmare. Foxes howled like madwomen. There was no local town. But soon the sheds became home – with plenty to eat. 'Have

148

you noticed?' Rewi took me aside one day. 'New Zealanders are big people. Your cooking is outstanding. But the meals need to be heavier.'

Today, walked away from the friendly-family-crowdedness into the hard sunlight edged with muted olive-greens and yellowy mud-creams along the river bank . . . Walked into timebends. The river snaking off into reach after reach of gentle zigzags, water coming down from Queensland, spreading its silt, then nosing toward a destination thousands of kilometres to the south.

For every hundred kilometres by road along the Darling, it was three hundred by river. The chug of the shed engine rose and fell as I followed the meanders, the river banks stately as an earl's parkland. Successive concertina-reaches of treeline drew me on. Newly shorn sheep stared from a few hundred metres away – five hundred rheumy stubborn gazes. How dared I intrude on what they had always known as theirs. Old river redgums marked the way, gnarled, wrinkled, massive. The river paddock was a well used home paddock but trees regenerated there. I tried to guess why: maybe because for months on end, in certain years, the river snaked around behind itself, creating islands, giving growth a chance to return . . . Came on a fat goanna clutching the girth of a redgum, its skin like the freckled bands of a sand painting, its powerful legs spotted yellow. A slim face peered down at me disdainfully, the narrowing-to-delicacy chain-mail tail just out of reach. A reptile close to a metre and a half long, looking immortal in its elevated hunting ground.

Swarms of mosquitoes drove me on . . . Feeling of sleepiness, dream, tired from work. The hot afternoon, elation of letting go: slithering focus of the grabbed fifty minutes. Tracked a wagtail from grass stem to grass stem, tame but elusive, hovering at knee height, just beyond reach. Found a store of fish traps in a hollow log, with wheeltracks leading away. (For every yellowbelly trapped in this part of the Darling, three carp were caught.) The river was rising by the hour, running a 'fresh'. At Nyngan a few weeks before, the Bogan had been a raging torrent. A freak storm had dumped four hundred millimetres on the district in a few hours. More than a thousand kilometres of meanders separated Gumbank from where the Bogan joined the Darling. Here came the same water again – flattened, smooth, implacable. Rafts of foam swept round the bends. Tree branches loosened from the banks bobbed in the current like stately barges. Along came a plastic meat tray. Glass wine flagons. Whole flotillas of beer cans – Reschs, Tooheys, West End, VB, Fourex, Fosters. I found a shire road barrier wedged in a tree from an earlier flood. This 'fresh' wouldn't go as high. Much of the debris was the rubbish of leisure seekers who'd come down the Darling by boat, months or years before.

I clambered down the steep, sheep-bitten bank with exposed tree roots like jug handles. Squatted by the water's edge. Jammed in a stick (would return tomorrow for a look). Did the same thing forty years ago: threw in a line on family picnics – caught catfish, perch, bony bream. No carp in the river then. Remembered the Darling flood of 1950. I was eight years old. Remembered the six weeks it took for the water to come down from Queensland, an excitement of waiting, like Christmas. Remembered blitz wagons touring Bourke calling for volunteers through loudspeakers. My father going out to fill sandbags on the levee banks, the Presbyterian minister doing his bit with an Irish-Catholic priest – Hugh Fraser McDonald offering Patrick Tracey a ride home in the Chev. 'Where to, Father?' 'First stop – the public bar.' Remembered the Aboriginal family camped in the gutted hotel across from the church, driven up from 'the common' by floodwaters. My brothers and I their 'friend boys', idlers in a swirl of time and meanings, playing billycarts. (The present moment immune from history.) Army 'ducks' rescuing tetchy old-timers from trees. Photographers from *Truth* swaggering into town, finding nothing newsworthy enough, so smashing windows in an old hut somewhere, inventing sensation. Remembered the dead muddy stink over the town as the floodwaters receded. I asked my mother not to bury me in Bourke if I died there. A boy died of rheumatic fever – Charlie Brown – and was buried in a sky-blue coffin from the now-demolished weatherboard church behind our house.

I wondered why I hated the river as a child. When I went farther west, visiting stations with my father, the stillness of the red sandhill country – a desert landscape of Sturt's pea, leopardwood, bloodwood, gidgee – gave time for thoughts to catch up to themselves . . . to meander . . . Somehow I hated the river with its bindii-carpets, its sudden frights of cattle crashing through overthick growth, the suspicion of enraged boars lurking about, the ugliness and foul odours of mud pools. Scrambling out after a swim was a mud-struggle. Floods brought corpses. Strange people were drawn to the river. Up Arcadian reaches, spirals of smoke betrayed loners camped on grassy banks. It was better not to go too close. Maybe they were just shearers between sheds. But maybe they were loonies. Childhood wasn't a good time to have an open mind about anything much.

I squatted on my haunches where a sharp bend of the river spilled over into a billabong. Watched a trickle of floodwater meander through burrs, dribble down cracks in silt. In a day or two the tiny flow would become a pouring rush. The billabong hung like a flattened question mark a few hundred metres east of the river. Its waters were shallow, mud-rimmed, puggy from hoofprints of sheep, cattle, wild pigs. A tangle of lignum hugged the shore – haunt of wild boars. Birds everywhere at the billabong – pelicans, ducks, cormorants, finches, wagtails, corellas, hawks – the shallow, motionless water thick with trapped waterlife. Carp made sluggish gulps.

I thought of another long walk taken on an afternoon like this, a couple of months earlier, at Alison Downs near the Queensland border. I had set the kitchen timer for three hours (leaving a big leg of mutton in the oven), pocketed a container of orange juice, and jammed my hat on my head. Away from the overgrazed holding paddocks it was the same sort of country I'd visited with my father, a place to recover lost dreams. My boots crunched on dry bark and sticks. To my left was a fence with a telegraph wire running along the top, and in the middle distance low red sandhills. I kept an eye on the telegraph wire fence, using it as a guide. Not that I thought I'd get lost – not me – I knew all the pitfalls. Emus appeared, a parent with seven almost fully grown chicks. They let me get close, then pounded away with feathers flouncing, hesitating only slightly as they ushered themselves through the fence, then wove up a slope of sand and disappeared into the low scrub of the near horizon.

I walked on through stands of dusty gidgee and shining-leaved bloodwoods. Corellas flashed their pink underwings. A clump of large, broad trees – coolabahs – created a vision of a watercourse. (Perhaps I clambered over another fence somewhere here. I don't remember.) My head was full of feeling as I brushed through the low-slung coolabah branches, entering a shaded lagoon. No water, of course – this was fringe desert country. Moving from tree to tree, I saw the old coolabah that stood in the yard of our childhood home in Bourke. The manse is not there any more – there's a cut-price motel where we rode our billycarts, an asphalt driveway where my father preached his sermons in the now-demolished weatherboard church – but here, forty years later, was tree after tree springing back through time. Low heavy limbs resting on the ground. The same coarse bark to clutch and tear away, to examine what was under and dream on – a universe of beetles and grubs under the dry matted fibre – and when I looked up, the same brittle convoluted ladder to the stars.

The dry lagoon twisted through the trees and came out after a few hundred metres into the intensified glare of afternoon. I could no longer see the fence with the telegraph line, but in my mind had fixed its location. The idea of getting lost wasn't even a whim to reject sardonically. I was happy out there under the burning, dry sun. I drained half my orange juice and picked out a circle to walk through in the trees up ahead. A tantalising promise seemed to draw me on. Dry blonded native grasses bent under a light breeze. Scattered gidgee, bloodwood and the slenderly beautiful leopard gum created a mirage of restfulness in the distance, an illusion of peace always just out of reach. After five generations in this country, my Scots-inherited blood rose to the bait that had deceived the first newcomers: easy to picture water farther on, just across that low rise there. Hard to compel the mind to stamp out the vision of a cottage, maybe a homestead, and a smoothly graded roadway leading to some cluster of human occupation. A small town in the scrub, even, and a roadhouse serving cold beer.

Looming on the left was a stand of dead gidgee. Gathered inside it was a family of five grey kangaroos. There couldn't have been much roo shooting on Alison Downs (despite the litter of spent shells in the dust around the shearers' quarters), because these roos were bold. They let me walk almost as close as the emus had, then the family bounded a retreat, while one held back – the male, I guessed – challenging me with a chesty bad-tempered grunt among the desolate dead trees.

That was all it took to dissolve my mood. I decided it was time to turn back. The circle through the trees back to the dry lagoon didn't take long – seemed hardly any time at all as I clambered over fallen logs and pushed through saucer-shaped depressions thick with scrub. Something on a grassy open space interested me: curious that I can't remember what it was. Animal tracks, ant lines, the stillness, the living heat, some tiny movement drawing my eyes one way, and my feet following, while in my mind I was always bearing back to the right . . . in the other direction.

The coolabahs at the dry lagoon loomed up where I expected them, but when I pushed through the lagoon wasn't there. Just a jumble of decaying logs, struggling saplings, humps of earth, signs of old tractor work, a ripping away at roots of woody shrubs. I angled my ear and listened for the sound of the wool compressor back at the shed. Nothing. Mentally I sorted things through – where the sun was positioned back when I started, where the last fence ran. It was like flipping through a stack of cards, watching for the right one to turn up. And it did. Up ahead, after a five-minute exploration, I saw a glitter of new fencing. Then I saw a telegraph line running along the fence line, and it didn't make sense. (The fence I'd used as my guide was an old one.) Sections of old fence could have been replaced by new, but when I followed the telegraph line to a cornerpost the line swung away from the fence altogether and marched off over the horizon.

I was lost. Same trees, same sky, same earth – all saying one thing but meaning another. I'd been skidded across into an ironically different bushscape. Being lost was like being trapped in a photograph of somewhere I knew, but with no way to grab the third dimension. I'd assumed that those telegraph lines of thick galvanised wire strung along rickety poles were hangovers from the era of boundary riders. In fact (I found later) they were phone lines in use. The scant scrubland was as deeply networked with blocked eyelines as anywhere else in Australia. My mistake to think I'd made a connection to things, that the maze of landscapes had welcomed me in, given me the right clues. The bush didn't care. I'd made a mockery of myself.

That leg of mutton in the oven back at the shearers' quarters – when it burned the alarm would go up.

By then it would be dark. I'd make a bed in the sand and moodily build a fire. I wouldn't be able to sleep for trying to invent some joke for when I was found, to counteract the one played on me, to cover my shame. At first light tomorrow the station's owner would get out his plane and come looking for me.

It didn't happen that way. I put the sun over my left shoulder (where it felt wrong), and tacked along the line of my shadow. There was nothing else I could do. Numb with suppressed panic, I trudged along for about twenty minutes, which – as it happened – was the total time I was lost. (The joke on me. After telling myself I couldn't get lost, it seemed I couldn't get lost properly.) I pushed aside a thorny bush. The sandhill where the emus disappeared stared me in the face. I turned my head. There was the same old piece of fenceline. I cupped an ear, catching the steady throb of the compressor engine at Alison Downs woolshed. An easy walk and I was back there.

On the banks of the Darling it was impossible to get lost. But when I looked back towards Gumbank shed – where the shed should have been – I heard nothing. The steady chug of the engine came from almost behind me. The river had twisted me round. Angling an ear, I located the sound exactly, and then stepping clear of the trees, caught glimpses of tin roofs across the bare open spaces beyond the river. I set a course back to the shearers' quarters in a straight line. Minutes from the riverbank, I rose onto an old flood terrace, then another . . . Red earth lines along the horizon to the east. A paddock of harsh herbage. Lignum in the hollows. The river barely existed any more – just a strip of trees slipping lower behind with every step. A walk of fifty minutes out, along the meanders, became thirteen back in a straight line. Dull pewter of galvanised roofs and I was soon into the shower, then back in the kitchen, turning the roast, stirring the soup, the evening full of chores till eight o'clock.

The Way of Wild Pigs

Henry G. Lamond

Wild pigs, still massing to plague proportions in inland Australia, were causing concern back in the 1960s, when Henry G. Lamond dissected their particular habits for Walkabout *magazine.*

From the August number of *Walkabout*, page 35, I quote a passage relating to the possible extermination of the cassowary in the Cape York Peninsula.

'The real menace lies in pigs that have overrun the jungles of Cape York and are rapidly exterminating everything that lives on or near the ground.'

This deals with pigs of the interior, of Central Queensland, in the great sheep areas. It makes only passing reference to the Basalt – that line which runs north of the railway from Charters Towers to Hughenden, a distance of two hundred or more miles. That land, with running springs and soft living for pigs, is one of their earthly paradises – the walls of the basalt are traced with pig pads even like the tracks of sheep in a paddock. Neither do I refer to the Flinders country, a land of artesian flows, plenty of water, another paradise for pigs, of which they take full advantage. This deals with pigs of the interior.

Years ago, and I don't know how long ago that was, I was reading an old book on zoology. I was struck by the quaint phraseology of one sentence: 'No large animal increaseth faster than ye pig.' It also made reference to the sow's lubricity which cannot be denied – and I looked up that word in the dictionary. It is the rate of increase which is alarming; the complacent manner in which we accept that increase as a thing of no account is also disturbing.

During 1905, when I was a passenger, the driver of the down-the-river coach drove his team a hundred yards or more, jolting over the Mitchell grass, to show us a rarity: a dead wild pig. Wild pigs were then so rare in that district that almost a price of admission was demanded to see one. And that was the centre of one of the great sheep areas of Queensland! For obvious reasons I cannot name the station and pin-point the spot. It can be taken that every word I write is literally correct. That was during 1905. And, less than thirty years later, on that same station, when the management decided the pigs were getting a bit thick, they shot a few to reduce the numbers – just the skimmings, as it were, to take the froth off the mobs. Three thousand pigs were shot – at least, at a shilling a snout, that was the number for which payment was made.

The pig's snout was taken as evidence of a dead pig. We know the two ears, the scalp, of a marsupial used to be regarded as a token; the two ears joined by a strip down the back and the tail is considered the scalp of the dingo. Snouts served for pigs. Though they were easy shooting, and no trouble to get, some bright sparks evolved a means of making snouts: they took preserved peaches, punched a couple of small holes in them, let them out in the sun to shrivel a bit, and there was a perfect pig's snout. Those fellows made quite a good thing out of it at a shilling a time until suspicion prompted a receiver to doubt them. I don't think he bit and tasted a snout to see if it was pig or peach; the distinguishing mark was the holes for hairs which were inside the nostrils – dried peaches did not have hairs inside the punch holes. It was quicker, and infinitely easier, for a man to go out and shoot a pig than for him to prick holes in imitation of non-existent hairs.

After that three thousand and odd had been skimmed a selector on that station, having an idle week to spare, and with the desire for a bob or two to jingle in his pocket, collected the payment on four hundred snouts – and there was not a preserved peach among them. He did not go off his 20,000-acre patch to do that. During 1913, when I was managing a big station a couple of hundred miles west of the property just mentioned – and still in sheep country – a sub-overseer and a jackeroo caused some amusement by their story of how they had seen a sow and a litter of piglets in the channels of the river – and those channels were interlacing billabongs about five miles wide. In their excitement, and carried away by the novelty, they had chased that sow and her litter. The part which caused the laugh was the mental picture of those two young men perched on the limb of a coolibah tree while that old sow fussily gathered her litter and left. She had treed them. That was 1913, and the area skirted what might be called a dry belt of the State.

A year or so ago I was yarning with an old kangaroo-shooter who worked on that station. He was, and is, one of the keenest students of natural history it has been my pleasure to meet. We talked of wild pigs, and of the two men being treed by a sow. As he had just come in from that country I asked him how many wild pigs there were now in the channels of the river. His reply gave his estimate: 'I'd back meself to shoot a thousand in a week, and there'd be so many left you wouldn't notice what I'd shot.'

That man was a crack shot. He could handle his rifle more surely than a clerk could swing a pen; but I think his arithmetic was subject to correction. To shoot a thousand in a week he would, approximately, have to shoot one every five minutes for seven days in a twelve-hour day. The pigs were in swarms – and we had better let it go at that. Yet, during 1913, they were in units!

Other instances of multiplication could be given. I saw a wild sow with a litter of half a dozen on the Georgina, just below Camooweal, during 1913. I saw a sow with a litter on the same river between Boulia and Urandangie, during 1918. I do not say, or claim, they have increased to the same extent in that extremely dry cattle country as they would in the softer sheep lands; but I know they have the nucleus for a start there. The scrubs of the coastal areas, with plenty of water and easy living, are alive with wild pigs.

It's perfectly obvious these pigs must eat to live. What do they eat? The pig comes under the same heading as man himself: it is omnivorous – it can live as a vegetarian; it can be happy with a diet of meat alone; it can mix them both to advantage. But it goes further than man: it doesn't care what state of decomposition its food may reach; it will still find it palatable. A pig is something of a synonym for a gross eater, a gluttonous feeder. That simile isn't misplaced: the pig is a big eater. As it must eat, as it will eat anything, and as it is a big eater, very simple conclusions provide us with the fact that the pigs in their thousands must eat quite a lot.

Years ago – and every word of this is true – a couple of partners owned a sheep property a few miles up the river from where that specimen pig used to be shown passengers by the coach driver. They had about 40,000 acres of really choice country. They intended to be pastoralists. Before they started on the land they owned a tank-sinking plant. They put down a tank on their property, and it was one of the biggest in the district at the time – over 30,000 cubic yards. When the property was fenced, a house built, some sheep bought, the tank filled, one of the partners took the plant and continued as a contract tank-sinker; the other stayed at home to look after the property and the sheep. They both had frugal minds: the fellow with the plant earned money with which to develop the property; the fellow who stayed at home bought some pigs and ran them as a side-line.

I visited that place several times. I saw a couple of hundred pigs which foraged about the homestead, wallowed in the mud at the edge of the water in the tank, and in the backwater, and which came when called to be fed scraps from the kitchen. I saw the sheep which came to the only water on the place, and I noticed how few lambs there were among those ewes.

Not long after my last visit the partners had a disagreement. The fellow who stayed at home left the district; the man who had the plant took over the management of the sheep property. This was his story:

'I thought there must be something wrong. At a time when we should be selling sheep, when others had sheep for sale, we had to buy some to keep up our numbers. Our country was as good as theirs; we had as much water as they had. Instead of the place keeping me I was keeping it – all the money I used to make from tank-sinking had to go back into the property. Our sheep didn't increase: that was the main trouble. I had a look at it. I saw those pigs. I saw ewes come to water with young lambs following them. I saw those ewes go out after having a drink, and no lambs went with them.'

In short, the partners fell out about the pigs. The man who loved the swine went away and took his pet pigs with him; the other fellow leased his plant and went to the property himself – and he shot any remaining pigs on sight.

That man has long since retired; his children and his grand-children now carry on the property; every year the officials in the

Taxation Department sharpen their pencils and smack their lips when his returns come in for assessment. The place has had additions made to it, and, comparatively speaking, it has been a gold mine since it was devoted to sheep. Pigs and sheep don't mix.

One of the strong points of the wild pig in the damage it does is that it leaves no trace. In the case mentioned the man who stayed at home challenged his partner to prove the pigs killed the lambs. That proof could not be obtained. The pig leaves no trace other than a few wisps of wool blowing away in the wind. I've seen a wether sheep bogged on the downs. I've pulled that fellow out and left him on his side, his legs clotted with mud, intending to deal with him in the morning. Next day when I went to that sheep there was nothing there other than pig tracks, a few tufts of wool sprayed about in the grass, a suspicious stain or two on the ground. The pigs left nothing – not even the smell.

On another occasion, nearly thirty years ago, I was managing a bit of a cattle station in North Queensland. There were quite a few pigs in that area, though it could not be classed as bad pig country. I know positively thirty-eight head of cattle were bogged in a certain waterhole. Those were grown cattle, steers and aged cows. The pigs did not leave a trace of them! They didn't even leave the bones to show where they had killed them. The bones were dragged out, carried over the plains, dropped when the pig satisfied himself it had taken all it wanted. In odd instances even the thigh bones had been crunched to extract the marrow. The only real evidences were skeleton skulls and pelvic bones. They scattered the other bones so no trace of their murders could be attached to them.

A dingo leaves evidence of its work; a blowfly wave shows where it has been among sheep; the pig eats all its evidence and scatters that which it cannot swallow.

Those are just two instances of pigs with sheep and cattle. They could be multiplied. Personally, and I claim to have taken some note of them, I wouldn't give threepence a dozen for weak calves in bad pig country – and most of the cattle country on the coast has hordes of pigs. In sheep country I know from experience what pigs will do with lambing ewes, and it matters but little how strong those ewes are – the lambs are always weak at birth; the protection a ewe can offer against a hungry pig is worthless. I have looked in the eyes of death in the shape of a charging boar pig, and it took some lively action on my part to dodge it. I know, had I gone down, my fate would have been the same as those cattle which had been bogged. Though I have no means of proving it, of course, nothing can make me think other than that quite a number of men who have disappeared entirely in the bush have been crippled. In pig country that would be all a pig needed to finish the work and leave no trace of what it had done.

Someone might claim the wild pig has some uses. Of course it has – it can be caught, put in a sty, fattened, sold or killed, and it makes quite good pork. But, usually, a wild pig killed in the bush is an awful dish to place before a man. It stinks; its flesh is detestable. Yet that same pig, fattened in a sty, makes good pork. I speak from experience: I've swung a knife and fork over much of it.

When comparing pigs and dingoes and trying to strike a balance between them and the damage they do, I reckon one dingo will outclass a pig – a dingo will kill for sport; the pig only kills to eat. Against that, and this is only a guess, I'd say a pig would need many times as much food as a dingo – and it rests with the inclinations and desires of the pig whether that food is beef, mutton, lily roots, other herbages and what not. Finally, and though this census must be vague and, possibly, so incorrect as to be ridiculous, I'd say there are at least a hundred wild pigs to every wild dog in the bush. They may be a thousand to one. Add to that the pig leaves no evidence of its crime and we begin to realise the debt it owes our pastoral industry.

As mentioned, men have reduced their numbers by shooting them. This isn't a treatise on how to shoot wild pigs; but I can say a man has to place his bullets carefully if he wishes to collect a snout. The usual poisons, strychnine and arsenic, aren't as effective as they might be with pigs, and I can't give any reason why they should not be. The stuff which does touch the spot is a poison with a phosphorus content. That puts paid to their accounts every time. Phosphorus poisoning is a horrible death to die – and I've seen animals die from it. Against that the pig is a horrible animal – and I refer to wild pigs with murder in their hearts, crime on their snouts. The trouble with the phosphorus poison is that, almost invariably, the pig dies in a waterhole. I am not chemist enough to say how many pigs, or how much phosphorus content of their stomachs, would be needed to poison a waterhole 600 yards long by 180 feet wide, by an average depth of ten to fifteen feet. I don't even know if enough phosphorus could be put into it to make it toxic. But I do know it doesn't take the bloated and burst bodies of too many dead pigs to pollute that water to such an extent that a man couldn't drink it, and to make it, at least, slightly unhealthy for stock. Using phosphorus a man would have to ride his waterholes every day and pull out dead bodies. A cumbersome boar pig, great in death, with a live weight of anything over 500 lb., is not easy to handle. It needs a draught horse to snig that fellow over the bank where the drainings from his body will not run back into the hole and pollute the water.

Now, and with at least one bright spot on the horizon, is the time to deal with the menace of the wild pigs in pastoral Queensland, and in certain areas, in other States as well. The floods this year have done damage running into any old sum the mind might conjure. They have also done much good. Wild pigs live mainly in the channels of those western rivers. Those channels are warm in winter, sheltered from the wind, close to food supplies near water. The pigs are not fools. They know what is good for them. Those recent floods must have drowned thousands, tens of thousands, perhaps hundreds of thousands. It gives a good base from which to start to keep the pest within reasonable bounds in the future.

Across Australia by Car

Geoffrey Dutton

Geoffrey Dutton relates the story of his father, Henry Hampden Dutton, and Murray Aunger following the Oodnadatta Railway and then the Overland Telegraph Line as they crossed Australia, south to north, encountering almost impassable difficulties of rock, sand and water.

In 1908 my father, Henry Hampden Dutton, and his mechanic, Murray Aunger, set out to drive the first motor car across Australia. In the 2100 miles south to north, from Adelaide to what was then called Port Darwin, there were probably 200 miles of roads. As for the rest, there were tracks over hard earth and mud, rocks, and sand, across dry riverbeds, huge sandhills, and tropical rivers.

There is a boundary beyond which enterprise crumbles into foolhardiness. Imagination, essential in conceiving any enterprise, has to be tested by truth in the shape of timetable, planning, a boring attention to detail. But the truly enterprising are those who are not daunted by failure. The best plans are subject to chance, to what insurance companies in a secular age still call Acts of God.

So my father, whom I shall call HHD ('Dutton' seems disrespectful, even though he has been dead for more than fifty years), had in 1908 already seen the collapse of all his plans. He and Aunger had set off earlier in 1907, and had completed some fifteen hundred miles of their journey when the transmission failed and could not be repaired without new parts. Also the wet season was upon them, and the monsoonal rains of tropical Northern Australia were turning the country into a swamp. So they had to abandon the car and return to Oodnadatta by horse and thence by rail to Adelaide.

In 1908 HHD and Aunger set off once more for Port Darwin in a 25-horsepower English Clement-Talbot (the first car had been 20/24 h.p.). Cans of petrol were sent ahead by donkey or camel. Unfortunately the Afghan camel drivers, ignorant of such things, often left the four-gallon cans in the fierce sun, where a number of them burst. As there was no town between tiny Oodnadatta and the mining outpost of Pine Creek, a thousand miles further north, supplies had to be sent ahead to the telegraph stations or cattle or sheep stations along the track. In all, petrol supplies were sent to thirteen depots, sometimes including such luxuries as sardines, tinned pineapple, and a bottle of brandy.

HHD was twenty-nine, Aunger a few years younger. The mechanic was a sturdy and highly intelligent man who later founded a successful business supplying motor accessories. HHD had already had quite an enterprising career. Born of pioneering land-holders who ran sheep in New South Wales and South Australia, he had a degree in geology from Oxford, had rowed in the Oxford Eight, and had hunted in Morocco, Newfoundland and Wyoming. He had a beautiful wife, Emily, and a son, John, born in 1906.

Extreme variations in terrain called for technological ingenuity. There was an extra set of wheels and tyres, known as Stepney wheels, which bolted on to the existing wheels to give extra traction when crossing sand or mud. There were rolls of coconut matting to be spread in front of the wheels when traversing sand. There were no mudguards, so thick grass or bushes would not jam the tyres, and the body consisted of a seat and a high box full of spares and equipment, with drums of water and the Stepney wheels tied to its top and sides.

On the first car, but not on the second, there was a canvas hood to keep off the sun. There were even brass acetylene lamps and a curved brass horn. In the box at the back was a Spanish Windlass by which a car bogged in mud or sand could be attached to a tree by a wire rope and hauled out. (One had to hope for a handy tree.) Strapped across the box behind the heads of driver and passenger was a 12-bore gun in a leather case, hopefully for shooting ducks and other game along the track. There were also eight tyres and tubes, spare tailshaft and back axles, goggles against dust storms, and a pick and shovel.

The second Talbot is still going strong, housed in the Birdwood Mill Motor Museum in South Australia, its brass radiator and lamps glistening, its wooden wheels still free of creaks or cracks. It has some odd features. The four cylinders are cast in two separate blocks. The fan revolves around a shaft bolted right through the immensely strong honeycomb of the radiator. On the dashboard there are glass tubes through which oil can be seen dripping down into the engine, at a pace to be adjusted by brass knobs. There is no speedometer, but the original mechanic who worked on the car at the Talbot agents in Adelaide told me, when he was a very old man, that each Talbot when properly tuned was required to cover a flying mile in one minute.

The Talbot has no self-starter, since it has no electrical gear outside the magneto. It is started by the crank handle; when cold, it requires four pulls with the ignition (which looks like an old-fashioned domestic light switch) turned off, then 'Contact!' and one sharp pull, and the low-revving engine with its huge flywheel chugs into steady life. When moving off from rest, the enterprising driver should beware: the clutch has a very small movement between stop and go. Too lusty a movement of the foot means a kangaroo hop and a stalled engine.

HHD liked giving his cars names. The 1907 20/24-horsepower Talbot was called Angelina; the 1908 25-horsepower model was the Overlander.

For the first journey, after they left Adelaide on 15 November 1907, crowds turned out along the way to wish them luck. On 26 November they left Anlaby, HHD's home, and had the best run, on made roads, of the whole journey: 160 miles to Quorn in just under eight hours.

They drove beside the railway line up to its terminus at Oodnadatta, 688 miles north of Adelaide, a funny little narrow-gauge line. HHD learnt to distrust the Afghans' and other stock drivers' comments on the way ahead. 'Good going' turned out to mean sandy country, which was soft for feet or hooves, but bad news for car tyres. 'Real crook country' meant hard, pebbly plains, across which the Talbot could happily cruise at forty-five miles an hour. Some hazards were particularly bad for cars.

The dry creek beds, for instance. The Alberga River, north of Oodnadatta, was one of the worst obstacles they met with in the entire journey. Dodging the trees, they rushed the quarter-mile-wide expanse of burning sand (that particular day it was 113 degrees in the shade) only to have the heavily laden Angelina sink up to the axles thirty yards from the bank. Then followed hours of sweaty work, jacking up the Talbot on the heavy boards brought for such emergencies, digging out the sand under the wheels and laying strips of coconut matting, fitting the Stepney wheels. When all else failed, the car had to be winched along by the Spanish Windlass.

To vary the torture, there were occasional, totally unexpected heavy rains, and Angelina had to be extricated from deep mud, the engine exhaust blowing bubbles in the water.

Then there would be the blessed relief of gibber country, dead-flat treeless plains covered with glittering ironstone pebbles, hated by the camels, loved by the Talbot.

Most of the way they were following the Overland Telegraph Line, which had been completed, after stupendous difficulties, in

1872. However, the tracks sometimes led away from the line, and once they were given bad directions and drove 130 miles out of their way.

Some of the rocky gorges were almost insuperable. Fortunately the Talbot had an immense ground clearance and could be coaxed along from rock to rock without demolishing the lower parts of engine and chassis. But such slow grinds were a terrible test of the engine in conditions of extreme heat, made much worse by the bare rocks on every side, with the cliffs keeping off any helpful breeze.

It remains a puzzle why HHD, having organised the enterprise so well, should have set off in summer. This meant travelling in conditions of extreme heat (Aunger's diary frequently reports temperatures of well over a hundred degrees) and also, north of the Tropic of Capricorn, facing the hazards of the heavy rains of the wet season.

Angelina coped amazingly well with the low-gear work over boulders and through sand. The worst obstacle of the whole journey came at the Depot Sandhills between Horseshoe Bend and Alice Springs. Splendid to look at, the deep red sand ceaselessly sculpted by the wind, these great drifts are often fifty feet high and cannot be avoided, as they run east and west parallel across the track. These parallel sandhills are a grave hazard even for four-wheel-drive vehicles.

A true enterprise must be infinitely flexible. Imagination must not only be tested by reality but be inventive, capable of modification. It was clear to HHD that the Talbot would never be able to cross the Depot Sandhills, even if coconut matting trails were laid. The angle was so steep and the sand so soft that the scrabbling wheels would pull the matting in and throw it out the back of the vehicle. It was extremely difficult to steer the Talbot in the heavy sand. Aunger's diary (HHD's has, alas, been lost) reads for 11 December: 'Only about 200 yards hard ground in seven miles, first five miles worst, has 13 bad hills all heavy loose sand.'

The problem was solved by donkeys. Together with camels,

donkeys were the heroes of early inland transport. Infinitely tough, able to survive in dry country on poor food, donkeys are also renowned for working intelligently together. Despite their small size, a team of twelve or fourteen donkeys can pull almost anything. The Talbot's Stepney wheels were fitted and strips of canvas wrapped around the twin tyres, and as the donkeys heaved, the engine roared and the wheels spun while they searched the sand for a grip. It was odd that despite the steepness of the sandhills the donkeys had also to tow the Talbot *down* the slopes, so soft was the hot sand.

Near the Depot Sandhills they passed His Majesty's Mail being carried by a string of six camels.

The arrival in Alice Springs was sensational. Where a flourishing large town now stands on the plain north of Heavitree Gap in the MacDonnell Ranges, in 1907 there was only a tiny township and, three miles away, the telegraph station. The first motor car ever seen in Alice Springs caused consternation. Horses bolted and were not seen for days. Aboriginal women climbed trees, clutching their screaming children. Aboriginal warriors confronted something too big and strange for boomerang or spear. The daughter of the telegraph stationmaster, who was about eight years old at the time, told me that the old descriptive term 'horseless carriage' was absolutely right; there was something utterly strange about this object on wheels which moved all by itself, needing no horse, camel or donkey.

The next telegraph station to the north, Barrow Creek, had been the scene of a massacre in 1874, when the natives attacked the whites stationed there and speared to death the stationmaster, a linesman, and an Aborigine working for the whites. Whatever the causes of the tragedy, and such attacks were seldom unprovoked, a terrible revenge was taken on the Aborigines. Nevertheless, by 1907 the tribes all along the route were very friendly. HHD was an ardent, talented photographer, and the Barrow Creek Aborigines had no objections to being photographed. The naked men and women were still carrying out their ceremonies and dances, living in wurlies made of boughs and leaves, an accommodation always shared with numerous dogs.

Not long before Barrow Creek they had passed Central Mount Stuart, at the heart of Australia, and now as they travelled toward Tennant Creek they were well past the Tropic of Capricorn. The bare plains of the Centre were giving way to the rank grass of the semi-tropics which was as high as the shoulders of the men in the Talbot in areas where water was lying. In other areas they found themselves among what they called ant hills (now more correctly known as termite mounds). Often ten or more feet high, these thousands of red monoliths give one the uncanny feeling that one is being watched. One is certainly not alone; the population of the visible ant hills alone runs into hundreds of millions.

The big termite mounds were easy to avoid. Smaller ones, like stumps, were a menace to tyres and undercarriage.

One day, following the steel posts of the telegraph line across a grassy plain, they were amazed to see what looked like a man on a bicycle coming toward them. And indeed it was: the remarkable Francis Birtles riding the first bicycle across Australia, from Port Darwin to Adelaide. A lean brown man in dusty shorts, with the barest minimum of equipment strapped to his machine, Birtles had the great advantage of being able to push his wheels over soft sand and through deep mud. They had a cup of tea together, then went off in opposite directions.

They were now moving from extreme dry heat into the downpour and steamy days of the wet. Aunger's diary reads: 'Heavy going . . . boggy . . . Very coarse sand.' There are ominous references to a failure of transmission bearings, which were replaced, and then to the collapse of the pinion in the differential.

Angelina had to be abandoned. The enterprise was at an end.

They had got as far as Edinburgh Flat, south of Tennant Creek. They tapped the overland telegraph line and called up Tennant Creek. Four riding horses and four packhorses were procured, and with a Mr Perry and an Aboriginal boy they set off on the long ride back to the rail-head at Oodnadatta, and thence to Adelaide.

Perhaps to be truly enterprising one needs to be disappointed, to be crossed in the full flush of adventure. To overcome consecutive difficulties, however severe, calls for a body and mind working together in harmony, in perfect training. It also calls for belief that the enterprise is possible and worth while. Ease up, and it becomes very difficult to resume. This is especially true when more than one person is involved.

In 1907 it had been a triangle, Angelina, Murray Aunger and HHD. The two men had to get on with each other under the most trying conditions of heat, discomfort and even despair. The mud of swamps or rivers after flash floods, the sand of dry rivers or parallel sandhills negated the basic principle of the motor car, the driving wheel. Most modern cars have wheels of fourteen to sixteen inches in diameter; the Talbot's were 24 inches. But even these huge old wheels (often with the Stepneys on) could spin and sink until the frame of the car had bottomed, sunk onto the mud or sand. The donkeys had saved them at the Depot Sandhills, but there were no other saviours available. All that was left was the skill of the men and the strength of the machinery.

After fifteen hundred miles of the most extreme conditions, the two men knew exactly how to use and conserve that strength. A mad revving of power could damage the engine or break an axle. A rock or a piece of ant hill at speed could break a spring. (The Talbot had no shock absorbers.) It was a major effort just to hold those huge wheels straight with the thick-rimmed steering wheel. In sandy country they would pull one way and then the other with a will of their own, rearing to seduce Angelina off the track and threatening to pile the car up.

And then there was always the consciousness of hundreds of moving parts in what was still a primitive piece of machinery. After all, it was only twenty-two years since Carl Benz had run his first automobile, a three-wheeler powered by a two-cycle, one-cylinder engine, and eighteen years since Gottlieb Daimler had first driven his four-wheel car with a chassis, rear engine, and four-speed drive.

It is amazing that in those few years something as strong and reliable as the Talbot was available to cross a continent on unmade tracks without breaking down. Also amazing was the durability of the pneumatic tyres, in the infancy of development. They had very few punctures, which is incredible given the presence along the track of stumps, rocks, ant hills and pieces of wood or root which in central Australian trees are iron-hard.

Now, as HHD and Aunger returned to Adelaide and Anlaby, HHD's sheep-station home, the whole enterprise sagged. Angelina was out there in the wilderness, an astonishing sight for tribes of wandering Aborigines, a totally inexplicable object in its complete remoteness from their lives and knowledge. Would they ignore it? Attack and attempt to destroy it? Keep away from it in fear? There was no way of telling.

To HHD it was clear that the enterprise could not be abandoned. Despite his commitment to new technology he was in some respects a very conservative man. He set great store by the family motto, *Servabo Fidem*, which may be translated as 'I will keep good faith; I will keep my word.'

The only solution was to set off again in another Talbot (by now any other make of car was unthinkable), collect Angelina, and drive the two vehicles on to Port Darwin.

He went down to Adelaide and bought the latest 25-horsepower model, with a slightly more powerful engine and modifications which gave more strength to the rear suspension. Although ultimately known as the Overlander, this car throughout the trip was called '474', that being her South Australian motor registration number. Angelina's was 319. Of course 474 had to be fitted out with all the same equipment as carried by Angelina, and petrol and supplies had once more to be sent ahead.

On 30 June 1908, HHD and Aunger set off once more on the two-thousand-mile track to Port Darwin. They had to do it all again – the sandy creek crossings, the rocky gorges, the Depot Sandhills, the easy runs across the gibber plains. They were driving in winter, and although the days were sunny there was often an icy wind, and 474, like Angelina, had no windshield. There are violent changes of temperature in central Australia, and the temperatures will go over 110 degrees in the shade by day and drop below freezing at night. On some mornings the water in the canvas water bags was frozen.

They had no trouble with 474, and the knowledge gained from their experiences on the first trip enabled them to make better time. On 16 July they reached Alice Springs, and finally through the long, dry grass and the light scrub they saw the outline of Angelina with its tarpaulin still tied down. After all those months she was untouched. But all around her in a ring was a circle of stamped-down grass and sand. The Aborigines had indeed found her but were so terrified of this strange apparition that they would not approach her, let alone touch her; instead they simply walked round and round her, watching.

Aunger stripped down the differential and installed the new pinion, and Angelina started without difficulty. Both automobiles were driven on to Tennant Creek. On the way they passed through an area of huge boulders, some split in two by frost, others perched on top of each other, and one weighing hundreds of tons balanced across a gap between two other boulders as if a giant had rested it there.

The shade of the wide verandas of Tennant Creek telegraph station was welcome, and from here HHD sent a message south to his wife, Emily, that Angelina was safe and they were on their way with both cars . . .

The Warramunga Aborigines at Tennant Creek, once they had got over their alarm at the sight of the two Talbots, were as friendly as those at Barrow Creek had been. They also were naked, although some of the men dressed up magnificently for the motorists in patterns of feathers and pipeclay with enormous headdresses four feet wide. HHD was allowed to photograph a group of a dozen native women in mourning, daubed all over in white pipeclay, sitting on the ground chanting . . .

By a strange conjunction of ancient and modern, the Aborigines, however unwittingly, were nearly the cause of the whole trans-Australian enterprise ending in tragedy. In the thick bush and high dry grass of northern Australia the Aborigines have from time immemorial set fires to flush out game and bring on new green growth. In some places the grass was so high that the Talbots were almost invisible. HHD and Aunger were following the telegraph line north of Daly Waters telegraph station when they realised that the black smoke they had been watching on the horizon was coming much closer. Soon they were circled by fires running with the extra wind generated by the flames. With the shade temperature at over ninety-five degrees, it already was unbearably hot before the fires reached them. They wrapped wet cloths around the carburettor, where petrol vapour could rise from the crude needle valve, and hoped that the cans of spare fuel would not explode. At times the vehicles had to stop while the flames went around them. Once they charged right through the flames to get upwind of the fire.

Water had never looked as beautiful as it did when they reached lily-covered lagoons and the great northern rivers – the Roper, the

Katherine, the Daly, the Adelaide – flowing by palms and white-trunked paperbarks. But water presented new problems. These were not flash-flood rivers as in the south; these waterways flowed all year round and were full of crocodiles and that most delicious of fish, barramundi. They had to be crossed, and there were no bridges.

The cars crossed the Katherine without much trouble at a ford between the long, tranquil reaches. But the Edith, as the Daly was called where it crossed the track between Elsey and Pine Creek, imposed severe difficulties. The river was four feet deep, over the wheels of the vehicles, and the only way to get across was to tie a tarpaulin across the radiator and back around the engine, and then charge the water 'all out', in HHD's phrase. A huge bow wave rose up in front as 474 roared in between the reeds and the paperbarks, but she made it with comparative ease. Angelina did her best, but the engine died when she was within six feet of the opposite bank. But 474 towed her out and they were both on their way again.

At Pine Creek, a railhead and old mining settlement some two hundred miles south of Port Darwin, HHD decided to give Angelina a rest and put her on the train to Port Darwin.

The country varied now between thick tropical growth near the rivers and open plains with the most majestic ant hills they had seen on the whole journey, some of them ten to twelve feet high, dwarfing 474. With the track, such as it was, quite overgrown, the Talbot had to push its way through thick grass up to six feet high. Only five miles from Port Darwin they had to scramble along a narrow path cut through dense jungle.

They reached Port Darwin on 20 August 1908. The Overlander, as 474 could now be justly called, had taken fifty-one days to cover 2100 miles across the continent. It had been the best of enterprises, one crowned with success after some difficulties, and a refusal to give in after the first failure.

HHD, Murray Aunger and the two Talbots went back to Adelaide by sea. Angelina was sold, and the Overlander went to Anlaby station where for many years she did the daily mail run to Kapunda, the local town. After that she was honourably retired and kept in a shed on the property.

There is a postscript to the Overlander's story. In 1941, in World War II, HHD's eldest son, John, was in the 9th Division, besieged in Tobruk in the North African campaign. As soldiers do, he was yarning with an old friend, Jimmy Gosse (grandson of the explorer who discovered Ayers Rock), about what they would do after the war. John thought of old 474 in the shed at Anlaby. He decided on a grand enterprise. He would completely overhaul her and with Jimmy and myself (the youngest brother, then a pilot in the RAAF), fifty years after the original journey the Overlander would once again cross Australia.

And so in 1958 the Talbot completed the journey, much of it over bad, unsealed roads, in the remarkable time of ten days. She is now, still in good running order, in the Birdwood Mill Museum in South Australia, awaiting her centenary journey in 2008.

The Flowers of Kosciusko

Edna Walling

*The renowned horticulturalist and garden designer Edna Walling
casts an appreciative eye over the beauty of the wildflowers on
the summit road at Mount Kosciusko, in the Southern Highlands
region of New South Wales.*

It was the month of February, and as we left Jindabyne, the steep little
township through which the Snowy River passes, we were all keeping
our fingers crossed and watching the clouds for fear lest they should
cover the sun just as we reached the flowers. It was fortunate, perhaps,
that a part of the road to the summit of Australia's highest mountain
was in the course of reconstruction, for it meant that we left the utility at Charlotte Pass (6039 feet above sea level) and tramped the rest
of the way on foot. This is undoubtedly the best thing to do.

Of speed the savour and the sting,
　　None but the weak deride;
But ah, the joy of lingering
　　About the countryside!
The swiftest wheel, the conquering run,
　　We count no privilege
Beside acquiring, in the sun,
　　The secret of the hedge.

Somehow you do not get the same feeling of this place unless you are *walking* along that mountain road. You would pass unnoticed that enchanting little valley, a miniature crevasse, where the Euphrasia in white and mauve (sometimes called Eyebright) and bluebells (*Wahlenbergia*) and the Alpine Leek-orchid (*Prasophyllum suttonii*) provided the first thrill of excitement. We came across the white gentian (*Gentiana diemensis*) – more like a crocus than a gentian – and drifts of a delightful dwarf mauve daisy, one of the Brachycomes, *Brachycome aculeata*, at the side of the road – hundreds of them.

Snow daisies (*Celmisia longifolia*) were everywhere. Probably on account of its size, this flower seems to be the most familiar of a very delightful collection; it has a certain architectural beauty with its glistening white flowers and silvery grey foliage.

A shining white everlasting, known sometimes as Hoary Sunray and scientifically as *Helipterum albicans*, is equally striking, forming a carpet on the summit, with nothing but the clouds to form a background for it. On the very top this everlasting and the Euphrasia predominate, the Snow Daisy usually being slightly further down.

Coming back to Charlotte Pass, where we intended to stay the night on the leeward side of some Snow Gums, we cut right down from the summit, avoiding the winding road and thus came upon a vast sea of Claytonia, or White Purslane, looking for all the world like hail on the ground.

At Charlotte Pass billowing masses of the white-flowered dwarf mint-bush, *Prostanthera cuneata*, cushioned the ground for mile upon mile, wrapping itself over the huge granite boulders in some places and spilling down to the edge of the roadway in others. This is a striking low-growing shrub that never failed to delight us; there was also *Kunzea muelleri*, with its little powder-puff flowers, of a fairly bright yellow, and short pine-like foliage, a dark green and yet almost greyish green in colour.

A tiny thing with grey foliage, a mere half inch high, *Ewartia rubigina* enthralled us, though it had never a flower; who could not be charmed with such a gem?

Following the rather common practice of fixing the mind upon the name of one species growing in particular localities (for use in conversation), we, in this country, have selected the Snow Daisy. In consequence one hears practically nothing about all the other delightful flowers growing in association with this daisy. You may ask, 'Are there any other flowers growing up there?' 'Oh yes, some everlastings,' they say after a little careful thought. And striking as these two white flowers certainly are, it is with great surprise and excitement that one comes across the Prostanthera binding many an acre of soil on these mountains, the Euphrasia, the Brachycomes (daisies in many species) and the Claytonia, to mention but a few of the delights amongst the plants that cover the ground here.

The narrow, gritty road leading to the summit of Mount Kosciusko is a merciful relief from the tarred highway, even if one merely squeezes by another car with nothing to spare at times.

It is said that fifty thousand square miles of this lovely alpine country will be affected by the Snowy River Hydro-Electric Scheme. In consequence one feels that one should end by saying, 'Go without delay to these flower-covered mountains.'

The Old Bush Fence

Bernard Cronin

Bernard Cronin muses on styles of fences 'with all their tottering shapes' which evolved through Australia's pioneering years. Some of them remain, 'wrinkled by a thousand suns and hard-bitten with frost and wind'.

Of the few remaining links with Australian origins, none perhaps has such power to evoke a colourful picture of the past as some corner of an ancient fence half hidden by a tangle of orchard grass, or standing sentinel on the bank of an outback waterhole. There is something fine and brave about these old red-gum or ironbark posts and rails, wrinkled by a thousand suns and hard-bitten with frost and wind; yet holding themselves, for all their tottering shapes, with something still of the spirit of the pioneer. They are eloquent of human courage and aspiration laid aside these many years. Their timbers are a sounding-board for long dead voices, the thunder of hoofs, the bourdon of grave days and lonely nights.

One puts a hand on them as on the shoulder of a dreaming friend, and is taken into the dream and given something of its patience and resolution.

It is a little astonishing to discover how slender are our records of Australian fences. One searches in vain the repositories of Australian history. All that can be gleaned is that, generally speaking, our fences began with the discovery of gold, around 1850, when shepherds deserted their flocks and herds to join in the rush to the diggings, and harassed pastoralists found nothing for it but to enclose their possessions. Yet in odd cases properties were fenced many years earlier. In Tasmania, for example, deadwood fences constructed as far back as 1822 are still in existence. The deadwood or brushwood fence was, in the nature of things, the first type of fence to be constructed in timbered country, as the stone fence was on untimbered but stone-strewn ground. The sequence appears to have developed on the lines following:

1. Brush fence: constructed of light timber and scrub.
2. Deadwood fence: constructed of piled deadwood of varying sizes.
3. The felled fence: here trees growing along boundaries were felled as nearly in line as possible and topped where required with broken or lopped limbs, and any gaps similarly stopped.
4. The chock-and-log fence: constructed of straight logs chocked at the ends. This type of fence was possible only in the country where straight spars of from nine inches to twelve inches in diameter, and up to fifteen feet in length, were available.
5. The post-and-rail fence: this generally began with two rails only; later, two and sometimes three extra rails were added. Often they were topped with a strand of plain or (on its hateful appearance, for there is no greater danger to stock) barbed wire.
6. The wire fence: constructed of several wires drawn taut and either stapled to the posts or run through holes bored in the posts. It became the practice, as timber for posts became more difficult to obtain, to space the posts further apart and staple the wire to intervening pickets.

7. The wire-and-picket fence: constructed of double wires top and bottom, with pickets twisted into them in a continuous line. This type of fence came in somewhere at the close of the nineteenth century. It never became popular and appears to have now completely disappeared. It caught fire easily and offered too much resistance to winds, among other disadvantages.

In between these main types were all kinds of odd fences, such as zig-zags, baskets, nailed-rails, and so on. They were more or less makeshifts and were replaced as opportunity offered.

There were, too, the fencing customs brought from the Old Country: the loose stone fence, the sunken or ditch fence, and the hedge fence. All these three types are still to be seen the length and breadth of Australia.

There is an amusing correspondence in a South Australian journal, *Farm and Garden*, 1858. The writer (who seems to have called forth little response) complains, in his opening letter, entitled 'Our Fences as they are, and our Hedges as they out to be,' that everywhere is to be met the 'same dull monotonous post-and-rail, or the more modern post-and-wire . . . a blot on the escutcheon of the province and a reproach to the fair fame of Adelaide . . . only fit for fuel.' Rather obscurely, he quotes Dr Johnson: 'A man who can't build a pigstye can pull down a palace,' and goes on to plead the cause of the live fence or hedge. He lists the following trees which he claims will form a fence par excellence: Gallaba, a species of mahogany; logwood, planted closely in rows; hibiscus; privet – 'a species of wild coffee'; bois-immortel – 'a tree with a bright scarlet flower'; Cape quince; prickly pear; and thorn.

In the following year South Australia entered into a discussion as to the most effectual and cheapest fence; a three-wire with a top rail or a post and three rails; which suggests that the live fence was deemed impractical on any large scale.

It may be fairly claimed that posts and rails brought to fencing something individual which it lacked formerly, and lacks to-day, despite the acknowledged utility of the modern fence. The post-and-rail fence is a subject for both artist and writer, which can hardly be said of any of it successors. It was, as we have seen, well established in South Australia in 1858, as it was in New South Wales and Victoria. We come across wire fences not long afterwards. In the *Australasian Farmer's Guide*, published in Melbourne by one Abraham Lincolne (curiously enough), dated 1869, the cost of plain wire for fences is given as £16 a ton for No. 5 and £20/10/- for No. 8.

One must not overlook the ancient slip-rails which kept company with so many of the post-and-rail fences, and brought inspiration to the poet and song-writer of last century. Nor the old swing gate beloved of the station children, set on an inverted beer bottle and held with leather hinges. In 1897 a bushman's charge for a 5 ft. 6 in. gate of the kind, made on the job, was from 7/6 to 10/-.

If romance has vanished from our fences we may take some consolation in figures. We possess, at any rate, the world's longest fence. It is in Western Australia, is 1200 miles long, and cost £400,000.

The Trouble with Merinos

A.B. 'Banjo' Paterson

*One of Australia's most famous writers, in poetry and prose,
A.B. 'Banjo' Paterson writes here on the difficult ways of the most
important animal in Australia, the merino sheep.*

The prosperity of Australia is absolutely based on a beast – the
merino sheep. If all sheep in the country were to die, the big banks
would collapse like card houses, the squatting securities, which are
their backbone, being gone. Business would perish, and the money
we owe to England would be as hopelessly lost to that nation as if we
were a South American state. The sheep, and the sheep alone, keeps
us going. On the back of this beneficent creature we all live. Knowing
this, people have got the impression that the merino sheep is a gentle,
bleating animal that gets its living without trouble to anybody, and
comes up every year to be shorn with a pleased smile upon its amiable
face. It is my purpose here, as one having experience, to exhibit the
merino sheep in its true light, so that the public may know what kind
of brute they are depending on.

And first let us give him what little credit is due. No one can
accuse him of being a ferocious animal. No one could ever say that a
sheep attacked him without provocation, though there is an old bush
story of a man who was discovered in the act of killing a neighbour's
wether. 'Hullo,' said the neighbour. 'What's this? Killing my sheep!

What have you got to say for yourself?' 'Yes,' said the man, with an air of virtuous indignation. 'I *am* killing your sheep. I'll kill *any* man's sheep that bites *me!*' But as a rule the merino refrains from using his teeth on people, and goes to work in another way.

The truth is that the merino sheep is a dangerous monomaniac, and his one idea is to ruin the man who owns him. With this object in view, he will display a talent for getting into trouble and a genius for dying that are almost incredible. If a mob of sheep see a bushfire closing round them, do they run away out of danger? Not at all; they rush round and round in a ring till the fire burns them up. If they are in a river bed, with a howling flood coming down, they will stubbornly refuse to cross three inches of water to save themselves. Dogs and men may bark and shriek, but the sheep won't move. They will wait there till the flood comes and drowns them all, and then their corpses go down the river on their backs with their feet in the air. A mob of sheep will crawl along a road slowly enough to exasperate a snail, but let a lamb get away from the mob in a bit of rough country, and a racehorse can't head him back again. If sheep are put into a big paddock with water in three corners of it, they will resolutely crowd in to the fourth corner and die of thirst. When sheep are being counted out at a gate, if a scrap of bark be left on the ground in the gateway, they will refuse to step over it until dogs and men have sweated and toiled and sworn and 'heeled 'em up', and 'spoke to 'em', and fairly jammed them at it. Then the first one will gather courage, rush at the fancied obstacle, spring over it about six feet in the air and dart away. The next does exactly the same, but jumps a bit higher. Then comes a rush of them following one another in wild bounds like antelopes, until one 'over-jumps himself' and alights on his head, a performance which nothing but a sheep could compass.

This frightens those still in the yard, and they stop running out, and the dogging and shrieking and hustling and tearing have to be gone through all over again. This on a red-hot day, mind you, with clouds of blinding dust about, with the yolk of wool irritating your eyes, and with, perhaps, three or four thousand sheep to put through. The delay throws out the man who is counting, and he forgets whether he left off at 45 or 95. The dogs, meanwhile, take the first chance to slip over the fence and hide in the shade somewhere. Then there are loud whistlings and oaths, and calls for Rover and Bluey, and at last a dirt-begrimed man jumps over the fence, unearths a dog and halls him back to work by the ear. The dog sets to barking and heeling 'em up again, and pretends that he thoroughly enjoys it, but he is looking out all the time for another chance to 'clear'. And *this* time he won't be discovered in a hurry.

To return to our muttons. There is a well-authenticated story of a shipload of sheep being lost once, because an old ram jumped overboard into the ocean, and all the rest followed him. No doubt they did, and were proud to do it. A sheep won't go through an open gate on his own responsibility, but he would gladly and proudly follow another sheep through the red-hot portals of Hades: and it makes no difference whether the leader goes voluntarily or is hauled struggling and kicking and fighting every inch of the way. For pure, sodden stupidity there is no animal like the merino sheep. A lamb will follow a bullock dray drawn by sixteen bullocks and driven by a profane 'colonial' with a whip, under the impression that this aggregate monstrosity is his mother. A ewe never knows her own lamb by sight, and apparently has no sense of colour. She can recognise her own lamb's voice half a mile off among a thousand other voices apparently exactly similar, but when she gets within five yards of her lamb she starts to smell all the lambs in reach, including the black ones, though her own may be a white lamb. The fiendish resemblance which one sheep bears to another is a great advantage to them in their struggles with their owners. It makes them more difficult to draft out of a strange flock, and much harder to tell when any are missing.

Concerning this resemblance between sheep, there is a story told of a fat Old Murrumbidgee squatter who gave a big price for a famous ram called, say, Sir Oliver. He took a friend out one day to inspect Sir Oliver, and overhauled that animal with a most impressive air of sheep wisdom. 'Look here,' he said, 'at the fineness of the wool. See the serrations in each thread of it. See the density of it. Look at the way his legs and belly are clothed – he's wool all over, that sheep. Grand animal, grand animal!' Then they went and had a drink, and the old squatter said, 'Now, I'll show you the difference between a champion ram and a second-rater.' So he caught a ram and pointed out his defects. 'See here – not half the serrations that other sheep had. No density of fleece to speak of. Bare-bellied as a pig, compared with Sir Oliver. Not that this isn't a fair sheep, but he'd be dear at one-tenth Sir Oliver's price. By the way, Johnson' (to his overseer) 'what ram *is* this?' 'That, sir,' replied the astounded functionary, 'that's Sir Oliver, sir!' And so it was.

There is another kind of sheep in Australia, as great a curse in his own way as the merino – namely, the cross-bred or half-merino-half-Leicester animal. The cross-bred will get through, under or over any fence you like to put in front of him. He is never satisfied on his owner's run, but always thinks other people's runs must be better, so he sets off to explore. He will strike a course, say, south-east, and so long as the fit takes him he will keep going south-east through all obstacles, rivers, fences, growing crops – anything. The merino relies on passive resistance for his success; the cross-bred carries the war into the enemy's camp, and becomes a living curse to his owner day and night. Once there was a man who was induced in a weak moment to buy twenty cross-bred rams, and from that hour the hand of fate was upon him. They got into all the paddocks they shouldn't have been in. They scattered themselves all over the run promiscuously. They got into the cultivation paddock and the vegetable garden at their own sweet will. And then they took to roving. In a body they visited the neighbouring stations, and played havoc with the sheep all over the district. The wretched owner was constantly getting fiery letters from his neighbours: 'Your . . . rams are here. Come and take them away at once', and he would have to go off nine or ten miles to drive them home. Any man who has tried to drive rams on a hot day knows what purgatory is. He was threatened with actions for trespass for scores of pounds damages every week. He tried shutting them up in the sheep yard. They got out and went back to the garden. Then he gaoled them in the calf pen. Out again and into a growing crop. Then he set a boy to watch them, but the boy went to sleep, and they were four miles away across country before he got on to their tracks. At length, when they happened accidentally to be at home on their owner's run, there came a huge flood. His sheep, mostly merinos, had plenty of time to get on to high ground and save their lives, but, of course, they didn't, and they were almost all drowned. The owner sat on a rise above the waste of waters and watched the dead animals go by. He was a ruined man. His hopes in life were gone. But he said, 'Thanks God, those rams are drowned, anyhow.' Just as he spoke there was a splashing in the water, and the twenty rams solemnly swam ashore and ranged themselves in front of him. They were the only survivors of thousands of sheep. He broke down utterly, and was taken to an asylum for insane paupers. The cross-breds had fulfilled their destiny.

The cross-bred drives his owner out of his mind, but the merino ruins his man with greater celerity. Nothing on earth will kill cross-breds, while nothing will keep merinos alive. If they are put on dry saltbush country they die of drought. If they are put on damp, well-watered country they die of worms, fluke, and foot rot. They die in the wet seasons and they die in the dry ones. The hard, resentful look which you may notice on the faces of all bushmen comes from a long course of dealing with merino sheep. It is the merino sheep which dominates the bush, and which gives Australian literature its melancholy tinge, and its despairing pathos. The poems about dying boundary riders and lonely graves under mournful she-oaks are the direct outcome of the author's too close association with that soul-destroying animal, the merino sheep. A man who could write anything cheerful after a day in the drafting yards would be a freak of nature.

Timbergetters and Scrub Dwellers

Eric Rolls

The Pilliga forest in north-central New South Wales gave an opportunity to men with no capital for an independent life as timbergetters and sleeper cutters. Eric Rolls went among the old-timers from the Depression years and in A Million Wild Acres *he recounted the skills involved and their memories of the harsh life. He also reported vividly on the wildlife in the forest.*

The forest gave opportunity to men with no capital for an independent life as timbergetters and sleeper cutters. The rabbit industry offered life without a boss to thousands, the forest to a few hundred. As the extending railways needed more and more sleepers, axemen set up camp by a creek in the ironbark forest. Some built houses for a wife and family and lived in the one place for fifteen years. When the near timber cut out, they rode bicycles to work.

A few worked with mates to 'give them a back down on the saw'. Most of them were so independent they worked alone and rigged a 'chinaman' or 'dummy' at the other end of the two-man crosscut saw. A flexible stick was driven into the ground and one end of the saw tied to it. In later years bands were cut from discarded rubber tyre tubes as straps to improve the action of the dummy.

The first sleeper cutters chopped the big ironbarks down with axes. So did the first fellers of pine. And, since it was hard work and bending made it harder, they chopped the trees off at a convenient height. The wastage in the stumps was huge and unthought of. Then the untidy butt was sawn off and the log was measured into eight foot lengths. The length of sleepers in New South Wales was always eight feet. The width and thickness varied but was usually nine inches by five inches. Metric sleepers are measured in millimetres, 2440 x 230 x 130. Two classes of sleepers were bought: square backs and round backs. A square back had to be all solid heart wood. A round back could have 'a bit of wane on it' – one end might run out into sapwood or even lack a few centimetres on each corner.

The sleeper cutter sawed the trunk into lengths until it was no longer big enough for sleepers. There was still much good timber left but he had no sale for it. He cut it off to rot.

He barked each length by bruising a line along one side with the back of his axe, rolling the log with a cant hook and bruising another line. He swung the axe heavily and if the season was good and the timber was sappy, the black heavy bark lifted off even a big log after he bruised four or five lines. The timber beneath is pinkish white, damp and pimply. A newly barked log looks like a woman stepping out of a hot bath into cold air, exposed, goosefleshed and a little surprised. In a dry time, when the trees are not growing, barking is a hard job. It seems to be glued on. There is little sapwood on good ironbark, perhaps twenty millimetres on a log ninety centimetres in diameter. Keegan of Baradine cut fifty-two sleepers from one tree, about 6.6 cubic metres of sleepers, and at least half of it would have been wasted in the slabs too small for sleepers. There is no such wastage in modern times. Trimmed sleeper offcuts are eagerly bought by graziers for yard building. The sleeper cutter sells them under a fictitious name and gets a good tax-free addition to his income.

The sleeper cutter often lit a kerosene lantern and sawed into the night. He liked to have a few lengths barked and ready for boarding out and billeting in the morning. A billet is a piece with a sleeper in it split off the main log. The board is his marker. It is a thin slab the size of a sleeper section. He studied the grain in the small end of a log, applied his board so the longer sides ran with the grain and pencilled round it. Then he took his chalked line, usually kept in a tobacco tin full of whiting, stretched it along the log and with one smart flick marked the line of his first cut. If he decided the log was a splitter, and many of the big ironbarks split well, he drove steel wedges into the bottom corners of his pencilled shape and, as the billet began to lift, he rolled the log with a cant hook and drove in wedges progressively along the chalked line. He always worked towards the big end to give room for error. He used wedges of various sizes, sometimes two together for greater leverage. One man who drove a thick wedge into a tight log reached down inside the crack to retrieve a small wedge. The big wedge popped, the split closed and trapped his hand. No one came. When his body was found weeks later the deep marks were still in the sand where he had scrabbled with his feet to try to drag in his axe. The blade lay no more than seven centimetres from the farthest stretch of his toes.

There were no sledgehammers for the early sleeper cutters to drive wedges. They made their own malls of Gunnedah Ironbark, an occasional cross between Narrow-leaf Ironbark and a box, probably Yellow Box. The timber has the hardness and weight of ironbark and the round grain of box. It will not split. Few are found. Logs of it were used sparingly and treasured for years. When fitted with a steel rim the mall face bulged over it and held it tight. As the mall wore the rim slipped down. They were superior to modern sledgehammers. The tops of the wedges did not mushroom under their impact.

If the grain was not true enough for wedge splitting, the sleeper cutter 'grooved in' and 'blocked out'. If he made a mistake and felled a tree with an exaggerated circular twist in the grain he abandoned it. Such trees could not be handled till the modern power saw was invented. Both grooving in and blocking out were done with a squaring axe, a long-bladed implement with an offset homemade handle and untidy wedges driven into the eye at different angles. It looked an awkward tool. But each sleeper cutter spent hours testing and setting it. If he was expert in its use, 'you could slide your bare bum down one of his sleepers and never get a splinter'. The inexpert often had to tidy up with the adze, a mattock-shaped axe that he swung between his straddled legs.

One side of the squaring axe was flat to cut a true face, the other bevelled to push the sliced-off chips away. The handle was offset so the sleeper cutter did not bark his knuckles on the billet. Left-handed axemen and right-handed axemen set it to opposite sides. Hard close-grained Motherumbah (*Acacia cheelii*) or Needle Bush (*A. rigens*) made favourite handles. The carved handle was boiled then bent to the desired set and pegged till it cooled. Alf Waterfield of Baradine, usually known as Whiskers, is remembered for the long-lasting handles he made. He told no one what timber he made them of.

Once the handle had the correct sideways set, it had to be adjusted with several wedges to suit the sleeper cutter's height so that the axe hit the billet squarely on the full edge. He tested the point of balance on a forefinger. He lifted the axe and let it fall under its own weight and tapped the wedges till the cut was perfect.

A sleeper cutter kept two squaring axes: a special one for the finishing work and another for grooving out. But although any sleeper cutter would say he used his second axe for cutting a groove, he never called it a grooving axe. Applied to the tool the word lost its meaning. He called it a 'groving axe' or a 'gruvving axe'. With it, in a log that would not split naturally, he cut a groove fifteen centimetres deep along the chalk line. When he first came into the district, Alf Water-field astonished the local cutters by lifting his squaring axe above his head and cutting with full force. It was usual to make a less confident half swing along the chalked line. Then the sleeper cutter finished splitting off the billet with mall and wedges, chocked it off the ground and squared the other side of the sleeper by blocking-in. He stood on top of the billet and used his felling axe to chop V-shaped notches into a second chalk line. He called the notches 'windows' and according to the toughness of the log he made them forty to eighty centimetres apart. Then he split off each block with his squaring axe. The squaring axe alone was usually sufficient to shape the other two sides.

Sleeper cutters soon found they could fell trees with the crosscut saw and thus save the time taken to square off the V-shaped end on the chopped butt. They made a first cut into the centre of the tree called a 'belly scarf' from the side they judged the tree would fall. They re-adjusted their dummies on the other side of the tree and sawed straight through in a horizontal plane about seventeen centimetres above the belly scarf which helped direct the fall and cushion it so the log did not split. The belly scarf also helped prevent a frightening 'whip back' when a tall evenly balanced tree jumped backwards off its stump and fell anywhere.

Some men cut extraordinary numbers of sleepers with a squaring axe. Oddle Edwards cut twenty-seven in one day on Wangen. His younger brother, Jim, averaged one hundred and fifteen a week for three weeks running. But they were the numbers boasted of, not the numbers averaged, and it was only possible when the sleeper cutter found a good big stand of free splitting timber. Usually he spent as long a time looking for timber as he did cutting. Bert Ruttley who classed himself as a good average cutter filled two drays a week for several years. A dray held sixteen. Loaded drays on the weekly trip to the railway depots could be heard coming ten kilometres away as they jolted in and out of the potholed tracks. The jarring shafts galled the horses. One man could bring in up to four drays at a time. He would drive two horses in the leading dray and hitch another on behind so he had spare horses to pull a bogged dray out of a sand monkey. The horses in the other drays, with promise of a good feed of chaff and oats at the end of the trip, willingly followed the first.

Sleeper cutters insist that sleepers cut with the squaring axe were superior because the axe closed the pores in the timber and protected it. The bruising shut of cut pores could have had only a temporary effect. Anyway the cells of timber run longitudinally. The early sleepers were superior because they were cut from selected trees. Nowadays any tree big enough is cut.

The food these men worked so hard on was rough enough. Jack Thompson and Jim Pullen who cut together often argued their preferences. Jim was a Salvation Army man and a slow talker. 'A ma-a-n when he's wo-o-rkin' needs plen-n-ty of sweet things such as bre-a-a-ad and ja-a-m and bre-a-a-ad and ho-n-n-ey.' His old mate, Jack, who had heard it often would stamp his feet till the dust flew. 'A man do not! A man when he's workin' needs somethin' substantial such as bread and fat.'

'I've eaten a lot of bread and dripping in my day,' old Ned Edwards of Baradine told me. 'There was never much meat about. The squatters would not sell it. We didn't like kangaroo and wild goat was awful. They ate too many gum leaves, and all you could taste was eucalyptus.' Ned was in his late eighties when I spoke to him in 1974. He boasted he had won sixty-four trophies at bowls, he had thirty-three grandchildren, and forty-four great-grandchildren, 'and a lot more to come yet, by Jesus!' School had always been too far away and he never learnt to write much but he taught himself to read just as his father had done. He had that brief spell of blacksmithing with Jack McCarty, he cut sleepers and bridge timber, he was a rouseabout in woolsheds and carried his swag between sheds, he was a shire maintenance man pugging the road between Baradine and Coonabarabran with a horse and tip dray. For many years he was head of the road gang in the Forestry Commission and with twenty-two men under him cleared and graded the first roads through the forest. They all pedalled out on bicycles early on Monday mornings with a week's supply of food in haversacks on their backs. He built Ned Edwards Bridge of round ironbark in the 1940s. The bridge is marked on Forestry Commission maps on Sixteen Foot Road in Pilliga East State Forest. The workmanship is outstanding. So is the quality of the timber. Almost forty years later the bridge was still as sound as when it was built.

Ned Edwards worked for several months on a fencing contract with Donald Magann, his cousin, who was trying to earn some money to improve the block of Baradine he had taken up. Donald's mother had been a housemaid for Mrs Fetherstonhaugh. He went to school till he was eleven, a common leaving age. Their boss on the fencing job was an uncle, Jack Munns, who had bought out several selectors on Goorianawa. They worked from daylight to dark then returned to their camp to cook the evening meal and enough food for the next day.

'He was a hard man,' said Ned. Donald Magann was present that morning. He also was nearing eighty-seven years old. 'The only way we could get a bit of a rest was by suggesting a game of mumble peg,' said Donald. 'He loved that game and would play for hours.' Both old men got out their pocket-knives and knelt on the verandah to show me how the game was played.

Mumble peg was played on sand or loose soil with two-bladed pocket knives. The longer pointed blade was opened fully, the shorter round-ended blade, usually known as the castrating blade, was opened at right angles. The first player pushed the short blade into the soil so that the knife stood up with the handle and long blade in a horizontal line. Then he flicked the handle and spun the knife into the air. He scored points according to how the knife landed: one hundred if the long blade speared into the ground, fifty if the short blade speared in and the knife returned to the starting position. He scored twenty if the knife stood upright on its handle, fifteen if it stood on both blades, ten if it fell on its back with the short blade poking in the air, five if supported by the handle and short blade. If it fell flat he scored nothing. The players flicked in turn and kept score.

They had meat on that job. Each night Donald cooked damper in one camp oven, Ned cooked the rest of the meal in another. 'We had meat, potato, pumpkin and jam,' said Ned. 'No jam,' said Donald, 'No bloody fear! Jam was too dear.' 'Honey!' said Ned remembering, 'a sixty pound tin of honey. Or Cockies' Joy, we used to go for that'. Golden syrup, the cockies' joy, was packed in the same bronze tin until the 1970s. It was the one treat the battling selector permitted himself.

The early camp ovens, the universal cooking utensil for both hearth and camp fire, show brilliant technique in casting and the making of metals. The walls are only three millimetres thick. It is difficult to get iron to fill such narrow moulds even when the freezing point is lowered by the addition of phosphorous. Metallurgy is now a science not a craft and some of the old arts have been lost. Modern metallurgists do not know how the old camp ovens were poured. Like anvils, they are still made but the walls are now six millimetres thick. The modern ovens burn everything the unfortunate cook puts in them.

The old camp ovens cooked deliciously but the bush worker's meals were monotonous. The evening meal usually cooked while he was at work. In the early morning he put potatoes, pumpkin, salt meat and a little water in his camp oven, covered it with the well-fitting lid, then dug a hole and threw in about four centimetres of hot coals. He settled the camp oven on to them and shovelled in more coals till they covered the lid. When he returned at night it was ready. All he had to do was make his damper. On a sheet of bark or the blade of a shovel he kneaded flour, salt, water and a pinch each of cream of tartar and baking soda. He dusted another camp oven with flour, put it on a low fire till the flour began to brown, then added his damper. It cooked in half an hour.

There are two species of Grey Kangaroos but they are not easily distinguished. The two species were confirmed by a study of blood samples in 1966. They might overlap in the Pilliga. One would expect to find the Forester or Eastern Grey Kangaroo (*Macropus giganteus*) but some of the hair samples studied by Hans Brunner were more typical of the Western Grey Kangaroo (*Macropus fuliginosus*). Many of the Grey Kangaroos lived in the forest where they had no access to open country. Their habits were changing in the 1970s. Bores and ground tanks supplied them with water in the northern and western sections of the forest, creek holes and permanent springs in the south. In many places they dug a metre or so to water in the sanded creeks and supplied wild pigs as well as themselves.

The bigger kangaroos are lavish with water. Through binoculars we watched a big buck Red-necked Wallaby on a sandy spit at one end of the Black Duck Waterholes on Borah Creek. For more than an hour he alternately bent down on four legs to drink and straightened up to groom himself with his tongue or soak his forearms and lower legs with saliva. Kangaroos sweat only at times of great exertion. Usually they depend on evaporation from special vascular structures to reduce body temperature. Even on mild spring days our pet Grey

Kangaroo frequently soaked his forearms and lower legs where networks of small veins spread beneath the skin. He never dipped them in his water bucket, he always drank first then wet them with saliva. It streamed from his mouth as he licked, far more liquid than he could have held in his mouth after drinking. As soon as his arms and legs were dripping wet the massive saliva flow stopped. When he groomed the rest of his body his tongue just kept normally moist.

Hairy thick-set Wallaroos changed their habits, too, and spread from the mountains into flat country, I disturbed one asleep in the middle of a flat paddock of wheat twenty-five kilometres from the nearest hills, an extraordinary place for a mountain-dweller to be found. The plentiful Red-necked Wallabies began to build up in the mid 1950s as cover increased and most of the Dingoes had been taken. Doggers stopped work in the forest in 1954.

In the early 1900s Dingoes were so plentiful they ran in packs. Billy Mills of Baradine counted twenty-four one morning at daylight in 1910 as they ran away from a dead beast on Dandry Creek. Marc Lubb remembered them in packs of ten to fifteen howling about his tent at night and coming into the firelight to steal food scraps thrown away after the evening meal.

In such numbers Dingoes outstrip their preferred food supply of native mammals and kill sheep. A determined effort was made to get rid of them in the 1940s. Any gaps in the landholders' high dog-proof fences were filled in right round the northern and eastern boundaries of the forest and professional doggers set to work with traps and poison. Sleeper cutters earned extra income shooting them for the scalp money placed on their heads. Many set trip guns across tracks to water. A rifle was lashed to a tree with the muzzle sighted at Dingo height. Then a wire tied to the trigger was stretched tightly across the track. Some men had up to six rifles set. It was dangerous to walk or ride along any but the main tracks.

A few Dingoes survived. In 1973 as we drove through old Gibbican in the Baradine State Forest a big red dog took off fast and straight from a Red-necked Wallaby run over by a truck on Mag's road. The dog had opened the Wallaby on the belly, not a place where a domestic dog would begin to feed. Mrs Jill Morphett of Uplands, Boggabri, on the eastern edge of the Pilliga Nature Reserve, watched through binoculars as a spotted yellow dog ran ahead of the Christmas Day fire in 1974. Tawny yellow, sometimes with spots, is one of the main colours of Dingoes. About a fortnight later Jack Taylor on Delwood, an adjoining property, found a ewe killed in the manner Dingoes kill. She was a strong shorn ewe. Her tracks and those of one dog led through the mud of a little creek to where she had been pulled down by the loin and her kidneys and kidney fat eaten. Another ewe nearby was still alive but so badly ripped about the loin her intestines dragged behind her as she walked.

We found two lots of droppings that were certainly dog and probably Dingo when collecting samples in 1974 for Hans Brunner to process. One had eaten a wild pig, the other a Brush-tailed Possum. Another dog, or possibly fox, had eaten part of a Spiny Anteater. The sharp spines of anteaters do not protect them as well as one would suppose. Among his collection Hans Brunner had the stomach of a Dingo that ate an anteater spines and all.

Pepper, our Beagle bitch, showed me how an anteater can be eaten. All food excited her but she was particularly excited by her own catches. When she nosed out an anteater she attacked cautiously at first. It was half-buried below a rotten pine branch. She felt its back with her paws then decided to dig under it. She dug quickly but the pine branch frustrated her so she bit hunks out of the rotten wood until it was nearly bitten through. Then she moved about thirty centimetres up the branch, seized it in her teeth, and propped one paw as a fulcrum in the hole she had chewed. She jerked backward with her head and pushed with her paw till the branch broke. She barked her pleasure, dragged it out of the way, then leapt back to dig under the anteater. By then it had wriggled itself almost out of sight. Pepper dug with all her energy but the anteater made little hunching movements and sank into the ground as fast as Pepper dug. She lay down panting and watched it for a while. Then she barked, cleared the dirt off its back, opened her mouth and struck downward with her top teeth. Three spines broke off. She leapt back, barked and came in again. Several more spines broke off. Blood ran from her mouth but she was too excited to feel pain. The third time she made it obvious she would soon break off enough spines to give her a clear bite. She was excited beyond obeying me so I picked her up and carried her away. Dingoes, bigger and stronger than Pepper, rake anteaters on to their backs and bite at the softer belly.

With a plentiful food supply anteaters are common in the forest. Signs are seen more often than the anteaters: dug-out ant holes, burrows in termite mounds, or piles of the peculiar sandy droppings of several ages under curved logs or in sandstone caves. Each wanders about in a home range of about forty hectares and returns to favourite night covers at irregular intervals. A range overlaps several others. At mating time the female drags her cloaca along the ground and soon collects a following of males attracted by the scent trail. Hollow logs have been found seemingly stuffed with Spiny Anteaters, a female and her coterie of males.

The hairs of Brush-tailed Possums were found in fox scats. Although their food supply has increased these possums are not as common as they were. In the 1930s thousands of possums were trapped for their skins with copper wire nooses on poles leant against trees. No possum could resist the easy way down the poles offered. Many more were poisoned with cyanide and flour. Yet the possums seemed to replace the numbers taken each year. Bushmen declare possums were devastated by myxomatosis in the 1950s along with rabbits. That did not happen but the observation that possums grew scarce then is undoubtedly sound. Almost certainly it was predation by foxes that reduced their numbers. Foxes had lived on rabbits ever since foxes were released in Australia. Then after eighty years their chief food supply had to be replaced suddenly.

Mrs Gwen Bower of Baradine was troubled by Brush-tailed Possums that lived between her roof and ceiling. They thrived on the fruit in her garden. When they grew too many and too noisy I lent her cage traps fitted with drop doors. The possums came readily to baits of pomegranate and honey and she caught them all in a few weeks. We released them among good food trees where there were no other possums.

The colony consisted of ten females of different ages, one young male, and one old male with a yellow belly. The young male was not mature or else the old male would not have tolerated him. Several times during the two years the possums were in residence Mrs Bower heard sharp fights in the ceiling. Each time a young male was found next morning crouched tightly in a corner where a verandah joined the house. Five times she heard prolonged fighting that continued for two or three nights and culminated in cries of pain that grew weaker and stopped abruptly. Each fight was followed a few days later by a bad smell above the ceiling, then the noise by night of something being dragged. The bad smells were transferred to a dense clump of bamboo at the bottom of the garden. Mrs Bower felt sure the old male killed any young males that did not willingly leave the colony and pulled them out of the house when they began to smell.

Out-of-town possums do not live in colonies. They lead solitary lives in defined territories with overlapping boundaries much like Spiny Anteaters.

Since there are few rabbits in dense parts of the forest far from settlement, fewer imported House Mice and, except near water, few imported rats, the foxes and feral cats that live in those places mostly eat native animals: insects in summer, small marsupials and native mice in winter. Food passes quickly through the stomachs of foxes and the hairs in their dung locate colonies of native mammals. Some of the marsupials eaten are rare enough but it is unlikely any species will be wiped out by this predation. What have suffered are the native cats that seek the same food as the foxes and feral cats. Some were still seen in the forest during the 1970s as a glimpse of something spotted in the headlights of a car. One was trapped in a Boggabri fowl-yard in 1972. The species is not known. They were probably the bigger Tiger Cats, creamy-brown with white spots that extend along the tail. The smaller native cats, now very rare, have no spots on the tail. They were creatures of the open eucalyptus forests and were once common. None of their original habitat is now available to them. If the forest has saved any it has saved them in a foreign atmosphere.

For more than forty years there have been reports of Panthers in the forest. Joe Rodgers who lived on Borah Creek twice saw a big black cat during the 1970s. He saw it once about thirty metres away just on dusk and again one night very clearly by spotlight. Several others who were with him saw it too. Joe is accustomed to estimating the weight of animals – his family breed pigs – and he judged it to weigh about fifty-five kilograms.

Big cats, black, tawny or striped, are persistently reported from many parts of Australia. Possibly seven different mammals are seen. The Pilliga cats might be Panthers. The creatures referred to as the Emmaville Panther are almost certainly Panthers. A circus trailer carrying two male Panthers and one female crashed off a New England road in 1959. The cage burst open and all three escaped.

Pumas are reported from the Grampians in Victoria. A few American airmen brought Pumas to Melbourne as cockpit pets during

World War II and released them in the mountains when they learnt it was against the law to bring them into Australia. But the Grampian Pumas are confused with the big feral cats sometimes seen there, twice the size of the biggest domestic cat. And elsewhere there are big yellow foxes that look different to other foxes, and Dingoes and feral dogs of unusual colours.

Among these reports of several mammals there are some that seem to describe a big marsupial cat and others that describe the Thylacine, or Tasmanian Tiger. A photograph of a supposed mainland Thylacine published in the *Sunday Telegraph* 27 March 1977 was no proof of its existence. The head looks foxlike – the massive jaws of the Thylacine are missing – and the stripes might have been painted on the body. The heavy tail is cocked to one side in a position that looks unnatural. The Thylacine uses its tail for balance like a kangaroo. It does not swish its tail about like a milking cow.

Early one morning in the Willala hills I heard three inexplicable noises. They were loud deep coughs with a rolling growl at the end, the sort of noise one would expect to hear when approaching the big cat cages at the Zoo, not near an Australian hill. The animal was no more than thirty metres away but the growth was so dense it was impossible to leave the graded fire trail I was walking along to look for it.

Cheating the Flames of Death

Gary Hughes

Gary Hughes wrote this immediate first-person report for his newspaper, The Australian, *after his family's remarkable survival in the Victorian bushfires of February 7 2009, which claimed 173 lives.*

They warn you it comes fast. But the word 'fast' doesn't come anywhere near describing it.

It comes at you like a runaway train. One minute you are preparing. The next you are fighting for your home. Then you are fighting for your life.

But it is not minutes that come between. It's more like seconds. The firestorm moves faster than you can think, let alone react.

For 25 years, we had lived on our hilltop in St Andrews, in the hills northeast of Melbourne.

You prepare like they tell you every summer.

You clear. You slash. You prime your fire pump. For 25 years, fires were something that you watched in the distance.

Until Saturday.

We had been watching the massive plume of smoke from the fire near Kilmore all afternoon; secure in the knowledge it was too far away to pose a danger.

Then suddenly there is smoke and flames across the valley, about a kilometre to the northwest, being driven towards you by the wind. Not too bad, you think.

I rush around the side of the house to start the petrol-powered fire pump to begin spraying the house, just in case.

When I get there, I suddenly see flames rushing towards the house from the west. The tongues of flame are in our front paddock, racing up the hill towards us across grass stubble I thought safe because it had been slashed.

In the seconds it takes me to register the flames, they are into a small stand of trees 50m from the house. Heat and embers drive at me like an open blast furnace. I run to shelter inside, like they tell you, until the fire front passes.

Inside are my wife, a 13-year-old girl we care for, and a menagerie of animals 'rescued' over the year by our veterinary-student daughter.

They call it 'ember attack'. Those words don't do it justice.

It is a fiery hailstorm from hell driving relentlessly at you. The wind and driving embers explore, like claws of a predator, every tiny gap in the house. Embers are blowing through the cracks around the closed doors and windows.

We frantically wipe at them with wet towels. We are fighting for all we own. We still have hope.

The house begins to fill with smoke. The smoke alarms start to scream. The smoke gets thicker.

I go outside to see if the fire front has passed. One of our two cars under a carport is burning. I rush inside to get keys for the second and reverse it out into an open area in front of the house to save it.

That simple act will save our lives. I rush back around the side of the house, where plastic plant pots are in flames. I turn on a garden hose. Nothing comes out.

I look back along its length and see where the flames have melted it. I try to pick up one of the carefully positioned plastic buckets of water I've left around the house. Its metal handle pulls away from the melted sides.

I rush back inside the house. The smoke is much thicker. I see flames behind the louvres of a door into a storage room, off the kitchen. I open the door and there is a fire burning fiercely.

I realise the house is gone. We are now fighting for our lives.

We retreat to the last room in the house, at the end of the building furthest from where the firestorm hit. We slam the door, shutting the room off from the rest of the house. The room is quickly filling with smoke. It's black, toxic smoke, different from the superheated smoke outside.

We start coughing and gasping for air. Life is rapidly beginning to narrow to a grim, but inevitable choice. Die from the toxic smoke inside. Die from the firestorm outside.

The room we are in has french doors opening on to the front veranda. Somewhere out of the chaos of thoughts surfaces recent media bushfire training I had done with the CFA. When there's nothing else, a car might save you.

I run the 30 or 40 steps to the car through the blast furnace. I wrench open the door to start the engine and turn on the airconditioning, as the CFA tells you, before going back for the others.

The key isn't in the ignition. Where in hell did I put it? I rush back to the house. By now the black, toxic smoke is so thick I can barely see the others. Everyone is coughing. Gasping. Choking. My wife is calling for one of our two small dogs, the gentle, loyal Gizmo, who has fled in terror.

I grope in my wife's handbag for her set of car keys. The smoke is so thick I can't see far enough to look into the bag. I find them by touch, thanks to a plastic spider key chain our daughter gave her as a joke. Our lives are saved by a plastic spider. I tell my wife time has run out. We have to get to the car. The choices have narrowed to just one option, just one slim chance to live.

Clutching the second of our two small dogs, we run to the car. I feel the radiant heat burning the back of my hand. The CFA training comes back again. Radiant heat kills.

The three of us are inside the car. I turn the key. It starts. We turn on the airconditioning and I reverse a little further away from the burning building. The flames are wrapped around the full fuel tank of the other car and I worry about it exploding.

We watch our home – our lives, everything we own – blazing fiercely just metres away. The heat builds. We try to drive down our driveway, but fallen branches block the way. I reverse back towards the house, but my wife warns me about sheets of red-hot roofing metal blowing towards us.

I drive back down, pushing the car through the branches. Further down the 400m drive, the flames have passed. But at the bottom, trees are burning.

We sit in the open, motor running and airconditioner turned on full. Behind us our home is aflame. We calmly watch from our hilltop, trapped in the sanctuary of our car, as first the house of one neighbour, then another, then another goes up in flames. One takes an agonisingly slow time to go, as the flames take a tenuous grip at one end and work their way slowly along the roof. Another at the bottom of our hill, more than a 100 years old and made of imported North American timber, explodes quickly in a plume of dark smoke.

All the while the car is being buffeted and battered by gale-force winds and bombarded by a hail of blackened material. It sounds like rocks hitting the car.

The house of our nearest neighbour, David, who owns a vineyard, has so far escaped. But a portable office attached to one wall is billowing smoke.

I leave the safety of the car and cross the fence. Where is the CFA, he frantically asks. With the CFA's help, perhaps he can save his house. What's their number, he asks me. I tell him we had already rung 000, before our own house burnt. Too many fires. Too few tankers. I leave him to his torment. I walk back towards our own house in a forlorn hope that by some miracle our missing dog may have survived in some unburned corner of the building.

Our home, everything we were, is a burning, twisted, blackened jumble. Our missing dog, Gizmo, Bobby our grumpy cockatoo, Zena the rescued galah that spoke Greek and imitated my whistle to call the dogs, our free-flying budgie nicknamed Lucky because he escaped a previous bushfire, are all gone. Killed in the inferno that almost claimed us as well.

I return to the car and spot the flashing lights of a CFA tanker through the blackened trees across the road. We drive down the freeway, I pull clear more fallen branches and we reach the main road. I walk across the road to the tanker and tell them if they are quick they might help David save his house. I still don't know if they did. We stop at a police checkpoint down the hill. They ask us where we've come from and what's happening up the road. I tell them there's no longer anything up the road.

We stop at the local CFA station in St Andrews. Two figures sit hunched in chairs, covered by wet towels for their serious burns. More neighbours. We hear that an old friend, two properties from us, is missing. A nurse wraps wet towels around superficial burns on my wife's leg and my hand.

We drive to my brother's house, which fate had spared, on the other side of St Andrews.

The thought occurs to me, where do you start when you've lost everything, even a way to identify yourself. Then I realise, of course, it doesn't matter. We escaped with our lives. Just. So many others didn't.

The Piners' Life

Richard Flanagan

Richard Flanagan revisits the life of a rare group of workers, the men who extracted the prized Huon pine from the rugged forest lands of river systems on the west coast of Tasmania.

For those who sought the golden wood, Huon pine, the inter-war period was to be the golden age. For over twenty years, upwards of a hundred men worked and lived up and down the many rivers that constitute the Gordon River system, felling, hauling, clearing and collecting the logs that kept the five sawmills and port of Strahan perpetually busy.

The boom had its origins in the improved log hauling techniques the piners had begun to use in this period. No longer were the large, long logs of pine man-handled through often dense scrub to skidways and chutes with only the assistance of long hand-spikes used in the manner of a crowbar. The piners now used block and tackle and, in the less remote areas, horse teams were employed. Horses were driven along the Eagle Creek track to work on the lower Franklin and were used as far up the Gordon as the Rocky Sprent River, where the Huon pine bridges built for their use still remain. These new hauling methods meant the piners could now log many areas that before had been thought worthless, either because they had been previously worked, or because the timber was too inaccessible and hence too expensive to get out to the river's flowing waters. These advances in efficiency, coupled with a depressed labour market and low wages, made it possible for a man to make relatively good money. In those grim times, when the average wage (if you were fortunate enough to have work) was about £3, a good piner could earn £6–£7 a week.

But the piners could not live complacently with the present, for such is the nature of the slow-growing tree that a second harvest lies centuries away, if at all. To all intents and purposes, pine is a 'one-off' product. So for thirty years the piners pushed further up the Gordon and its tributaries in search of the new stands of pine that were the lifeblood of their livelihood. As they roamed and, in the course of their searchings, discovered, a tremendous spirit of exploration grew among these men. Charlie Abel, a son of Barnes Abel, recalled how his father would often suddenly decide to head off and explore: 'Often the old bloke would take a mad fit on himself and he'd say "We'll go and look for some timber", and away we'd go . . . I don't suppose anybody knows those rivers better than we do'.

These days little is remembered of the great exploratory feats of the piners. Not being publicists, belonging to no city bushwalking club or conservation group, their stories were told only to one another, hence only enduring to the graves of those who had created them. In historical and general books and articles on the West, the piners are given at best only token recognition, while at worst they are dismissed as vandals, hell-bent on destroying the environment. In consequence, many people now believe that true exploration of the rivers began in 1958 with John Hawkins' descent of the Franklin, and Olegas Truchanas' descent of the Gordon. Yet the Morrison brothers had been down the Franklin nearly two decades before John Hawkins' successful attempt, while Olegas Truchanas' trip had for its inspiration an old account he had read of an exploration led by Barnes Abel up the Gordon in 1928. Nowadays little is left of even the names they gave to the rivers' many features as they pulled their punts upriver:

the names Slippery Guts Rapid, Long Tom Rapid, Red Hills, Smith's Creek, Smith's Weekly Creek and Big Bastard Rapid are now all gone. Deception Gorge is now called the Great Ravine, while Devil's Hole has the more prosaic title of Big Fall.

In the piner's heyday, though, the valleys and gorges had rung with these names and the names of the families that worked the rivers: the Abels, the Dohertys, and the Morrisons, the Finns and the Grinings; they had rung with the feats of the men of those families: epic stories such as when Charlie and his brother, Basil Abel, rowed from the First Split on the Gordon through to Strahan to get an appendix victim to safety; or when Charlie and Basil's father, Barnes Abel, once walked form Tullah to Port Davey in four days to prove he knew the country better than any living man.

The life of the piners was extremely demanding, not only physically, as they had to work weeks on end in dangerous conditions in the cold and wet forests, but also mentally, in the self-imposed isolation. It could often be months between seeing people other than those in one's own gang. Barnes Abel, for example, went up the Gordon in the latter half of 1939 and built himself a hut of King Billy pine, in which he lived through that summer and much of the ensuing harsh winter. When he returned to Strahan in mid-1940 he was to find the world had been at war for over half a year. The piners, however, did not regard the conditions of their work as extraordinary or hard, but simply viewed all the disasters and delights that befell them as a way of life. As Charlie Abel remarked:

it was just a job, that's all it was. It was nothing out of the ordinary because you rowed up the Gordon, way up to the top end, up the Splits there, and it took you a month to get your tucker there for three months – well we didn't take any notice, it was just in a day's work.

The job finished when the gang had enough logs or was running out of food. Then they would start the long return trip to Strahan. If they were on a small, dry river such as the Rocky Sprent, the piners would leave the logs till a flood would, with luck, wash them out. If they were on a major river, they would collect all their logs at one point and these would then be let go. As the logs drifted with the current, two of the gang would be in a punt at the front ready to catch them, and two men would come behind clearing logs out of eddies, hauling others out of trees and snags 'and whenever night fell on you, that's where you stopped – up on the banks of the river, and if it were too bloody wet you sat up all night . . .' The slow journey downstream might take up to a week before the logs reached a point on the Gordon where they could be collected into a raft and towed to Strahan by little steam launches such as the *Kathleen* and the *Lynx*.

When the men reached Strahan many would go on a wild spree. The legendary 'Bunny' Doherty, whose reputation for hard work was only surpassed by his reputation for hard drink, once walked into a Strahan hotel carrying an axe by his side. The barman attempted to make conversation with Bunny about his axe and enquired politely if he could have a look at it. The piner responded by embedding the axe in the bar top, and then casually asking for a drink.

But after the drinking and carousing were over the men generally returned to the rivers. It was more than the money that attracted them, it was the lure of the river life itself. Arthur Doherty, who worked the rivers in his youth, recalled some of his impressions:

There are some things in your life that you will never ever forget, and one of them is Lifebuoy soap – that's carbolic – you wash on a cold, frosty morning outside the camp, you wash yourself and it's got a smell of its own. The other thing is horse manure. You've got a horse stable, and the smell of that first thing of a frosty morning is something terrific. There are such things – I suppose everything has its own smell – but if you are pulling on to a skidway, a muddy sassafras skidway, with the bark coming off it, and you go on to that and the horses start to plonk through the icy mud and the smell rises – there's something about that smell – it's not a bad smell – it's just a beautiful earthy smell and they are the sort of things that if I live to be ninety will still come back to me . . . and I suppose there are a lot of people that never had the privilege of smelling that sort of thing.

Long before the rivers of the South-West were household words, the piners knew and held deep feelings for the country through which they flowed. They loved and hated the rivers but were never indifferent to them. The rivers could make or break a man. A flash flood might wash all a gang's logs out as soon as they left a site and the piners would be in good money. Alternatively, it might take two or even three years before logs with their brands would be seen drifting in the Big Eddy on the lower Gordon. For the men who were only paid by the mill when it received the logs it could be a grim wait, especially if they had families. The piners knew and respected the awesome might of a land where the rivers could change in appearance overnight from a gentle stream to a wild, stormswept torrent, ready to trap the careless and unwary.

James Fenton, who battled similar conditions exploring the North-West interior in the mid-nineteenth century, wrote:

when one comes to live on salt pork and damper for twelve months at a time, the sentimental is pretty sure to vanish before the stern realities of life. Nevertheless there really is fascinating charm in exploring the primitive forests . . . Go into it however and spend a day toiling and fighting to make headway through its impenetrable mazes and you will discover that 'a thing of beauty is not a joy for ever'.

The 'stern realities' of the piners' lives certainly tempered many of their romantic and sentimental excesses towards nature. But by placing the feelings they had firmly in reality, it added a depth and breadth to their beliefs that many modern environmentalists will never know. Thus it was with deep conviction that Reg Morrison said, 'The Gordon and her tributaries are my life, financially and in every other way. If they dam her it would be like cutting off the blood to my body'.

For such men the rivers meant far more than just an enjoyable, adventurous holiday. 'The old man', said Charlie Abel, 'stood on the beach at Lake Pedder years before that Truchanas chap was even thought of, but he didn't say anything – well, that and the rivers – it was a way of life then'.

It was a hard life, and some found it too much and left. During the Depression a number of North-West Coast bushmen came down to Strahan to make their fortune pining. Harry Smith called them the 'bog-oranges' because some had been potato diggers, and the name stuck. Most 'bog-oranges' found the rainforest too difficult and confusing to work in and threw their jobs in. A few stayed on and became good piners, equally adept at rowing a punt, using an axe with either hand, and finding their way in the bush as those who had been on the rivers all their lives.

Most piners would start full-time work in a family gang at the age of thirteen or fourteen, after finishing their schooling. The boys grew up quickly. By the age of sixteen they were treated as men and expected to do an equivalent amount of work.

Gangs would generally consist of four to six men who would live in a camp of semi-permanent nature near the river. There would be a hut with low log walls, roofed with canvas, with an entrance at one end and a fireplace and chimney at the other. Up the chimney would go freshly carved axe handles to be hardened in the evening smoke the same way Aborigines harden their spears in the fire. Sometimes new flannel shirts would also be thrust up the chimney. In good weather, a piner wore one flannel tucked into his dungaree trousers. In cold weather, such as the winter of 1931 when the snow lay down the banks of the Gordon to its mouth, they pulled on the outer flannel, slightly larger and looser, leaving it untucked. After a new flannel had been left up the chimney for a few days, it was considered thoroughly enough waterproofed by the smoke to be worn.

Some camps had more solid huts, such as the one the Abels built on the Upper Jane in the early 1930s. Balfour Johnston, an early bushwalker, saw the hut in 1935 and was much impressed by it, giving a detailed description of what he saw:

> Constructed in the American log cabin style, this hut was built entirely of Huon pine logs and palings. It was some forty feet long and fifteen feet wide. There were no rooms, and the entire end of the hut was one huge fireplace. We marvelled at the hardiness and endurance of these pine cutters. The hut was crammed with provisions and equipment, bags of flour, onions, sides of bacon, and tinned goods of every description. There were three iron camp ovens, one dozen axes, huge blocks and hundreds of feet of rope. All this had been carried in on their backs over twenty-one miles of difficult mountainous country from the West Coast road. Later we learnt that they had been packing for nine consecutive months.

Unlike normal hardwood logging, where most of the time is spent felling, many of the piners' days were spent in such work as packing or boating supplies and gear in, finding new sites of pine, building

217

new camps, building skidways out of the greasy 'sassy' saplings, then hauling and shooting the Huon pine down such skidways into the river. The splash of the pine log in the water did not signify the end of the piner's labours. After a flood he would have to go upriver and clear snagged logs and later collect all the logs together in a boom. If the logs had come down a particularly rough river, such as the Jane or the Rocky Sprent, the shattered, pulped ends would have to be sawn off to leave a clean cut. Whatever they were doing they did it from daylight to dark. Rising with first light they would go outside into the chill morning air and quickly wash with carbolic soap, then have a breakfast of perhaps 'powdery', a form of bread cooked in a camp oven, eaten smeared with jam or golden syrup which was known as 'tear-arse'. And if the gang was going logging, they would start rowing their punt slowly up or down the quiet river, trying to pick out and distinguish landmarks through the heavy mist that lay all round so that they would know when they had come to a particular belt of pine. Then, with axe and crosscut saw, which in the hands of skilled men cuts faster than a chainsaw, they began the proper work of felling the Huon pine.

The piners' life was dangerous, tough and often miserable, yet in the beauty and grandeur of the rivers lay rewards for them far richer than any miller's cheque could offer. Such was the world of the men who were to open up the Gordon River country.

Head Stockman at Wave Hill

Tom Cole

*Tom Cole, a legend of outback life, recounts the trials and tribula-
tions of his period as manager at Wave Hill, a huge cattle property
owned by the Vesteys, an English firm with vast station holdings
in Australia.*

The Ambroses were busy getting the stores and supplies needed for
Banka Banka, while I filled in my time at O'Shea's pub. Tim O'Shea
had four attractive daughters and I was completely infatuated with
two of them. I was beginning to find out that I had some hitherto
unsuspected talent for getting into difficulties without realising it.
This was an area which, over a wide span of years, was to sidetrack
and divert me to a considerable extent. However, looking back and
recalling some of the alarming situations in which I found myself it
appeared I was twice blessed – my talent for getting into difficulties
was shaded, but only just, by a flash of genius which got me out. In
this case it might be said I was saved by the bell.

One day I was approached by an elderly gent who introduced
himself as Alex Moray. I knew instantly who he was, pastoral inspector for Vesteys, controlling all the firm's cattle stations. He came
straight to the point; he wanted a head stockman for Wave Hill, one
of Vesteys' larger properties. He had been talking to the Ambroses
and they had recommended me, for which I was grateful.

I accepted with alacrity. Paddy and Jim were quite happy to look after my horses until I could make arrangements to get them; they also said that they would see that Bill Crowson, whose horses I had brought from Anthony's Lagoon, would get them back.

Everything fell into place nicely and two days later I was on Bob McLennan's mail truck heading for Wave Hill, 300 miles to the west. McLennan, the mail contractor, was a Gallipoli veteran and a seasoned warrior in many other fields. In the dry season he battled his way over what was not much more than a bridle track in an old truck that testified clearly to the rugged conditions. Dropping mail at Willeroo, the first stop, 100 miles from Katherine, then another thirty to Delamere, then seventy miles to Victoria River Downs completed the first day.

Pigeon Hole, an outstation of VRD, was next and finally Wave Hill. The round trip was 600 miles. There were other stations – Inverway, Limbunya, – further out whose mail he carried, but they had to make their own arrangements: there was only a bridle track. A native stockman and a couple of pack horses had to ride to Wave Hill: for them it was a couple of hundred miles there and back.

In the wet season, roughly from November until March, the roads were impassable for any kind of vehicle. McLennan would then muster his horses, ten or fifteen pack horses and half a dozen saddle horses for himself and his two horse tailers; perhaps a couple extra if he had a passenger. Sometimes he did; there was no charge, but whoever it may have been certainly earned the ride.

Of the pack horses, two especially selected for their tranquillity carried a few dozen bottles of rum, the sales of which supplemented his income.

The principal rivers, such as the King, Battle Creek, Victoria River, perhaps one or two others, would often have to be swum, and at this he was an expert.

The crossing place would be carefully selected according to the force of the current, the most important feature being a gently shelving bank on the other side, enabling the horses to get out easily. Having decided on that, the water would be entered about half a mile upstream. If they missed the landing place they could be carried for miles downstream before they found another place suitable to leave the water, and sometimes they would find their way back to the side form which they had started.

The mail, rations, swags and gear would be packed into an enormous tarpaulin and tied at the top like a huge plum pudding. It was dragged into the water and floated with surprising buoyancy, pushed to the other side by two men swimming beside it, keeping it upright. A couple of trips were usually enough to get everything across.

At night the tarpaulin was slung between two trees and served as a shelter. In those latitudes, it rained more at night. The mail, the packs and saddles, McLennan, his horse tailers and any passenger slept under it. The mail was always kept dry, the men were nearly always wet and the mail was never late.

Bob told me that in all the years he had carried the mail to Wave Hill he had had only one serious mishap, when a crocodile took one of his horses crossing the King River. He was paid £400 a year and, as Bob explained to me, the rum sales were 'fruit for the sideboard'.

And so I came to Wave Hill.

Vesteys owned seventeen cattle stations, from Western Australia in an almost unbroken chain to the Overland Telegraph Line. Totaling something in excess of 40,000 square miles, they were but a fraction of this multinational company's interests.

Headed by Lord Vestey, the firm had substantial interests in Africa, Latin America, meatworks scattered around the world like confetti; and the Blue Star Line, one of the world's largest shipping companies, flew the Vestey house flag.

This vast empire was one of the most successful in the world, judging by the publicity given to what must have been one of the most ingenious accounting systems ever devised. It enabled Vesteys, while accumulating massive profits, to completely escape the demands of the British taxation authorities.

Among the tongue-in-cheek criticisms of this legal villainy one could detect a distinct note of jealousy, not unmixed with admiration and, if the press reports of the day are to be believed, it caused a serious fracture in a friendship between the polo-playing young Lord Vestey and a prominent member of the British Royal House (which, I suppose, is understandable, the latter being the recipient of substantial largesse garnered from such sources).

Wave Hill Station was the jewel in the crown of the Australian pastoral division. Being head stockman there carried a certain amount of prestige; it gave me a lot of satisfaction to take over the camp of such a famous station.

It was first taken up by the incomparable Nat 'Bluey' Buchanan in 1885. I have always thought of Bluey Buchanan as one of the finest and most courageous bushmen Australia has known, and it is unfortunate that more of his exploits have not been recorded. He rode with Landsborough in one of the earlier searches for Burke and Wills. He was with Cornish exploring the Diamantina River in 1861. He formed Mt Cornish Station, then the largest cattle station in the world, for the Landsborough Pastoral Company.

In 1887 he piloted 1200 head of cattle through country that was then unknown to Europeans, from Aramac in Queensland to a station called Glencoe, 100 or so miles south of Darwin. This property had been taken up by two partners, Travers and Gibson, who had a station called Punjab at Aramac. Travers came with the cattle but unfortunately was speared by the blacks on the Limmen River, a little more than halfway to their destination. Bluey buried him there and continued – there was nothing else he could do.

Shortly after this the surviving partner, Gibson, was discouraged enough to sell Glencoe to Fisher and Lyons, who had formed the North Australian Pastoral Company. They had already taken up the mighty Victoria River Downs. However, they were sufficiently impressed with Glencoe to commission Bluey Buchanan to oversee the buying and moving of 20,000 cattle from Queensland to Glencoe.

This must surely stand today as one of the greatest droving feats of all time: the number of cattle, the distance, the unknown terrain. It took nearly four years from the time they started and there are several astonishing features to this tremendous movement of cattle.

Fisher and Lyons, like Travers and Gibson, must have been deceived by the apparent potential of the country; one can only assume that they saw it after the first storms, when a lush growth of grass appears. They could not have been aware of what it was like a few weeks later when torrential rains were flooding the country, the gentle creeks turned to raging torrents and spear grass an impenetrable ten feet high. Twenty thousand head of cattle!

Even allowing for their lack of knowledge of the country, and endeavouring to see it through their eyes at that time, it is still difficult to believe that it was carried through with such determination. We are all experts in hindsight, especially in the area of other people's failures, but it has always seemed to me that a strong streak of sheer insanity ran through the operation. Victoria River Downs, with its beautiful Mitchell and Flinders grass downs, lay empty. And to cap it all, ticks reared their bloodshot heads and the dreadful redwater fever added to the decimation of those 20,000 cattle.

Forlornly they gathered up what was left of their herd and took them to Victoria River Downs. Meanwhile, Bluey Buchanan had taken up Wave Hill.

The Buchanan clan was then strong in the Territory and the Kimberleys. Among them were Bluey's wife's brothers, the Gordons: his nephews the Farquharsons, who had helped him blaze the trail with the Glencoe cattle, had stayed and pressed on further west. Hughie, Harry and Archie Farquharson had taken up a couple of thousand square miles on the headwaters of the Victoria River and Sturt's Creek and called it Inverway. Then there was Gordon Downs, Flora Valley, Birrandudu; they were all associated one way or another. It was a mighty saga.

Vesteys swept through the country in 1913 like a ravenous lion and the owners, all with empty pockets and open arms, welcomed them – the pot of gold at the end of the rainbow had, for them, materialised at last.

A meatworks was built in Darwin and in 1914 they were all ready to go when war broke out. The Blue Star Line came into Darwin regularly and took meat away. Its ships were sometimes torpedoed, of course, but the British Government looked after that for them. Their contribution to the war effort was considerable; their profits massive.

After the war, things went badly for Vesteys; industrial troubles piled up in Darwin and eventually the meatworks closed altogether. The bullocks that used to go north were then turned eastward, 70,000 of them every year, starting in March.

This was when Wave Hill really came into its own. Beautiful land and ideally situated, it became an important link in the chain. All the bullocks from their properties to the west – Margaret River, Lower Sturt, Flora Valley, Gordon Downs, The Turner, Ord River, Mistake Creek, Waterloo, Limbunya and more. They all came to Wave Hill where they were rested for a year. It was a tremendous operation. After a year's spell they were walked to Queensland, and the drovers who brought the cattle from the west carried on with a fresh mob.

I introduced myself to the manager, Alex McGugan, a man of few words. He pointed out my quarters with the remark that he didn't think I'd be seeing much of them, which I took as a hint that he didn't expect to see much of me around the station area. After saying that he'd see me first thing in the morning to take me out to the stock camp, he left me to my own devices.

I made the acquaintance of the storekeeper, the saddler, the blacksmith-cum-mechanic and a well borer. I was trying to get as much information about Wave Hill as possible. One thing they all agreed on was that McGugan was 'an odd sort of a bastard', and apparently he'd had quite a few men through his hands in a fairly short space of time. I was the third head stockman he'd had for the Number One Camp that year . . . and it was only July!

There were three stock camps; Number One, Number Two, and Catfish. Number Two and Catfish were outstations and consequently didn't come into contact with the manager much which, it would seem, made for a better relationship.

As I was well aware, the storekeeper was the most important individual on stations owned by companies whose headquarters were in some distant city. He did all the ordering of supplies, calculating the quantity of rations required, the numerous items that kept the wheels of industry revolving. With the nearest source of supplies 300 miles away, the calculations had to be correct to the last ball of hemp for the saddler, the last handful of horseshoe nails for the stock camps. It was he who knew exactly how many calves were branded three years ago and who, after figuring the number of females to be deducted less the accepted mortality rate, would come up with a figure for the number of bullocks the stock camp would be expected to muster. They were never far out. And it was he who advised the distant general manager of a lot of other details. He was frequently known – not always affectionately – as a 'company man'.

Vesteys was very much the big company organisation and figures were its life blood; always a mystery to, and usually detested by lowly ringers and stockmen. When calves were branded the tally was cut into a stick, one by one with a castrating knife, at the branding fire. After adding them up and dividing them by two – half females, half males – they were entered into a book most meticulously with what appeared to be, to quote Banjo Paterson, 'a thumbnail dipped in tar'. Sydney managers frequently developed apoplexy from such minor matters.

I wandered down to the blacksmith's shop and made the acquaintance of a genial old fellow who was busy repairing a pump rod. In between drilling and bolting he explained to me that he was 'a bit of bloody everything'.

'I'm the windmill expert,' indicating the pump rod; 'I'm supposed to know all about that bloody contraption,' pointing to a truck (the inevitable Model T Ford), 'not to mention blacksmith,' nodding to a sheet of iron swinging from a rafter, on which was painted in letters of black:

Toiling rejoicing sorrowing
Onward through life he goes
Each morning sees some task begun
Each evening sees its close.

Unless a bloody bore breaks down
And water's running low
No matter whether night or day
This bastard's gotta go.

I laughed and asked him where the second verse came from, and he modestly said, 'Me.'

'Last time old Moray was here he took a photograph of it and said he was going to send it to the big wheel in London – Lord Vestey I s'pose.'

Another fine character was an old Aborigine named Charcoal, who was just about pensioned off. He looked after the manager's horses, which wouldn't have put any great strain on him: managers never rode anywhere they could get their utility to go.

Charcoal told me he came from Newcastle Waters. He was just a piccaninny when Bluey Buchanan came through with a mob of cattle, giving his horse a drink at the big waterhole where the Newcastle Waters homestead is now.

Charcoal said: 'I was sitting under a tree crying. My father had just given me a belting, I bin playing 'round with a quee-i [young lubra].' He laughed at the recollection, 'She was the wrong skin [totem], I was playing with wrong side, wrong kind play too.' He chuckled at the memory: 'Old Man Bluey said, "You like come long me?" I said, "Ui, me like", so he picked me up and carried me in front of him on his horse.'

Charcoal was quiet for a while, enjoying the memories. Then he said: 'I never bin on a horse before, first I liked it, then I got big fright and cried – he was taking me away from my momma and my poppa and my country. But old man Bluey was good to me: gave me plenty tucker, then we come up long Wave Hill and I saw the big river, plenty fish, plenty turtle, plenty duck, full up bush tucker – more better than Newcastle Waters, and I played with quee-is and no one belted me.'

He told me Buchanan became a father to him; he accompanied Bluey wherever he went. 'Bluey learn me everything,' he said, 'show me how to shoot a gun, the Myall blackfellas used to spear plenty cattle, got plenty cheeky.'

He told me they were attacked once by the Myall blacks. He said a friend had warned him they were planning to spear them and loot the store, but when he told Bluey he laughed and said: 'They all talk-talk 'bout spearem me fella, all gammon.'

Charcoal said, 'I told him, "I dunno, they talk-talk plenty, me tink-tink plenty."'

He said Sam Croker was working with them at the time and they were about to start a horse muster. He got the saddle horses in from the paddock and Bluey, Sam and Charcoal rode down the river together. 'We took Winchesters with us, we nearly always took our guns, we were way down the river. Bluey and Sam were riding in the lead, my horse was a bit lazy, I'd dropped back a bit. We came to a clump of paperbark saplings an' my horse shied real bad, I look round an' four Myalls had jumped out of the saplings an' they all had long shovel spears.

'I sing out, "look out Bluey, Sam look out, Myall blackfella here an' I galloped into the scrub an' got my gun out, it was under my saddle flap, there were some more Myalls in the scrub an' they ran away, they all had spears but got fright, some ran into the river, some fella run all about. I heard some shots, an' I shot him dead. Then me an' Blue an' Sam got together again an' I asked them how they got on an' Bluey said "We give 'em the biggest fright they ever had in their life before, they won't come back."

'Then I said: "Well I gave one a fright that won't come back because I shot him dead!" Then Bluey got real cross with me, I thought he was going to belt me, I never seen him that cross before. He said: "You shot one of those poor bastards dead? Jesus Christ! You shouldn't have done that!" He was real mad at me, he said we'd better go and have a look at the poor bastard, he mightn't be dead. So I took them to where I'd shot him. He was real dead, no gammon; my bullet had gone through his head. Bluey told me I'd have to bury him but the ground was terrible hard an' I got some friends and we made a big fire an' cooked him up to nothing.'

I could well believe Charcoal's story; Buchanan was known as a very humane man and treated the blacks, whether they worked for him or not, extremely well – a lot better than most.

Some time later Charcoal showed me the tree the Myall had climbed. If it hadn't changed much since then he wouldn't have had much chance of escaping.

McGugan took me out to my new command, which was camped on the Camfield River about twenty-five miles from the station. On the way he gave me a rundown on my duties. Number One Camp was the bullock camp and didn't have much branding to do, except towards the end of the year on the Camfield, sometimes meeting Pigeon Hole, an outstation of Victoria River Downs, for a boundary muster. The Wave Hill herd was about 30,000; the mustering and branding of these was taken care of by Number Two and Catfish camps. Wave Hill was a depot for bullocks coming from the western stations and Number One received them from the drovers, turned them out into the paddock where they would be rested for a year, and the drovers would be given a fresh mob – always 1350 – which they would take to a company station in Queensland, a walk of 800 miles.

The camp usually handled about 30,000 to 40,000 bullocks in a season. This sounds a very formidable figure, but not as daunting as it appears. The head stockman would know exactly when a drover was due. He would take delivery of the drover's bullocks, count them, turn them into a paddock, count a fresh mob over to him, all in one day. In some cases the drover might ask for a day's spell, but the schedule was a fairly tight one with mobs arriving four or five days apart.

We got to the stock camp at midday and after a brief exchange McGugan left. Whatever bonds of friendship there may have been once were now conspicuously absent.

I thought Gordon Smith, the outgoing head stockman, was a good type and though I was taking his job, I knew nothing of the circumstances of his departure. He greeted me warmly and together we went over details of the camp. He had the working horses rounded up, and we looked through the horse book. It seemed there were about 150 working horses; fifty to sixty were in work at a time, roughly five or six weeks between changes. They were very good horses and had been well looked after; they were all well shod and their backs were good. (In a badly run camp, saddle sores were frequently prominent.) all the saddlery was in good condition and everything was nice and tidy.

There were nine Aboriginal stockmen, a young jackeroo and a Chinese cook. Smith said all the stockmen were good, the jackeroo was a nice lad, he said 'but don't let him out of your sight, don't let him get away on his own in the bush.' He went on to say that he'd sent him out on his own once to look at a waterhole and it took almost the entire camp a day and a half to find him. 'If you put him in a shithouse, turned him 'round three times and closed the door he'd never find his way out!' I made a mental note of this disability.

He said old Ah Ping was a good cook but hated getting on a horse, which of course he had to do when the camp was moved. 'Make sure he's always got a quiet horse, one that'll wait for him when he falls off. One thing about Chinese cooks,' he went on to say, 'they never complain – you can fuck them about, pack up in the middle of the night, they'll never say a word. A white man would never stand it.'

Gordon Smith stayed another day. I found him a very likeable bloke; he didn't say much but clearly he hadn't got on with the manager.

I ran the Wave Hill camp for the rest of that year and found McGugan a very difficult man to work for. In November I brought my camp into the station for a change of horses. We were busy pulling the shoes off before turning them out, it was stinking hot, I was strug-gling with a mare who was being twice as obstinate getting her shoes pulled off as she was when they were being put on: McGugan didn't choose an ideal time to come over to the horse yard and criticise.

I hadn't seen him coming and had just torn my hand on a bent horseshoe nail. I suddenly heard his voice: ' What are you doing in at the station, Cole? You're s'posed to be mustering Cattle Creek.'

'Well I'm not mustering Cattle fucking Creek because it's dry from one end to the other. Consequently there are no cattle there to muster, the reason for that being because they like to be somewhere they can get a drink now and then.'

But he wasn't going to be beaten as easily as that. 'Well, that may be, but I don't think you need a change of horses. Your horses are in very good condition – they're good for another couple of weeks.'

At this stage I knew it was all over for me at Wave Hill. I climbed up and sat on the top rail, looking down at him from what I thought was a position of advantage. 'I am head stockman of this camp,' I said. 'I am not going to work the horses into the ground, and if I'm not capable of deciding when they need a change then I'm not capable of running a camp . . . and you can stick the whole lot, one horse at a time, up your fundamental orifice!' Which I thought was a very good expression.

He turned and walked away. As he did so I heard him mutter, 'Jesus Christ, I've got a line of fence and number seven bore up there now!' Apparently a fencer and another man who was pumping at number seven bore had pulled out and told him something similar. It was the first flash of humour I'd ever heard from him. I don't know whether it was intentional.

Fettlers – A Particular Breed

Robin Bromby

The lonely life of the outback railway fettler, patrolling and maintaining the lines often along hundreds of kilometres of uninhabited country, led to a particular breed of hardy bushman, as seen by railway historian Robin Bromby.

All the railway systems had fettlers, thousands of them across Australia. These were the men who were responsible for a given length of rail – they are also known as lengthsmen for this reason, or track repairers or gangers – and their lives were spent travelling along that section making sure it was in good condition and fixing anything that was wrong. It was not much of a job: you worked hard, really hard, in all weathers; lived in tents either permanently or when you were away from home; and often your water had to be delivered by train. The West Australian Government Railways' working timetable of 1953 for the Laverton and Leonora branches instructed staff that 'water for Permanent Way Gangs, must as far as possible, be supplied on Down journey' (that is, on the trip outward from Kalgoorlie, not on the return journey) and that Train 191, which ran two days a week, 'may stop at 402-Mile Post . . . to set down provisions'. In the 1940s, the narrow gauge goods trains that ran on the Central Australia Railway would often depart with a wagon load of sheep; these were for the gangs along the line and the train would stop at each fettler settlement and drop off the next week's meat supply.

The list of equipment used by a typical fettler gang testified to the backbreaking work involved. They would either carry with them or have in their huts rail tongs, spiking hammers, picks, shovels, crowbars, ballast forks, hand augers (a tool for boring holes in wood or in soil), dog-spike lifters, rail jacks and long-handled spanners.

Cec Townsley, who took a job as a fettler on the Injune branch in Queensland after coming back to Australia from service in World War II, did not last all that long. As Cec puts it, after the army years of living in tents in the middle of nowhere, he did not feel like doing the same thing for Queensland Railways, and threw in the railway work in favour of a job based in Roma.

His experience would have been typical. In very hot weather, the gang of six men of which Cec was part would pitch their tent out on the job. Otherwise, they slept in a goods shed which had been built with walls of galvanised tin (no wonder they slept out in tents during hot weather) although the ganger, the man in charge, did have a house at one of the stations along the line. The first job each morning was to 'run the line' of that section for which they had responsibility to check for any problems. Otherwise, most of the time was spent lifting and packing sleepers or replacing any that were beyond their useful life. The worst part of the job was working Saturdays as well which meant that, because there was no train after they finished their shift, anyone without their own transport was stranded in the camp for the weekend.

There were not too many trains on the Injune branch, traffic varying over the years from three a week up to nine. Yet even such a lightly used branch required considerable manpower. It was, at 100.6 km, on the longer side as far as Queensland branches were concerned but there was not a great deal of difficult country even though there were fifty-three bridges, most of them small. Yet in 1932, five gangs of fettlers were stationed along the branch, one each based at Minka, Orallo and Injune, with two others based at small sidings.

Every fettler, to a greater or lesser extent, knew how vulnerable they were on their small trolleys if they came around a curve and found themselves face-to-face with an oncoming train. There were no walkie-talkies in those days; many country stations were not connected to the telephone system. While a ganger might know the timing of the daily mixed, a livestock or wheat special could catch them by surprise. Life was made even more risky if there were any tunnels on the line in such a circumstance.

When they were not replacing sleepers, the fettler – if they were located in one of the parts of Australia with lush vegetation – would regularly chip the weeds along the permanent way with a shovel, or they might have a can slung over their back containing weed killer and a spray gun. The gang would also have beaters, a doubled up piece of canvas attached to a pole, used to control burn offs of long grass alongside the railway line. They could also turn their hands to farm work when local property owners needed help; they could do such tasks as sewing wheat bags or being roustabouts in the shearing sheds. No doubt the money helped, but for the farmers it was a solution to a labour problem at the times of the year when everyone on the land needed to find more pairs of hands.

There were many who spent their working lives at this task. Others were blow-ins: men looking to make a few quid before moving on elsewhere, taking the job because it was the only one on offer; or men on their way to something better. William Morris (Billy) Hughes worked as a fettler in Queensland (among other jobs like stockman, bookseller and ship's cook, until he was taken on by the Australian Workers' Union). Edward Mabo, of the famed Native Title case, was one, as was the writer and poet Roland Robinson after arriving as an immigrant in 1921. The Australian writer Xavier Herbert (his real name was Alfred Jackson) worked on the narrow gauge North Australia Railway, being based at Rum Jungle south of Darwin. In the 1920s, Herbert used his experiences on the railway and in Rum Jungle for his portrayal of the town of Black Adder Creek in his classic *Capricornia*. In that book, he describes train day (in those days, it ran once every two weeks):

> Train day was special to the people living on the railway, particularly to the fettlers, to whom the train brought not only mail and stores and news from civilisation in the form of gossip, but wages for the past fortnight's work and liquor for the next fortnight's drinking.

The luckier ones were stationed in towns, but many lived with their families at remote wayside stops, often camping out when away on overnight trips. Lloyd Holmes recalled when, on a 1955 journey from Albury to Culcairn in New South Wales, he spotted from the carriage window at Table Top station a scene that stayed in his mind. There, beside the goods shed, sat a fettler's wife sitting outside the family's white calico tent peddling on her sewing machine.

> Somehow this unlikely domestic scene typified the spirit of the then New South Wales Government Railways: here she was, no electricity, no running water, no amenities to soften life, no protection from the heat and cold but a thin layer of canvas, kids probably temporarily enrolled in the nearby school, and she was sewing away merrily for her family.

Or the fettler and his family might be comfortable on location if given railway department houses. However, Norman Sibraa was not one of these when he was posted to Jerilderie in the Riverina region of New South Wales in the late 1950s.

As his daughter Norma Gowans remembers it, there was no railway house available in Jerilderie when the two parents with their eight children (there would soon be two more) arrived from the former posting at Yenda on the Temora-Roto line. So they set up house in the Jerilderie goods shed and Norman put in an application for a tent. When that arrived – it was a large, marquee-style tent – bags were nailed to the ground to make a floor. Norman's wife was then able to sweep up the dust that blew in and so keep the place as tidy as she could. The children slept in the large tent, but the parents had a smaller one next to it which served as their bedroom. The family showered once a week, using water from the locomotive watering tank at the station. There was an outside lavatory and from time to time Norman would dig a new hole and move the shelter on to it. Each Sunday, the kids would go to the local tip looking for food scraps dumped by the local greengrocer. The children's tasks during the week included carrying home food and supplies from the local shops hauled in old sugar bags. Norma also had the job of walking along the line on payday to pick up her father's pay packet from the station. During the week, their mother would walk more than half a mile to wash the family's clothes. She did that every weekday, with Norma given the job on Saturdays. They might have lived in a tent with bags for flooring, but there were no dirty clothes left lying around. The wet laundry was carried back from the creek and hung to dry on a wire strung between two trees. (Mind you, it was not only fettlers that endured such conditions. In the mid-1950s, the important station of Albury at the change of gauge with Victoria had, in its yards, a tent town. Here drivers, firemen, guards and their families lived in small tents with water taken from a community tap. Each staff member had six shillings a week deducted from their pay for being provided with a tent and water. How the train crews on night duty slept during the day, with all the noise of the yard, remains a mystery. But the use of tents on the New South Wales railway network lasted in to the 1970s.)

Norma remembers that the locals were good to the family; when there was a local ball or other function, leftover food would be delivered to the tent. The only pullovers they had during the cold Riverina winters were the ones that formed part of their school uniforms, and they had to take these off as soon as arriving home so that the jumpers would last as long as possible. Norma said this experience has given a lifetime ability to cope with the cold. (She also says her own children can scarcely believe her accounts of childhood on the railway just forty-five years ago, so different has life become.) Eventually, the family moved to Finley and Norman was able to acquire a railway house which was eventually purchased; his widow continues to live there.

In 1971 Norman's son, Noel, joined the fettler gang based at Finley. It was a job that, despite the backbreaking work, the heat in summer and the cold in winter, Noel still looks back on with affection. He lost the job when the line was closed down and the government railways laid-off the staff.

But at least the Sibraa family lived where there was a school. Not so in August 1939 at Menindee on the line to Broken Hill. A reporter from Sydney's *Daily Telegraph* filed this report from the settlement:

Living along the railway line between Menindee and Ivanhoe are 30 children of school age without any educational facilities. They are mostly children of rail workers. Most of them cannot read or write. On Saturday I interviewed many of the children and their parents. In seven shacks which I visited I saw no reading matter but popular periodicals. One mother of six children said: 'I don't know enough about learning to take correspondence lessons with the children. Anyhow, what with floods and dust storms and looking after the children I don't get enough time. Nearly all the children here are suffering from sandy blight and malnutrition'. At one siding, Kaleentha, there are 17 children of school age who haven't had a school lesson since they came to the area.

Being a fettler meant keeping the line open. Occasionally there was variation, such as changing a set of points at one of the stations, but otherwise – day in, day out – the job of the fettler was to change sleepers under the rails. When a line had two wheat trains a day, each hauling between thirty or forty wagons as the Narrendera-Tocumwal line did, each of those in turn carrying 70 tonnes of grain, the track took a hammering. The fettler crew usually comprised eight men who would ride out each day on their rail trike with its petrol motor (in later years the gang was provided with a truck – comparative luxury as they no longer had to melt the frost on the rails in the winter to allow the trike to gain traction). Noel recalls that there was no shade along his gang's section of the Tocumwal line; it was searing heat in the summer, freezing cold in the depths of winter. You had to be fit. This is why Noel, when he applied for the job, was given a rail pass to Sydney where he went through the same sort of physical tests that the military employ to check new recruits. He was given a chest x-ray, and the doctors looked for potential problems such as a hernia or bad back. That sort of fitness was needed, as men on the fettler gangs were expected to be able to use large tong-like instruments to pull out sleepers that needed replacing, then use a shovel to clean the sleeper trench of any debris before sliding the new one in. The hardest jobs were done by the younger men in the gang; those in their fifties simply no longer had the muscle to haul a sleeper out of its trench. Noel makes the point that modern occupational health and safety rules would never allow such work practices now. If the sleepers needing replacement were scattered along the line, the gang could manage between fifteen and twenty a day; if the replacements were targeted for one continuous section of track, then they might manage fifty a day. For the big jobs on the Tocumwal line, a large workforce would be rounded up from railway stations as far away as Griffith or Leeton. More than two hundred men would assemble and work along a section changing all those sleepers that a foreman had marked with chalk or paint.

Further down the line at Finley, oral history records compiled by the local railway museum indicate that, in the 1930s and 1940s, fettlers and their families were living in tents at the station. Cooking was either done outside (the children would have to hold an umbrella over the fire when it rained) or inside the tents using a small cast iron stove with a flue up through a hole in the canvas.

Fettlers would also check the evenness of the track level by sighting along the tops of rails and packing the ballast under low spots (which were known as 'holes in the road'). The distance between the two rails was known as 'the four foot' in New South Wales where standard gauge applies and 'the five foot' in Victoria where broad gauge ruled. Devotion to the job was high; weeds in the ballast were seen as an affront to the gang looking after that section. The man responsible for driving the spike into the sleeper, using the spike hammer, was expected to be able to complete the task with three hits – any more invited derision from the rest of the gang.

Crocodile Hunters

Malcolm Douglas

Trekking in the wilds of Arnhem Land, Malcolm Douglas and David Oldmeadow watch a dawn corroboree, witness the excitement over a crocodile kill and savour one of the great untouched and unspoilt regions of Australia.

We found the swamp people camped beneath a large drooping palm tree. It was a happy meeting with everyone wanting to hear all the news from Nangalala. There were about twenty altogether, most of them from Nangalala, but one family had come from Mirrngadja. Milparoo had an infected eye and kept wiping it with an old handkerchief. He told us that a stick had caused the injury a few nights before when he was hunting crocodiles. Bundalil was in a happy mood and I had never seen him looking better. I set up the camera and filmed the events with it on automatic control. I tried to get a close-up of one of the children from Mirrngadja, but she covered her face with her arms and hung her head. I kept filming, but she ran to her mother, who was very amused and laughed at her daughter's shyness. The young mother's smile showed a gap where one of her front teeth had been knocked out to make her more attractive. A primitive custom that has now almost stopped.

These Aborigines are some of the last of their race living on their own tribal lands. Today they wear a few clothes and the younger men are using rifles more often than spears, but their methods of food gathering and day to day living have changed little in hundreds of years. Our main reason for coming to the Arafura this time was to live with these people and record on film their crocodile hunting technique and methods of food gathering. We certainly did not realise as we sat on the ground talking to Gooday-Gooday and Milparoo that the film we were to get in the next week would excite and amaze tens of thousands of people throughout Australia.

Making camp was just a matter of finding some bare ground, preferably in the shade, and hanging our mosquito nets. Dry grass was cut and spread out on the ground for sleeping and eating on. Food consisted of porridge and coffee in the morning and native food for the rest of the day. We added rice to our meals so that Dave would have sufficient carbohydrate to balance his insulin. There is never any shortage of food in the swamp. It is just a matter of hunting or collecting it. The Aborigines living in the billabong eat tortoise, water bird, fish, mussels, lily bulbs, and file snakes. The file snake was one of the most interesting reptiles that we came across in the swamp. It gets its name from the rough skin resembling a rasp or file. It has a peculiar puglike head and very small eyes. An aquatic, it is incapable of controlling its movements on land; there it looks like a gigantic and sluggish worm. In the water it is extremely active and agile. It is non-venomous but very powerful and, if roughly handled, will turn sharply and inflict severe wounds with its large teeth.

The men offered to show us how they catch these snakes and this led to one of the most amazing experiences of our trip.

It was still cool and pleasant when we left the camp and began crashing through the tall, still reeds towards the backwaters of the billabong. The reeds gave way to a small clearing where the whole party stopped and began picking berries from small bushes about two feet high. The little green fruit tasted very similar to tomatoes and we ate until the supply was exhausted. Once again we pushed through the swamp grass until we reached the backwater. Thick water hyacinth completely covered the surface like a heavy bright green blanket. The men waded in, pushing their way through the tangled weed. I followed cautiously, holding the camera high above the water, and at the same time noting a very recent crocodile slide on the far bank. I mentioned the slide to a group in front of me, but no one seemed to care. It was assumed that the crocodile would move on to quieter water with so much activity.

The men spread out until they were evenly spaced across the lagoon. In unison they ducked under the hyacinth. Wading behind them I made slow progress with the camera. My biggest worry was the many submerged trees on the bottom. If I tripped and ended up in the water, the camera would be ruined.

Heads appeared, grasping for air, then down they went again, driving the snakes and tortoises ahead of them towards the dead end of the backwater. A fish leapt into the air in panic. Milparoo appeared grasping a long necked tortoise. He quickly broke its neck and flung it to the women waiting along the bank. Then under he went again, the heaving movement of the water hyacinth following his progress. Nulmarmar rose beside me with five-feet of fighting, struggling snake; its jaws were held tightly in his strong fingers. He pushed the reptile's head into his mouth. Gripping it in his teeth he pulled; a firm quick tug, that broke the snake's spinal column. It, too, was thrown to the excited women on the bank. Fascinated, I kept the camera rolling.

As the men neared the end of the backwater the quarry really panicked, doubling back to deep water. As quickly as they brushed past the hunters they were grabbed and their necks broken. The women and children ran along the banks picking up the kill and stuffing the reptiles into dilly bags. One of the older boys watched his father kill a snake, then he copied everything that the old man had done. The snake's head went into his mouth and he snapped its spine. I filmed the sequence as I knew that he was one of the few Aboriginal children today learning the old ways of survival. The number of snakes and tortoises amazed me. It was not long before the dilly bags were overflowing and the men began throwing snakes at one another in mock battle.

From the bank, the cry went up: 'Yindi Jenna.' Everyone scrambled out of the water and head for the reeds. A large goanna had been sighted by the children and the hunt had swung from the water to the land. Nulmarmar grabbed his spear and woomera and followed the excited cries of the children. Out in a clearing the old goanna stopped for a minute, his mouth open in anger, his long tongue flicking in and out. Nulmarmar whipped the spear through the air and the point buried in the goanna's back. He was upon it in an instant and killed it with his woomera. Normally goannas are run down or hunted up a tree, but with all the swamp reed around the hunters did not want to take the risk of the goanna getting away.

Back at the camp the men relaxed while the women did the cooking. The snakes and tortoises were simply thrown onto the coals until roughly cooked, then they were flicked from the fire and handed to us as we sat in the shade. Everyone attacked the flesh as though they had not eaten for days. A tortoise was my choice and it was extremely rich and oily. I ripped the shell apart to get at the rich yellow fat. Few animals in the bush have any fat on them and one yearns for the taste of fatty meat. I enjoyed the neck most of all as I found parts of the body were a bit strong.

Some of the tortoises and snakes were kept alive in string bags. In the afternoon everyone slept while Dave and I built a hide in a clump of cumbungi out in a patch of open water. We cut bundles of reeds and stuck them upright in the mud just in front of the cumbungi. I climbed in behind the reeds and cleared a small area, making just enough room for me to sit with the tripod and camera. Then over my head we constructed a roof of reeds and the retreat was complete. The idea was to leave the hide for a few days and let the birds become used to its presence before I made any attempt to use it.

Evenings in the Arafura swamp are never forgotten. In the short time between sundown and dark the sky is filled with the sounds of the birds. Thousands of them leave the relative safety of the open water and spread out across the grassy plains to feed. The most common of all are the whistlers. They come flying in low over the palms and the familiar whistling sound of their wings fills the sky. There are also wood duck and black duck and Burdekin duck and teal and pigmy geese and magpie geese, the night herons, and all the other birds of the darkness. They fly over and disappear into the evening sky.

During The Wet, when the rains pour down and all the billabongs overflow and join together forming one vast inland mass of water, the estuarine crocodiles move from one waterhole to the next, enjoying the freedom and knowing no enemy. But when the dry season comes and the waters recede until only the permanent waterholes are left, man hunts the crocodile for his skin. The professional white hunters are not allowed into the Arafura so there are still sufficient crocodiles for the Aborigines to hunt commercially. During the day the men stalk through the swamp grasses, their shot guns loaded with solid lead cartridges, watching for the crocodiles to surface among the lilies. But at night or in a new area when the reptiles are quiet, the Aborigines use dugout canoes and harpoons. Milparoo and Gooday-Gooday are masters of this technique. When there is no moon to light up the water, they paddle up and down the billabong with torch and harpoon at the ready looking for the ruby red eyes. It takes skill, patience and teamwork to hunt crocodiles from a dugout canoe. Gooday-Gooday always sits in the rear of the canoe paddling and Milparoo stands balanced in the front holding his long five-celled torch. Once a crocodile is sighted he signals speed and direction to his paddler, places the torch between his teeth, and is careful to keep the beam on the crocodile's eyes. He raises his harpoon, twelve feet long with a detachable head. Silently they move closer, the paddle making no noise as it slips into the water. The crocodile, watching the light beam, hangs suspended in the water. They move close enough to see the body of the crocodile, motionless, just under the surface, with only its nose and eyes above the water. It is over ten feet long, almost too big for them to handle, but Milparoo drives the harpoon home, aiming for the centre of the nervous system at the back of the skull. The crocodile dives for the bottom, twisting and turning in a frantic effort to escape. The rope attached to the barb slices through the water. Milparoo squats in the front of the canoe and hangs on. The desperate reptile tows the canoe through the waterlily weed and out into the open water. For more than half an hour the fight continues. Slowly the hunters pull in more and more rope until the crocodile is just ahead of the bow. This is the critical time. One mistake and they would end up in the water with the snapping jaws and lashing tail. They wait until the crocodile is exhausted and then it surfaces for air. Gooday-Gooday works the canoe into position alongside it and Milparoo smashes a tomahawk down between the wounded reptile's eyes. Gooday-Gooday paddles away quickly from the tail thrashing the water. When the crocodile is dead they haul it alongside and it is towed back to camp. They then set out for another. Not every crocodile is caught: a few break away from the harpoon and learn to be wary of the light. As soon as the beam hits them, they dive and will not be seen again all night.

Games of the Bush Children

Mary Fullerton

In her record of what it was like to grow up in a pioneering family in the 'big bush' of Gippsland, Mary Fullerton recalled the inventive, and sometimes dangerous, games played by children living in isolation.

When we played at being pack-horses, the wood we carried was in bundles on our backs, as we saw the men load the horses when preparing them for the trips up the mountain track, whither our father's team went frequently in front of the whip of a hunch-shouldered driver. These were certainly games suggested by our environment, as I have since seen the children of miners in an up-country town setting forth with their picks and shovels and 'crib tins' to the play that was their father's work. Ours was a world specially designed for such games as these, indoors or out. There were barns and sheds everywhere, and haystacks and standing crops, and farther afield the ambush about the creek, and the bush itself. I remember once tunnelling into a haystack so deeply to make a good hiding of it, that I almost smothered; and once Fred hid himself so recklessly amongst some bags of chaff in a barn that after a time, in response to his involuntary movements, an avalanche of bags descended upon him, so that all the ambushed ones within hearing of his muffled cries had to emerge from their several hiding-places to render the struggler first-aid.

I make serious claim to our having, if not invented, at least developed in pursuit of this same game of hide-and-seek the art of camouflage so much heard of today. To find Red Riding Hood in our wood, where most objects suggested her, was a pretty puzzle for a searcher. Annie's striped pinafore swishing forth from a scrub clump by no means proclaimed, though it suggested, the immediate presence there of Annie herself. Nor did the crown of Dick's hat peeping above a fallen log necessarily mean that the curly head and mischievous brown face of its owner were reconnoitring below it. I remember to this hour the experience of literally seeing stars where stars were not. The perils of blind man's buff played on a half-cleared landscape where abound stumps of felled trees as high as one's face are not to be minimized. To come with bandaged eyes hastily into contact with one of these is to bring about the immediate necessity for a bandage nose. Blind man's buff is more suited to an environment where nothing more solid than chairs and tables is to be encountered. It was a bitter day for my tomboy pride that on which it was borne in upon me that there is a tyranny of garments – that the child of the skirted sex is, becoming subject to the skirt, thereby tamed. Moral lectures from certain aunts used to the more 'correct' ways of little town girls had in their sundry administerings failed to curtail the athletic ventures of Claribel and myself. There was not a tree, dared by the boys, along whose limbs we too had not sung and clung. A lengthened frock was the real reformer. It was, though, a bitter day when a trammelling skirt reduced me to inferior place in the matter of 'vaulting with the pole'. Tournaments of this diverting exercise Dick and I often had, and for long I could clear a height at which he boggled or brought down the barrier. And then a new skirt of more generous length brought me my Waterloo. Was it, I wonder, symbol and epitome of much in woman's race of life? I rebelled sorely, I know, and smarted at my cousin's derisive and triumphant laughter when my flying sails brought my downfall. It was the same in running. I was no more the peer of the boys, and for a year or so had the further chagrin of seeing Claribel, my yet unfettered junior, surpass me in such sport.

Very early we came to cricket – or cricket came to us. I cannot remember how old I was when I first stood defending an old kerosene-tin from the onslaughts of a rag ball. That A.H. of whom I have before spoken was a born cricketer; he gave us the lore of it, not, I fancy, as a drilled-in lesson, but bawled to us bit by bit as the exigencies of the game in progress necessitated. The boys admitted us willingly enough to what in those days at least was regarded by divine right as exclusively a masculine game. We were grateful, knowing this, till experience lessened our gratitude, as we began to notice how much in the field we were, running, running after flying balls amid stentorian urgings to yet swifter flight; how seldom bowling, or with the bat. We mutinied at last, Claribel and I and our two younger of the non-cricketing sex. Whereupon the astonishing discovery was made that no kerosene-tin was for long safe when I, ball in hand, opposed it. It was a disconcerting discovery to Dick especially when, on my first essay, amid a barbaric roar from his brothers, the 'wicket' he guarded tintinnabulated his defeat. And thus from inglorious scouting, from stopgaps and makeshifts, we were promoted on our merits to the glory of full-fledged cricketers on equal terms with the boys. I remember a black eye from a smart ball once, and bruised shins often; but who cared when glory went with such wounds? Claribel and I finally achieved the great distinction of taking part in a full-dress match on a prepared sward, and with the actual regulation tools of the game.

There was one great occasion on which we all gave demonstration of our skill and prowess. It was on a birthday of the assertive Dick, when to 'sports' he had arranged in his own honour certain relatives were bidden. Besides the cricket match there were general sports all more or less strenuous and designed to call forth the applause of the admiring elders, whose part it was to show their amazement and approval, and incidentally to provide and spread the goodly picnic under the 'grandstand' box-tree. It was as if we had prepared and rehearsed for that day from the hours of our infancy. The games, great and small, important and trivial, were gone through as the culmination of a long apprenticeship. Our repertoire was interrupted only by the picnic (no irrelevancy that!) and ended by nightfall. We ran through the whole gamut, it seems to me, and used every muscle of our bodies in the display. It was a great day, and stands out in my memory – with its aftermath of aches. Fred had a sprained ankle for his remembrance. Tree-climbing being on the sports list he must, in scorn of older folks' warnings, go to the extreme end of a half-rotten limb of the gum-tree he had scaled. The law of gravitation did the rest. My uncle supplied the befitting philosophy, while he bound a handkerchief round the injured leg, congratulatory that it was not a fractured bone.

There was a waterhole that lay – or, should one say, that stood? – neutrally midway between our house and the home of my cousins in a paddock where rushes and tussocks introduced one to its brink. This old pre-historic waterhole was never known to dry up, and was haunted by things of interest, both imaginary and real. Eels of a coarse flavour lived in its depths, and sometimes consented to take the worm dropped to them at our peril no less than at the peril of worm and eel. Such was the waterhole, fear of whose mythological monsters kept us, as toddlers, I verily believe, from a watery grave, thereby justifying the pious fraud of our elders in so peopling it with the brutes of fable. Its existence lent suggestions for aquatic sports of various kinds. Mossy logs of antiquity, deliciously risky for venturing foot, thrust up their pachydermatous backs here and there over its surface. Wildfowl used to come and flirt tentatively with its reeded edges. There were willows planted modernly, and native vegetation planted anciently. There were waterlilies and duckweed on its murky waters, and lush islands of rushes here and there well away from its edges. There the domestic geese and duck fancied an unmolested reign, being of insular tastes – especially in the laying season. Instinct perhaps it was that suggested to them that, deposited there, their eggs had a better chance of becoming the oar-footed young of their dreams; fluffy babies, capable, when their time came, of reaching the big world past the sedgy shore. But instinct, doing its best for the preservation of the species, could not provide against the ingenuity of young human despoilers. Many a nest's contents we got, unaddled still by brooding, and bore them home. We had for such ventures a wonderful raft, which usually allowed itself to be cumbrously paddled to the desired island. As often as not it threatened to turn turtle or otherwise take itself and its passengers from the face of the waters. Then the bright eyes of danger would look suddenly forth at the hardy mariners aboard, and tense moments would follow. More than once a cold plunge had been the rower's fate, while the rest of us, according to the depth of the water where the disaster occurred, cheered, jeered, or feared from the margin. To gain the alluring water-lilies, too, many an embarking on that rude raft was undertaken; our mothers loved to set the sweet blooms in a shallow dish of water for indoor adornment, and that afforded excuse enough for any rashness in the enterprise of obtaining them. Little they ever knew how near to tragedy our pious desire to consider the lilies at close quarters sometimes brought us. There were times when an unwary pair of wildfowl made temporary home at the waterhole; and more than once we abstracted their eggs from the secret nest, and made a foolish hen foster-mother to strange wild creatures that soon, turning like divining rods to their true ele-ment, made her a thing of nerves. Later, with fierce ingratitude, such broods invariably further followed their nature by taking to the bush.

We used to stilt-walk about a certain quaggy portion of the water-hole paddock. Certainly to walk in that part at most seasons of the year, even in stout boots, would have meant wet feet, but across that rushy, reedy patch no road ran anywhere, and nothing but the spirit of childhood called us there at all, by stilt or foot. Still, there we went. I remember one day taking a 'short cut' to my cousin's house by that route. I had been sent to borrow some sugar. Whether my errand required hasty execution I do not remember, but I made my marshy detour on my stilts, and left them hidden somewhere before I reached my journey's end, proceeding by their cumbersome means again on the return trip with my borrowed sugar. I reached home muddy and sugarless; some will-o'-the-wisp of that marsh sprited away my sweet burden; but, then, what can one expect when one's stilts go suddenly deep into crabholes?

We had, under the teaching of other children, once we started to go to school, a whole galaxy of new games; that is, games new to us, though old as childhood, most of them. Of these I do not speak; there was never the romance and fascination about them as there was about those learned or invented by our isolated selves.

The Brumby Mare

Brian Taylor

Drover, saddler, stockman and all-round bushman, Brian Taylor recalls his dramatic encounter with a beautiful brumby mare at Wallabadah Station in New South Wales.

No sooner had I juddered my way across the wooden-railed cattle grid, off the Garnet road and into Wallabadah Station, than I knew something extraordinary was happening out on the flat.

It was still early morning, and the ironbark trees were casting long shadows towards me on the powdery vehicle tracks. Over to the east, a great cloud of dust-filtered yellow light hovered over a big mob of Brahman cattle. Driving quite slowly so as not to disturb the mob, I went as close as I could, then stopped the motor to observe exactly what was going on.

There were about 150 head of breeders in the mob. They had formed in a circle, which was about fifty to sixty yards across, all facing inwards and watching most attentively. As the dust cleared a little, momentarily, I saw two calves in gladiatorial combat; they were all of three days old, as the umbilical cords had not completely withered. One was a magnificent white, the other an apricot and yellow with a white head. They were all ears, legs and loose skin, but hearts as big as bulls.

First head to head, then head to flank, they charged, bunted, hooked instinctively as though they had horns of massive proportions. Dust that had accumulated on this traditional cattle camp was being dug up and hurled into the air with rare abandon, quite out of proportion to the size of those doing the stirring and digging.

Reaching a state of temporary exhaustion, there was mutual consent to a pause, just for a breather, then it was on again. The spectators gave approval with the occasional nodding of heads and swishing of tails, but the attention to combat was constant. There was definitely no intervention, for this was real grown-up cattle business, being decided and sorted out. That's where I left them, with the cloud of dust and sunlit haze rising even higher.

This property was only fifty square miles, but a great place to do a couple of days' mustering, run the cattle through the yards or shoe the horses up for the work ahead. It's always a pleasure to poke about a good piece of country, well run, with good stock. Besides, this place has quite historical background, in that many of the clearings have sizeable stone fireplaces, remnants of military encampments for soldiers heading to the New Guinea campaign.

That day I had three horses to shoe, then it would be out to the shady verandah to drink tea and tangle with some of Merle's magnificent scones, listen to the daughters playing duet piano, or watch them ride the station pet, a full-grown silver Brahman bull, about the lawn. The same bull, with bucking straps and a Condamine bell swinging under his belly, was unrideable at the Mareeba rodeo.

It was a good feeling to be made welcome and to know that I was contributing towards the running of this lovely place. I took pride in shoeing the station horses, one of which we had taken down to Ted Cunningham's Bowen River races and rodeo weekend. The mare had won the seven furlongs and the mile in good company. To ride the same mare through the timber, to the lead of a running mob, was exhilarating to say the least.

After smoko Mick said, 'Right, I want to take you up to the yards and show you some brumbies that those fellows from the Millstream ran on the weekend, from the scrub and timber country up on the goat track stock route.'

The horses were in the wire yard, and hanging in one corner. They did not like where they were and wanted to go home. They stood stock still, not wanting to be seen, these hijacked refugees from the wild. I walked around them and they trotted close-shouldered into the timber post-and-rail forcing yard. Mick opened the gate under the capped rail and they went through and up towards the pound yard.

They milled around, not knowing which way to turn, and then wheeled in the dusty yard and faced us where we had climbed the seven-foot high panel of rails to get a good look at them. They knew they were boxed in, throwing their heads and manes, snorting and swishing their tails as they suffered the agony of confinement.

In quiet tones we discussed whether or not they would make saddle-horses.

'Tell you what, Mick,' I said, 'I'll run that big roan mare up into the pound, if you could fetch a rope for us. I'll put a rope on her and see how she handles.'

'Right,' said Mick, 'she might have just a touch of clumper, but I agree she's worth a look.'

I went around and opened the yard up. Being the leader, she was first through. I blocked up and shut the gate. Walking back to open the other gate for the rest to go back to the wire yard, I was thinking about the mare and how she moved. She was in great condition, legs looked clean, no scars anywhere to speak of, no brands or saddle marks. She was a brumby for sure. She'd look all right settled down, with her tail pulled and her feet tidied up.

When I got back to the yard, Mick was still on his way from the saddle shed with some gear, so there was time to have a real good look. She had great stature, front legs well spaced out, held her head well, lively clean face, good eye – not too much white showing, and watching me most intently. It is very important, and an advantage, to handle an unbroken horse that has good focus.

'Hang on to the halter, Mick. I won't be needing that just yet. Just give us the rope.'

With that, I slid through the rails real gently, so as not to cause alarm, coiled the rope comfortably in my left hand and stood still for a considerable time. The yard being quite small, the mare stood her ground in questioning anticipation. From then on, it would be a two-way search for a communion on safe ground.

She shook her head, stamped a front foot and pawed the sand in defiance. After several repeats of this, and no reaction from me, she appeared to relax a little. I commenced to talk gently and quietly, maintaining the same tone of voice. Just when I thought I was getting through, she began to behave restlessly again, throwing the sand.

'Phew!' I thought, 'this is tight.' Never had I felt such tension. I could have thrown the rope and handled her that way, but I just had a feeling that I was going to put my hand on this horse.

In spite of being a brumby, she had a special stamp about her that deserved a different approach to the 'catch 'em and tie 'em up' method. The words of a long-passed ringer mate, one of my early tutors, rekindled in my ear: 'You've got 'bout as much chance as a celluloid cat chasing an asbestos rat in Hell.'

'No worries Jim, old mate, I've got this one in hand', I said to myself, as I inched ever so positively, yet cautiously, towards the mare.

The concentration was so intense; it all came down to indirect eye contact and smell, I guess. Closer, ever closer, I became aware of the salt sweaty smell of her body. I inched one boot slowly and softly through the sand, followed a little later by the other, hardly bending at the knees and all the while keeping the balls of my feet as firm as possible on the ground for balance – or, should the need arise, to leap in any direction to avoid being run over.

The mare's face was about four feet away now, and ever so slowly I began lifting my right arm. With the elbow akimbo and fingers half clenched, the back of my hand was slowly rising up to the level of her muzzle.

The mare's hot breath hit me in the face as she snorted and shook her head. Pausing momentarily before gaining contact again, I noticed that her ears were forward, which was quite an encouraging sign. Not so my hand, which was now beginning to shake, ever so little. I was becoming increasingly aware that my whole being was reacting to the tension building in that yard; I was entering a realm I had never been in before. So close now, I could feel the power of this horse.

My continued sweet-talking in monotone seemed to help me as well. With hand held close, not too far away from her nostril so she could smell me, I noticed the hair on her flaring nostrils was quivering and damp. The mare was either going to succumb and accept my touch, or leap straight at me. I was in no position to avoid the charge, and I remembered a horse I had faced that had reared up and belted me about the head and upper body with its front feet.

It was no man's land now. We were at each end of a very short fuse. Two against one, for it seemed that there was both my intense psychological mind game and my body reacting with quavering voice to the demands of progress and keeping control. She was watching, watching my every movement, sensing, yet seeming now to accept her predicament, while displaying a proud, defiant eye. I would have liked to cup my hand over her eye and soothe her down. Time, time, just a little more time.

When I felt the time was right, I moved the back of my fingers ever so close to the cheek under the eye, feeling the hair. Then ever so slowly, I opened my hand a little so as to gently rub her face. Unblinking for long periods of time, all of me was now aching from rigidity. Soon it would be all over. Finally I would put my hand comfortingly on her face and soothe away all her fears, then perhaps walk away for a time.

'This is it!' With such softness as I was able, I breathed out ever so gently, anticipating a wonderful conclusion, and put my hand down, lightly until firmly, onto her face, and looked into the gallant eyes of this yet untamed brumby mare. With a great spasm and a couple of throws of her head, she dropped dead at my feet.

I cannot begin to describe the horror, nor the pain of anguish I experienced then, as I stood back from what had just happened. Pathetic, soul-destroying grief. In disbelief I looped the rope over my shoulder and climbed the rails, took out the makings and tried to roll a smoke. That was a waste of time, as my hands were shaking so much that the tobacco just fell away. Never have I been so disturbed at an animal dying as I was about that beautiful brumby mare. Unbelievable.

Mick joined me on the top rail. 'Well, you never gonna handle any more fresh horses for me, young fellow!'

I turned and looked along the rail at Mick. He was sitting there, with the heels of his riding boots hooked on the second top rail, his chin on his chest, his shoulders rounded and his battered hat pulled down over his eyes. With one hand on the rail and the other running slowly over the stubble on his face, he looked a very sad man. He was trying to find the right words, one friend to another.

Mick slowly lifted his gaze towards me, from the catastrophe that was sprawled grotesquely on the sand in front of us, and our eyes met. In that instant, I recognised something in my friend I had never seen before. There was a mutual acknowledgment, and then he said, 'Let's go and have a drinka-tea.'

The Horse Will Save You

Leo Rosten (as told to John Ross)

An old bushman and farmer, Leo Rosten was still winning show trophies with his draught horses when he spoke to John Ross about his life around the Upper Macleay region in northern New South Wales, and a desperate escape from floodwater.

Oh well, I've been to every show around the coast and I've never been anywhere yet when I didn't come away with something. Got a few championships.

I started in the 1940s, but I had a break after then, for a good while. I always had a desire to parade a draught stallion in Kempsey Show Ring from when I was a little fella. I have paraded them on that ground 20 times. That's not too bad.

I have had horses down at Taree, Wingham, up as far as Coffs Harbour and Bellingen . . . all those places. In the finish it gets too expensive carting them about, so I stick to Kempsey now.

When you go to a show you accept what the judge says, even though you know he doesn't know what he is talking about, quite often. You say nothing otherwise you only make a bad name for yourself.

I was born on a dairy farm my father rented in the Upper Macleay Valley, up on what is called Second Flat. Strangely enough, most of that's been washed away in the 1949–50 floods.

I always wanted to go to Queensland, but the father died when I was 16 and I had to stop home and look after the mother a bit. When I could have went I was too old, so I was satisfied with droving, working on properties, and train droving. The 1949–50 floods knocked us about a lot. I went working at the mill then, and had three years there. I've done a lot of log falling too. Anything that was hard work, I suppose I've done. It never hurt me.

I think it was 1995 I come down to Kempsey. I got hurt up there, both eyes got injured with wire and it took me a good while before I could even see at all out of one. A bit of wire let go around the post – we were never provided with any protective gear or anything like that, which we should have been. They got a verdict against them now. You can get a verdict all you like, but you have got to get the money. That's the trouble.

Everywhere I went I always like to be on my own, do it the way I wanted to do it. I suppose that might have become a bit of a reputation, because they always said 'you'll have to let him handle it his way'. But you can always learn though . . . the fella who knows everything about everything hasn't been born yet.

The last property I managed was across the river from Bellbrook and I worked on my own there, done all the cattle work, all the branding – done it all myself. The boss, I used to tell him to get out of the road, he was only a bloody nuisance. He accepted that.

The funny thing with city people, even the way they move will irritate stock. They have either got to be in a hurry and singing out or something. The stock get used to you – this old fella is listening to me, what do you reckon Prince?

I only have six horses at the moment, and that's too many. I was hoping to get hold of a bit of country, if I ever get any dough out of these fellas.

This injury was 1995; previous to that this eye was injured in

1983. It's only half sight, they can't do any more with this one. This one is dilated all the time, you can't stand the glare. That's why I have to wear the glare glasses. Anyway, there are a lot of people worse off than me.

I worked at the saleyards for 50 or 60 years I think, and done all the rodeos. You get hard work at the rodeos, but they retired me from that. They didn't want to see me get hurt.

I still work them. I'm the chalky and the timekeeper now. I'm still in contact with the people, that's the main thing.

I used to do all the sales down the river, Willawarrin and all those. But the little local sales are all folded up now. It is a big selling centre at Kempsey. I used to be the night watchman too.

It's all beef now, but dairying was the main item on the Lower Macleay at one time. We had the milk boats, trucks and all sorts.

Most of the up-river went from beef cattle to dairying when the bottom fell out of beef cattle after the 1914–1918 war. Anywhere they had a bit of land at all, they started dairying. They had the Toorooka Butter Factory, Kempsey Butter Factory and then there is Nestlés. The first dairying I remember was out at Collombatti. I think we were getting sixpence halfpenny a pound for the butter in the Depression. Toorooka got sixpence farthing because they allowed a farthing freight to bring it from there down to the boat.

The wharf was in the same street as Preen's engineering place, you'd see this big boat pull in there. The boat used to go up to Belgrave Falls. Then they built the wooden bridge at Kempsey and the ocean-going boat couldn't get up there, so they had drogues to go up there and pick up produce from the wharves. They had a paddle-wheeler to bring it down here. But the shipping was just about on its knees when the '49 flood came and filled all the river up with silt. That flood was a shock because the previous flood had been before the turn of the century.

The old entrance used to be at Stuarts Point. Then, when the new entrance broke, it was a lot closer or shorter down-river to the ocean. The cry went up: 'We'll never get any more floods now with the new entrance.' Well, they had a couple of minor floods and they came up and went down, and people thought, 'We're right'.

The '49 showed them just how wrong they could be. It was a shock. I forget how many houses were washed away, and they were down on Glenrock like pumpkins, bits and pieces broke up everywhere.

About six people died. It was amazing that there wasn't more. But anyway the people who know everything – 'You won't get another one for a hundred years' – ten months afterwards we got a bigger one, and 13 years after that we got one nearly as big. In the meantime there was a heap of little floods. Since we lived down the river, the land we were on was never completely covered. I think we had a flood just about every month of the year, through the years. But we were reasonably happy down there . . . you go back and clean up.

The first one we didn't know anything about down-river. It come so fast. I was always grateful to a chap named Clarrie Everson – I had our stock all rounded up and I reckoned I was going to shift out the next morning, and he rode out past where we lived to get some of his stock and said: 'Don't be here after dark.' Well that was good enough for me – he knew the country. When I saw the place last there was hundreds of acres of land above water. Next morning it was just a sea of water, from Clybucca to the sandhills out here.

I got the dairy herd out, but I didn't get the pigs all out, lost a good few of them. Anyway, the only way of getting out was the horse and dray, across a swamp to the Hathead Road. I took the stock out and loaded the wife into the dray with horse, two little kiddies and a litter of young pigs and whatever else you could get in. There was a short cut out to the road that you go across the swamp and I said to her, 'Now, whatever happens,' I said, 'the old horse – Bill, we call him – he won't hurt you.'

The water was halfway up to the front board of the dray, and it was raining and bitterly cold. They had to cross a bridge that was under water, with no guideposts. To miss the bridge was to tip the dray in the creek. After that there was a narrow track to higher land, and safety. Aileen said later she could see nothing but a moving mass of cattle and horses – thousands of heads in the water.

Later, I got out to within an ace of getting onto the Hathead Road and couldn't get any further, the water got too deep. I said to the fellas there, 'Has Aileen come through?' 'Yes,' they said. They went out and led the horse through for her. Anyhow, when I got there it was getting dark and too late to do any more and they said: 'We'll put the pigs on the verandah if it gets too high.' That was all right . . . the next morning the pigs are up on the roof of the dairy.

If I had dry clothes . . . oh, I was as cold as two frogs . . . I would have stayed there with them, and Mum would have never known what happened. But anyway, that was all right. When I caught up with her again she said: 'I couldn't see where we were going.' But anyway she said, 'Old Bill took me through.'

Well, I said: 'I told you he would know where to go.' That's how much faith you had in a good horse.

Anyway, there's another story attached to that of the dog on a pig's back.

The dog must have got bamboozled and missed me out on the Hathead Road and he went back home. There was no-one there, so he went up the lane about a mile to where he used to wait for me if I was away.

It appears that the pig came from somewhere and got in Lyle Ward's laundry. It was an open laundry with a bench. Lyle said: 'When I got up in the morning there was a pig on the bench and a dog on top of the pig, out of the water.' He said there was a couple of fellas with him there and they didn't believe him, and he said, 'Come and have a look at it.'

I was getting a bit anxious about the dog and thought, 'He's gone.' Several days after I was in Kingstown and Lyle was walking about looking for me. He said the last he saw of the dog it was sitting up on the top of the corner post in the stockyard out of the flood. The dog, he was a great mate of the young John, who was only about two years old. When we got him out to John – well, the reunion was touching.

I think my great-great-grandfather had horses in the first place, but I had me own team. I'd have had four or five draughts when I went to Kinsale and I've bred about 20. I've worked other people's horses.

The draughthorses weren't as popular in the bush as the bullocks, because horses are very much thinner in the skin and some of them get a bit excited if they get into a bad position. Whereas a bullock, he doesn't care much. But for road work the horses were quicker than the bullocks.

There was no tractors about. There were plenty of sleepers to be cut and you'd cut a track in to get the sleepers out to load on a truck.

In the Depression they reduced the sleeper cutters to 10 sleepers a week. Just kept them alive. They came back to two shillings a sleeper, so that meant the bushworkers got a pound a week. And they lived on it, shot pigeons and did a bit of fishing in the creeks, and they lived.

There are a few draughthorses still working, but they will never come back to where they were. They can still be used in combination with tractors. There is nothing, I don't reckon, like the draughthorse to clean corn, or pull corn, either. There are one or two out there with small areas. They work the draughthorses, quite a few down around the Manning.

Well I'll tell you something now, I always loved the draughthorses, or any horse. I sent a mare down to Ken Drury, to his horse called Samson, and he had him in the team that he used to go round the shows with. Anyway, he always told me how good a mare she was in the lead, and I thought, 'Oh yeah.' Anyway, I was down at Wingham, and he always worked her in the near-side lead. With a leader . . . they have got to tighten the chain and lead your team . . . straighten your team out. When I saw how she straightened the team out, she just about pulled the lot of them out into the river.

Well, the old feeling that I thought was dead came to the surface, and I said to one of my mates afterwards: 'Why is it that I feel that way?' And he said, 'Look, you have to be an Australian to understand that.'

My Wild Life

A.B. Facey

A.B. Facey, in his remarkable book A Fortunate Life, *recalled some happier experiences in his times as an orphan who started work at the age of eight on the rough Western Australian frontier.*

Two days later, Charlie got a letter advising him that his Sunshine harvester had been forwarded to Cuballing, the nearest railway siding. This siding, on the Great Southern railway running from Perth to Albany, was twenty-four miles away.

The following day Charlie and I started on our way to bring the harvester home. We put a horse in the sulky, and loaded on all the harness and gear we would require to haul the harvester. It took four horses to pull it while it was working stripping the crop, but two could pull it easily at other times. We took all of one day to get to Cuballing, then rested the horses for a day before setting off for home. Charlie drove the harvester and I drove the sulky, keeping just a few yards behind.

New year came and went; the Muttons returned home to the Goldfields and Charlie and I were busy carting hay. Charlie was the stack builder. He said he hadn't learnt how they built stack in Australia, but when he was a boy in England he worked on a farm and knew how the stacks were built there. He said the only difference was that the hay over there was loose and had to be packed in rows whereas here it was in sheaves and should be easier to handle. He built a beautiful haystack.

Carting hay was very hard work for me. I had to pitch the hay sheaves up to Charlie, one at a time, while he stacked them on the cart. When we got the cart loaded and into the haystack yard, I had to pitch the sheaves from the cart down to Charlie who put them into position on the stack. This knocked me out and on hot days it was worse. It took us two weeks to cart the hay.

Then Charlie started harvesting. He had one hundred acres to strip, and as his harvester was one of the first to come to the district, there were many farmers coming to see how it worked. Some of the farmers were amazed at the results of his method, which was wonderful compared with the older way of harvesting. Charlie drove the harvester and it took him a little over two weeks, working Sundays as well, to harvest the hundred acres of wheat. He was delayed a lot having to stop and show the many interested farmers how it worked. Charlie got just over four hundred bags from the one hundred acres, which was a good return because a lot of the wheat had been eaten by parrots, jays, kangaroos and other bush animals.

I had to sew the wheat bags up when they were filled by the harvester. A man with eight horses and a large box-wagon carted the wheat to Cuballing. He charged one and sixpence a bag and he used to cart sixty bags each load. This was the first year that the wheat bag sizes had been reduced from four bushels to three bushels, so sixty bags would be near enough to five tons.

The contractor would bring back a load of superphosphate after delivering each load of wheat. He could bring sixty bags back each time and charged one shilling a bag. The superphosphate ('super' it was commonly called) was a new kind of artificial fertiliser subsidised by the Government and delivered to the settler's nearest railway siding. The freight was only five shillings per ton. It was a boon to the settlers, in some instances improving the crop by forty percent.

In the evenings, after dinner, I usually helped Mrs Bibby to wash the dishes, then went to my room. One night as I was saying goodnight, Charlie said, 'Wait Bert, I want to tell you something. Sit down. I've been thinking about you and how you have worked and looked after the stock, and we haven't forgotten Boxing Day. We look like getting a good price for our wheat, so we have decided to raise your wages to fifteen shillings a week and full keep, starting one week before Christmas.' This thrilled me and I felt so pleased I didn't know what to say.

I thanked Charlie and Mrs Bibby for the raise in my wages and told them how pleased I was and how happy I felt. Charlie said how sorry he was about getting drunk and that it wouldn't happen again. He said that they hadn't seen Mr Mutton for about four years and made the mistake of drinking wine and whisky with beer. He finished by saying, 'It cost us dearly.'

Burning-off season opened and several neighbours came to help put the fire through the chopped and burnt down timber like they had helped Frank the year before. When one of our neighbours wanted help with putting a fire through, we always helped them. This co-operation went on with all the new settlers, and they used to meet at each other's places from time to time to discuss and exchange ideas on farming, clearing, fencing and stock. My Uncle was the one who gave advice on all kinds of stock and stock issues.

That burning season, Charlie had what was known as a 'good burn'. This term was used when the undergrowth, scrub and timber burnt freely and left only the large logs and stumps. We then started on the clearing. Charlie and I worked hard and long hours six days a week from the middle of February through to the end of the first week in April. During that period we cleared the one hundred and thirty acres that we had chopped and burnt down during the previous August, September and October.

Just after the clearing was finished we had a storm with heavy rains. This softened the ground and Charlie started ploughing the new land. He had bought a disc plough which was better for working new land and was much quicker than a stump-jump plough. A disc plough could also be used for working up land that had long grass or straw on it. It was driven with six horses and covered a strip four feet eight inches wide, which was more than twice as much as a three-furrow stump-jump plough.

During ploughing and putting in the crop, my job was looking after the stock and picking up any roots pulled up by the plough. I would cart these to the house as they made good firewood.

The only time we worked on Sundays was harvest time. I had Sundays off at other times, except I had to look after the stock, and fill up the wood-box in the kitchen for Mrs Bibby. I never had any young people to play with apart from an occasional trip over to Uncle's to see Grandma. On these visits I would always join in games with my cousins. Otherwise I had no young company, so I used to take my rifle and walk in the bush. Sometimes I got a shot at a 'roo and many times I would find a quiet spot and sit down and keep quiet and watch the birds and the small animals.

The birds used to fascinate me. There were so many different kinds and most of them were friends of the farmer. The bush in those days was alive with them, their beautiful noises were something you had to hear to believe.

The martin sparrow went in packs of hundreds; it lived on small insects and made its nest in hollow limbs of large trees. It was very pretty, about the size of a canary, and had a black head, brown feathers along the sides and back, light grey underneath its body and around the neck, and bright brown under its wings. When flying, its tail-feathers were spread like a small hawk.

Then there was the willy wagtail, which had a black head and back, and a white underbody – a very lively little bird with a long wedged tail. The blue wren was a small bird with a beautiful blue body. And there was the little brown and grey tom tit. There were hundreds of these, flitting in and out of the scrub and bushes. The woodpecker was bigger than the wagtail and would run up any tree by digging its sharp claws into the wood.

There were hundreds of the common magpie, and also the ground-lark, a small grey and light brown bird that wouldn't sit on a tree, but flew from ground to ground. The brown bush quail was also a ground to ground bird. The bronze-winged pigeon lived on seeds and such like and was good to eat – it was half the size of a chicken. The robin red breast was a very pretty little bird with a scarlet red marking on its breast. The peewit was a light brown bird with some black streakings on its back and wings, and a white breast marked with a U-shaped black half circle.

The plover was the same size as the peewit and had much the same markings but it was a ground to ground bird. It had a cunning way of concealing its nest out in an open patch of cleared ground. The nest and eggs looked the same colour as the ground – you could walk on the nest without knowing. The blue bird was about the size of the peewit too, but had a black head and a very light blue body. This bird was sometimes called a storm bird on account of it appearing more frequently just before the weather turned stormy. It had a very beautiful whistle-like call. There was also the parakeet which always flew in large mobs. It had pretty colouring – green, brown and red – and resembled a parrot but was very small like a canary.

There were also the night birds such as the curlew – a ground bird with extra long legs – and the owl, which lived on bush mice and rats. Also the mo-poke, which had much the same habits as the owl. There were also large flocks of black cockatoos, always making a terrible noise. They were a very large bird and the noise they made was deafening, particularly when in flight.

There were many other birds which were the enemy of the farmer. These included the ring neck parrot, which was also known as the 'twenty-eight', and was one of the most beautiful birds to look at. The name twenty-eight came from the noise it made when frightened and flying from danger. It was most destructive on cereal crops and fruit. Another parrot, smaller and of different markings, was the rosella. This bird was also destructive on cereal crops and fruits, as was the jay bird.

There were also two small species of birds that were destructive. One was the silver eye, a small bird about the size of a tom tit, grey with silver coloured rings around its eyes. It lived on flowers, sucking the honey or nectar out, and also on fruit. It was very damaging to grapes or any fruit near ripe. The other small bird was the greeneye. This was dusty green in colour and had the same habits as the silver eye.

There were, and are, many other varieties that are hard to describe. They made the bush a beautiful place and helped one forget about loneliness.

The wild animals were also quite a study for anyone who had to live with them, and sat quietly to watch their habits. They lived in a world of fear and danger, always watching, listening and smelling for some scent of trouble.

The birds and animals of the bush were all great company and very nice to see and hear. I loved the bush.

Charlie finished ploughing the new land and then started on ploughing the land that had been cropped the year before. He then did the seeding, finishing at the end of the third week in June.

After seeding, Charlie and Mrs Bibby went away for a fortnight's holiday, leaving me in charge of the farm and stock. They drove to Narrogin by horse and sulky, and took a train to Perth.

Charlie told me before he went that he had some business to

attend to in Perth, and Mrs Bibby wanted to do some shopping. He said, 'All you have to do while we are away is look after everything. Never mind anything else. You are the general manager while we are away.' Mrs Bibby cooked me plenty of food before they went and she told me to have lots of eggs. When the meat she had left was finished I was to go over to the neighbours' place about four miles away. She had arranged for the woman there to supply me with whatever I wanted in the way of bread and meat. She said I could ride over on Prince. He was a very quiet horse and I used to ride him around the farm sometimes.

So, with these instructions, they set off on their much-needed holiday. I felt very proud of myself – my fourteenth birthday wasn't until next month but they had enough confidence in me to leave me to look after their possessions. I was a little scared at first, but soon settled to doing the daily chores. At night I used to roam around with my rifle and make sure everything was safe. I even put an extra wire around the sheep gate in case the dingoes troubled them.

The Brightest Place on Earth

Tim Flannery

Tim Flannery, as a young scientist studying for his Masters degree in Geology, joined an expedition to Lake Frome in South Australia and saw, in the salt crust, the 'brightest place on earth'.

From space the dazzling white salt-crust of South Australia's Lake Frome is said to be the brightest spot on Earth. Lying just east of the Flinders Ranges, the lake occupies a sunken region of saltpans and sand dunes unknown to most Australians, for it is dwarfed in both reputation and size by its westerly neighbour, Lake Eyre. But the Frome Basin is important, for here, through a process of wetting, drying and relentlessly blowing wind, the lakes have eaten deep into rocks laid down 20 to 40 million years ago – the middle of the Cainozoic era, the age of mammals.

Fresh outcrops of fossil-bearing rocks in the Frome Basin are the brightest shade of green to be seen in that arid region, and the fossils of moisture-loving creatures entombed there testify to an inland that was once verdant. That vanished landscape was a place I very much needed to understand, for I suspected that it was in some superannuated Centralian rainforest that kangaroos took their first hop.

The opportunity to visit came in the late 1970s courtesy of Tom Rich, who was mounting an expedition to Lake Tarkarooloo – one of the smaller salt lakes in the region, and the location of a previous dig.

I had begun my Masters studies in geology, while Tom was pursuing his dream of finding mammals from the age of the dinosaurs. Things were going badly on that front, however, and Tom felt an obligation to his employer, the Museum of Victoria, and to his country of adoption, to provide something more than his arid wanderings in Mesozoic-aged rocks had yielded. Working on the oldest mammal-bearing sediments then known in Australia would at least provide some public benefit, Tom believed, so he planned several extended periods of field work there.

Our expedition consisted of half a dozen volunteers packed into two Land Rovers, and we drove from Melbourne via Broken Hill through a countryside that had received heavy rains. On leaving the highway and entering the maze of dirt tracks that led to the lake we found ourselves in a sort of Eden. Immense fields of daisies blanketed the sandy soil, filling each swale from horizon to horizon with bright golden flowers, while the dune crests were a great mass of purple. Meandering lines of gold and purple as far as the eye could see were punctuated only by skeletal mulgas, whose deep roots would not taste the slowly percolating water for months to come, and which served to remind us of the usual order of things out here.

It seemed a violation to drive or walk over that carpet of blooms, for you crushed delicate flowers and stems at every step. And the scent of desert dust was replaced with a sweet smell of nectar and young, green growth – a heady perfume that became overwhelming as evening approached. Instead of retiring to bed with the travel-weary on our first night, something drew me into the darkening desert. Crossing one dune after another, with the light of the campfire left far behind, the sky seemed so vast and studded with stars that my mind could liken it only to a great city at night seen from the air. The stars sparkled with such vitality that you felt you could reach out and touch them, and the dizzying, sweet night-scent of a billion daisies had reached fever pitch, a billion sexual organs frantically courting a moth to their delicate stamens before the drying soil shrivelled them, robbing them of their fertility. For moths – indeed insects of any sort – were rare on that still night, for too brief a time had elapsed following the rains for them to migrate or complete their life cycle.

At first I did not notice the moon breach the horizon at my back. But as I watched it rise in the sky I witnessed a miracle in the golden fields before me. Each gilded flowerhead was turning its face to the light of the moon, until they formed a field of shimmering gold, the twice-reflected light making it seem as if the land was illuminated from below. I could not think of sleep, so I lay down among the fleshy young daisies, embraced by their scent and the still-warm air, to watch the watchers as they tracked the great silver orb on her steady journey to the far horizon.

You can live a lifetime in the Centre and never see a really big wet. The one in 1974 had filled Lake Eyre by dumping enough rain to nourish a rainforest, an event never before witnessed in living memory. But wets, both great and small, are just bounteous punctuation marks of uncertain frequency and duration in a country that nine years out of ten can stifle all but the most superbly adapted desert specialists. On that trip all I saw of red kangaroos were piles of bleached foot-bones discarded by roo shooters at gates, for the great reds that flourish in that area had dispersed far and wide to feast on the green pick.

A big male red kangaroo can exceed ninety kilograms, and there is barely an ounce of fat on his frame. As red as the sands of the Centre (the female is a smoky blue-grey – almost the colour of galahs' wings), he is the creature most people conjure up with the word 'kangaroo'. He may stand taller than you, and look down his long Roman nose at you with large brown eyes, through lashes whose length and beauty would make a diva envious. The musculature of his upper body, visible through the fine, pale fur, is that of a wrestler, while the span of his hands with their five long, sharp claws, may far exceed your own. His lower body is the essence of elegance, his long, slender legs looking almost surreal as he props himself on toes and tail-tip. If attacked, he will defend himself – with his back to a tree if possible, by grappling you close, then kicking out with both feet while balanced on his tail.

But the real miracle of the red kangaroo is more difficult to see, for the species is built to endure the erratic rhythms of the inland, when nothing can be wasted and no opportunity missed. Perhaps because of their need to travel great distances reds are not very social animals, living in smaller groups than other plains-dwelling species. But this self-reliance pays off when somehow, in the vastness of the inland, they detect that rain has fallen. Then they will move, even from an area that they have lived in all of their life, to the invisible green feast beyond the horizon. With their no-nonsense approach to life they have also dispensed with elaborate courtship. Their preliminaries to mating are rudimentary even by kangaroo standards, consisting of a golden shower (the female urinates on the male's nose), and some sniffing and pawing of the female's tail-base by the male. She favours the largest and most powerful mate she can find, and the pair copulate just once (as opposed to the repeated efforts of other kangaroos) for a brief ten to fifteen minutes.

As if they have stripped down every aspect of their existence in pursuit of flexibility and rapid growth, this business-like approach to life continues after conception. The very day she gives birth, the female red kangaroo will eject her older joey (if she has one) permanently from the pouch, and copulate so she can conceive again. Except in the most severe drought the female is never without a pouch-young. Most of her babies, however, never reach maturity, for unless conditions are favourable there is insufficient milk to feed the growing joey after it is more than a few months old. If no rain falls it is sacrificed and the next joey takes its place. The constant replacement of her growing young by the mother red kangaroo may seem brutal, but consider the sheer efficiency of this system compared with our own. Human conception is often the business of many months, while gestation takes nine months and lactation (in traditional societies) three to four years. Droughts would have come and gone, and come again, before our species had completed one reproductive cycle.

If the young red kangaroo gets past this critical juncture it grows rapidly, making its first forays from the safety of the pouch 100 days in advance of its grey-kangaroo cousins, and is weaned at about twelve months rather than eighteen months as with the grey. Having reached independence, however, the rush is over. Reds reach sexual maturity at the same age as other kangaroos, and may live longer. The oldest kangaroo on record is a male red who was tagged when fully grown in western New South Wales, and shot twenty-seven years later and over 300 kilometres away in South Australia. In effect the life of the red kangaroo mimics the rhythms of the inland; they rush to independence in the brief good season, but then live long enough to see another great wet that will carry their line onwards.

The adult red displays other abilities that have ensured its survival. An adult male is not bothered by a single dingo, for he can outrun a dog or even a horse, and if caught is likely to beat the wild dog in a fight. Nor does competition for food in a drought usually worry them, for they can go without drinking far longer than any domestic stock, allowing them to feed over a wider area. Their food requirements, furthermore, are not overly demanding: a red kangaroo thrives on two-thirds the food required by a similar-sized sheep, and can get by with even less in a dry summer. At such times reds can eat saltbush without ever becoming too thirsty, and they can avoid the need to urinate by recycling urea through their saliva and into their stomachs, where it is converted into food. And then, if distant rain falls, they will all move off, leaving grey kangaroos and sheep alike to perish around shrinking and depleted waterholes, to return to a field of bones when the drought has broken.

An absence of older fossils indicates that the red kangaroo sprang into existence in the past million years. There is no doubt that it is loosely related to the antilopine kangaroo (*Macropus antilopinus*) of Australia's tropical north, and may have developed from some isolated population of antilopines living on the desert margins. An Australia without reds is unimaginable, but weather shifts predicted for the continent as a result of global climate change offer a sobering reminder of how delicate the balance of life is. Many climatologists calculate that over this century the number of very hot days will increase dramatically, as will the length and severity of droughts. At the same time, rainfall over much of southern Australia will decrease – perhaps by as much as 40 per cent. Red kangaroos are creatures born of the climatic oscillations that characterise Australia, but extreme swings in climate could have disastrous consequences, for reds rely on the odd good year to replenish their numbers, and if these become too widely spaced the population will crash.

The year I first visited the Frome Basin, 1978, was a good one for reds, with few young perishing that season. Yet the ground around the lake was still parched and barren. We chose to camp beside a clump of tortured-looking coolibahs, the only shade in the area. The area that Tom intended to work ('Tom O's Quarry') was around ten kilometres from the camp, so each morning we would make lunch and drive to the site. The place was a couple of knee-deep holes a few metres across, located beside a dry salt lake, itself set in a horizontal landscape of salt scalds, samphire and grey-green clay. We would sit there scratching cautiously at the sides of the excavation, hoping to uncover some treasure – maybe the jawbone of some long-extinct koala. But such finds are as rare as gold nuggets, and a succession of the more common fossil fishbones, crocodile teeth and turtle shell fragments provided the only excitement for days on end.

By 10 am the sun had heated the air in the pits to uncomfortable levels, and at 11 we would rise to brush the dust, salt and mud from our skin and break for a cup of tea. It was then that we would confront the full force of those undersized devils of the outback, *Musca vetustissima* (in Latin 'most hairy fly'), aka the bush fly. It is much like the house fly but smaller, more persistent and far fonder of orifices – each time any of us opened our mouths to speak, the son of a maggot born on a dungheap would dart inside. Because we were host to hundreds if not thousands of these irritants, we seemed destined to swallow a fair proportion of the horde each day. Although it is possible that some entomologist actually counted the hairs on the bush fly to ensure the appropriateness of its Latin name, it seems far more likely that instead they merely estimated its hirsuteness from the tortuous tickling that these licorice-tinctured insects inflict on the oesophagus.

Tom was well prepared for this particular torment, for he had recently returned from Saudi Arabia, where he had acquired the full Bedouin outfit of *thobe* and *gutra*. He was much taken with the Arabs and their way of life (though references to Noah and the flood made his search for dinosaur bones a touchy subject) and he saw nothing wrong with donning the white *thobe*, which stretched from neck to ankle, nor wrapping his head in the red-and-white checked fabric known as the *gutra*. Thus swaddled, Tom sat unperturbed, immune to heat and flies alike as he scratched for enlightenment in the quarries of Tarkarooloo, with only his American accent betraying him as a newcomer to Arabia Deserta.

After a week of unproductive torment the clouds grew dark and threatening and the wind began to gust. Tom decided that it was time for us pansies to return to camp. He had, however, just discovered two splendid fossilised turtle carapaces which he intended to excavate and encase in a plaster jacket before the storm struck. He asked that one of us return in two hours, conditions permitting, to pick him and his turtles up. If the rain bucketed down, though, we should not bother – the walk back to camp was a pleasant stroll for one encased in *thobe* and *gutra*.

When he turned up later that day, Tom told us that after we upped stakes he heard of a wheezing old truck bump along the track to the quarry – the first visitor at the remote location. As the battered vehicle drew near it slowed to a halt and its driver, a rabbit shooter who sat propped between his rifle and a slab of Victoria Bitter, stared at Tom, who had entirely forgotten the strangeness of his habiliments, and asked in a tremulous voice, 'What are you doin' out here, mate?' The thunder pealed and the first fat drops of rain began to fall as the swaddled figure, without car, hose or even camel to support him, replied in a broad American accent, 'I'm digging for turtles.' At this the rabbiter gulped, turned mechanically away, and drove on up the track.

Back at camp we were sure that we were in for a soaking. I wandered out among the dry cane-grass on a sand-dune, where between thunderclaps I heard something deep underground. It was the unmistakable croaking of frogs, yet below the surface the sand was still as dry as a mummy's handshake. That afternoon the heavens opened and we copped four centimetres of rain in a couple of hours. I poked my head out of my tent in the fading light to discover that we were now camped in an inland sea populated with thousands of frogs. Their croaking was deafening, for they were everywhere. I wanted a close look, so I placed three in a billy that I hung from a coolibah, there to await inspection by the light of day.

The raucous croaking made it almost impossible to sleep, but about midnight a distinct shift in the sound occurred. Earlier it had come from all around, but now it was distinctly louder just north of my tent. The frogs were concentrating in one spot, and by morning all croaks – except for the three amplified ones coming from my billy – emanated from the one place. Beyond the camp the water still lay in a broad sheet, so I had no idea what brought the frogs together. In a few days, however, their strategy became clear. As the water receded, one pool after another dried up until there was only one left – exactly where the frogs had migrated that first night. Just what prescience led them to the spot is still a mystery to me. The next morning I discovered that my three captives were pale, flabby, golfball-sized creatures, bright of eye and with a determined turn to their wide mouths. I later identified them as water-holding frogs (*Cyclorana platycephalus*). They are among the hardiest of all amphibians and live buried in a state of animation for years in the salty inland deserts, then emerge during a wet to feed and reproduce before diminishing puddles drain away into the sand.

Ceremony

Ros Moriarty

*In an emotional journey across country and culture Ros Moriarty,
a white woman married to an Aboriginal man, travels in the
Tanami Desert, Northern Territory, to perform ceremony with
Annie and other matriarchs of her husband's family.*

It is eleven o'clock by the time we drive in from the mine to Borroloola.
We find Annie and Thelma at the fuel pump at the edge of town. Ready,
anxious to go. We drive together to where more than twenty women
are sitting with bags and mattresses on a cement verandah. They are all
John's relations. Greetings begin again, and their hugs are warm and
welcoming. I realise with relief I am not an intruder. I am a daughter-
in-law, expected on the journey. Three other vehicles are loading up.
We will drive in convoy. It is midday before everything is tied down on
top of the cars, and we farewell John and Tim. I can tell John is happy
I am doing this. Happy I am accepted. He feels deeply about it. My
skin doesn't feel white here, and the women's doesn't seem black.

We stop at the store on the way out, buy more torches, load up
with water and juices. A fifty-dollar note is all the town's cultural fund
has distributed to each of the travelling women for the week. It's all
gone by the end of the road out – given from the car windows to kids
ambling along to the Borroloola Show. 'Can't go there with nothing
in their pockets!'

We head out along the Carpentaria Highway. I have three passengers – Annie, Thelma and Dinah Norman Marrngawi. No personal names now – just kin names. It's the law. A name may belong to someone who died. Can't use it. 'You call me Yuwani, and her too,' Annie says, nodding towards Dinah. 'Mother-in-law.' She moves on to Thelma – 'You call her Baba – sister. She is Nangala. Same skin as you. She's your sister.'

Yuwani Annie starts to sing softly as we leave the town behind. The songs are in language. Baba Thelma and Yuwani Dinah join in. Gentle clapping of the beat. There is great contentment to be heading bush. Earlier this generation, the exodus from the summer camp would have been on foot, weeks of walking together stretching ahead. Catching small game, gathering seeds and berries in the cool of morning. Resting in the shade through the afternoon until the sting of the day's heat softened in the dusk, and the cooking fires burned down. Stories and songs providing a backdrop to the convivial preparation of food. Knowledge and nourishment being passed down with surety to every new generation, as clans crossed the land to sacred corroboree grounds. Now culture moves on wheels, and ceremony time is merely a pause in town life's sedentary routine.

We drive five hours, with a couple of fuel stops. One at Heartbreak – a crossroads stop an hour from Borroloola – the other at Hi-Way Inn, Daly Waters, at the junction of the Carpentaria and Stuart highways, north of Tennant Creek and Alice Springs. They are the same stops we made for years on the five-day drive from Adelaide, and on more recent fly-drive trips via Darwin. The convoy leaders are setting a cracking pace considering the state of the road. The sealed part of the road is narrow – just one car-width. The edge is loose red gravel. Even so, it is better to pull off the road to let semitrailers and cars with caravans pass. Safer to give them a wide berth than risk their tyres throwing up a stone to shatter the windscreen. Stock graze unfenced, and as twilight comes kangaroos may leap in front of the vehicle without warning. Eagles with enormous wingspans are already picking at recent road kill.

We drive into the western sky. The setting sun casts a golden glow of reflection on the top of the tree canopy that flanks the road. Trunks glow red. The sky turns powder pink above a layer of spongy blue on the horizon, deepening as the light fades. We are quiet in the car as the calmness of night drifts in.

We cross the Stuart Highway, and turn onto a dirt road in the dark. I have no idea how far it is to our destination, or even precisely where it is from here. Or where we'll be sleeping tonight. I am more than happy to leave the planning to others. I am open to whatever the week will bring. At the moment, I am a driver, a daughter-in-law and a sister. It is an invigorating change from my life in the city, planning every quick-paced move of my job and the household.

The unsealed road is deeply corrugated. The car shudders violently, and neither slowing down nor speeding up seems to make it more comfortable. Two more vehicles have joined the convoy – meeting of the tribes has begun. We pull up in a line behind each other on the road verge. We wait an hour, maybe more, for another vehicle to catch up, then we make camp for the night at a railway siding. A clearing of stony red dirt by a train crossing on the main north–south line from Darwin to Adelaide. Tarps are pulled off the tops of vehicles, and swags and mattresses are thrown down in family and clan groups so we can go to bed. Everyone's too tired for dinner. There will be food for breakfast.

The vehicles are parked in a semicircle to flank the campground for thirty-five women and two small girls. The black sky is crystal clear overhead. No city lights here to dilute the darkness. I settle down into my swag, pulling the edge of my sleeping bag up under my chin. I throw the insect netting over my head to enclose my pillow.

It is entirely pleasurable, a familiar feeling from the countless nights on the roadside, in dry creek beds and in the scrub, where John has taken us before.

The women chat and sing a little as they curl up on mattresses and swags around the fires. It is quiet here without the fights and noise of the town camps. Peaceful. 'No humbug here,' Annie tells me. It's like the exciting start of family treks out bush when they were just girls, and days of being together stretched out ahead. When the seasons and nature's cycles guided them to new hunting grounds, to birthing camps, or to life-affirming ceremonies. As they settle down to sleep, the dancing days ahead are the threads of anticipation that tie these sisters and nieces, mothers and grandmothers, aunties and mothers-in-law so strongly together.

Above us, the Milky Way is a slash of sheer silver gossamer, studded with diamonds. The stars of other constellations are in sharp focus, stretching far out into the heavens. Two trains blaze past in the night, sirens and headlights blaring as the signal bells ring on the road next to us. They pierce the total silence and wake some of the campers. There is quiet talking, singing. The pitch-dark explodes again a little later to the headlights of a semitrailer roaring past on the track, its load shaking with the corrugations. Then perfect quiet settles until dawn.

Wilderness – A Personal Account

Chris Bell

Photographer Chris Bell spends days on an alpine plateau in the Central Plateau of Tasmania, a place he has come to love like no other. As he describes his surrounds, the threat of weather and the intricate natural encounters, we understand his view that solitude is 'aloneness', as distinct from loneliness.

From the top of the mountain I can see clear into forever. In the creamy, diffused light there is no horizon. Sky merges into land, the distant mountains float.

Scattered across the pavements of fractured rock, out-of-season gentians spring from sheltered cracks, withered stragglers hanging on to the last, as gentians do. Far below, another world away, the valleys tinkle with the chirruping calls of the Crescent Honeyeater. With its black breast-crescent, yellow wing-patch and spirited calls, the 'crescent' is the voice of the Tasmanian mountains – the music of the wilderness.

This morning there was a snap frost and the waterfalls and creeks have all but frozen. The water barely moves, dribbling in pulses over the crystalled lips of knobbly rock. I run my hand over the stone, greeting the place that has become everything to me. Out here little changes; I find comfort in that.

Once, I came here just for the mountains; like anyone else who first ventures into this realm, I saw only the obvious. Returning again and again, I have established an intimacy with Nature formerly unknown to me. What I want to talk about here is that feeling and why it is important to me. To do this, I'll have to give away a few secrets about this special place.

Perched high in the Central Highlands is an alpine plateau, spacious and wild. Though ringed by impressive ridges and towering cliffs, the feeling here is subtle, rather than grand. It is a gentle place, a fragile place, where glassy pools are cradled by containing walls of cushion plants, and flowers sway from rock ledges. At night you are soothed to rest by the echoes of chattering frogs and the whispering trickles of a creek. This is not only the place where I began my first excursions into the wilderness, but it is also where I began to explore my own mind.

I have come to love this place as no other. It is secluded and safe, lying beyond the reach of reckless hands. This remote range, tucked away in one of the wettest corners of our wooded isle, has become almost a shrine to me. It was here that I first became conscious of the depth of wilderness, of its subversive ability to de-program and to recast our thinking.

I generally return here alone. For me, entering wilderness accompanied means perhaps seeing only a portion of what it offers – we see the 'scenery', but can miss the profundity. To be receptive to all its facets one should reflect from the perspective of solitude.

Solitude is 'aloneness', as distinct from loneliness. In loneliness we discover nothing, but in solitude lies the mechanism – if we take the opportunity – for seeing beyond some of those maxims which are taken to be the cornerstones of our civilisation, yet which so often are nothing but the causes of our derailment. In a state of isolation we can evaluate, more carefully and deliberately than at other times, why we arrive at the values we have. Perhaps only in solitude can we cast off the tethers that limit our thinking.

On the slopes of this mountain lies a goblin forest of gnarled and contorted Myrtles; they are caked in moss so soft that you can't pass them by without touching it to confirm that such a thing indeed exists. The twisty forest is ideal habitat for the smaller and generally unseen birds that bob around on the scaly trunks, hanging upside down, and filling the air with the warbling song that makes these rather plain birds so appealing. On my way here, I rested among fallen branches caked in mushrooms; my exhaustion was soon forgotten as I watched a Scrub Tit flitting around on the mossy fronds, pouring out its musical trill. Once you've savoured this call, you can never turn your back on the wilderness; the bonds have begun.

I seek cover high in an open bowl – a cirque-like depression which offers shelter from the raging westerlies that go hand in hand with these mountains. Drenching fronts from this quarter dump some of the heaviest rain in Tasmania, and keep these places as they are. If you don't like the rain, you can't love these mountains.

Beneath the final summit block, trickling creeks rush from the open slopes to form a graceful tracery over the damp and spongy turf. It is a natural blending of water, rock and flowers, the essential elements of an alpine garden. I feel at my best here.

On the edge of this protected scoop, colossal shafts of unbroken rock plunge to the tinkling forests. To stand on the edge of these spooky cliffs as echoing bird calls drift up the shaded walls is one of the most calming sensations I know. The rock here is dolerite, an ancient rock from deep within the Earth. For shape, dolerite has no rival, being cast in an appealing array of columns and blocks; and in the flood of light at dawn or dusk these walls are infernos.

Whenever I return here I begin by 'doing the rounds', reacquainting myself with the place. I wander round the familiar rock pools and animated boulders, letting myself open up again and confessing that I've been away too long.

In my ramblings I'm suddenly almost swept off my feet in shock – SWOOSH . . . I scan what's left of the sky and glimpse the blurred traces of what look like shooting stars disappearing into the gathering mist. The silhouettes – and speed – are unmistakable. If the magnificence of flight is embodied in a single bird, it is in these sleek little strangers from the northern hemisphere. Needletails (Spine-tailed Swifts) are perhaps the most aerial of birds, spending almost all their time on the wing; it is thought they may actually *sleep* on the wing, catching rest as they fall, with wings folded, before regaining their graceful flight. They are marvels of the bird world – among my favourites.

The mist has crept right down now, obscuring the other side of the bowl. When the weather sets in like this, the place feels wholly detached from everything. I'm wonderfully alone, just me and the rocks. Immersed in this comforting shroud, I imagine for a while there is total harmony in the world: how can there be so many divisions out there, when here there are none? While this feeling is illusory, the impression is real enough; it's sufficient reason to keep returning.

It's turned bitingly cold and the swifts have fled; only drifting snowflakes remain, braving the air like day-moths.

Summer or winter, the snow is always a welcome attraction. I like the calming effect of the feathery crystals coasting to earth. When it snows out here I'm excited, continually unzipping the tent door – every five minutes – just to see how things have changed.

I've always been fascinated by snow; it is, after all, a minor miracle. Many childhood memories revolve around jumping into deep drifts – head first – and coming home saturated and freezing. I used to watch it decorate everything it touched; and secretly, I still get a thrill out of the way these soft, spidery crystals of water can make almost everything unmanageable. Men shelter, physical work grinds to a halt. Snow humbles.

After several days of whiteout I venture out into the world of magic. Cornices festoon the cliff edges, framing a vista of Earth's most beautiful work, floating on fog. Swirling whorls of wind-blown ice crystals – spindrift – smoke over the soaring columns of silvered dolerite, almost obscuring the snow clouds piling above.

It strikes me very clearly now that these clouds are essentially the same clouds as those which roll over the Arctic slopes and saturate the Amazon Basin. There is a universality about them which links the wild places to us all and, for me, reaffirms my intuitive belief that dotted lines are for guarded minds; like birds wild and free, clouds know no boundaries and make a mockery of ours. Clouds also strengthen our grasp of the notion that wild places should exist for their own sake, not ours.

Suddenly a Wedge-tailed Eagle appears, drifting like a leaf over the powdered slopes; it banks and rolls among the frigid clouds, taking in everything.

The Dingo

Bill Harney

*The origins of the much maligned wild dog of Australia, the dingo,
is the subject of fascinated conjecture by Bill Harney as he traces
its connection to Aboriginal legend, and discusses its qualities and
its use as a hunting dog.*

'Give a dog a bad name' is a truism for the dingo that has come about
from bitter experience with many pastoralists in this land. That is the
economic angle of the story, yet there is another side to this strange
animal that makes it a truly remarkable object for observation. Where
did it come from? Who brought it here? When did it arrive?

At first observation the answer seems to be a mystery hidden in
the past, yet listen to the native's rituals and hear his legends, and out
of it all comes a fairly complete picture of its arrival and origin.

Aboriginal ritual is bound up in the wanderings of their Culture
Heroes, and the songs of their totems tell the story of the dingo's
coming in the dreamtime.

In the Kunapippi legend and ritual, the story is enacted by the
Kundi-Djumindju tribesmen of how their ancestors came into this
land by canoe and landed near the Victoria River. By mimicry the
tribesmen enact the scene – the canoes coming ashore, the old Earth
Mother with her sacred stick coming up the beach, and amidst the
dancers painted with the symbols of the dingo totems are the men

who perform the story of the coming of the dingo. First they leap as a dog does when it jumps from a canoe, now the dancers roll upon the sand, and then with perfect mimicry they shake themselves and lift up their legs as the Song-man chants the story of their coming in the dreamtime.

The dingo is important in some aboriginal rituals. Legends amidst the Waddaman and surrounding tribes mention the dingo as the head-man of subincision. His party introduced reincarnation into the land, and from a pocket in his ear he is said to have produced the stone knife, and by doing this replaced the wooden knife that was formally used by the original inhabitants.

Native legends record that the dingo made the Katherine River – possibly the path of their migration – and near the old crossing two miles above the present township, and on the right bank of the river, are the large stone Dreamings that belong to the subincised Dingo clan.

How long has the dingo been in this land? The answer lies in the varying names for the dingo amidst the fifty tribes of the northern territory. In few instances are the names similar, and this fact alone points to the antiquity of the dingo with man in Australia. Names alter slowly when used as trade, as witness the Malayan names for rice, wooden canoes and steel blades that have not altered over the last one hundred and fifty years since the northern traders introduced these things into this country. The *lama*, or steel spear head, is called by the same name on the coastal belt of Arnhem Land or along the edges of the desert, even into Western Australia.

Here then are two methods of approach to the dingo's origin. Legends and ritual record how one lot came ashore with a migration near the shores of Cambridge Gulf facing the Timor Sea. The different names for the same animal point to its coming many years ago.

Why did the black man bring the dingo into this land? Maybe as a watchdog or companion, and also as a means of hunting, for early records show that the aborigines had dingoes with them during the hunt. To-day amidst the primitive people the dingo can still be seen with the hunters, and aboriginal customs show us that the native did use the dingo.

On Bathurst Island, the 'Diaminni' (dingo), as distinct from the 'Wonginni' (domesticated dog of the white people), is spoken of by the aborigines as the rightful owner of the land, and food was always left at the kill for this one-time friend of man.

These 'Diaminni' always hunted in pairs, and when hunting the wallaby they would drive it towards and over the high cliffs on the southern shores. By neat team-work and closing in upon their prey at the right time they would force it over the cliffs, to be dashed to death on the rocks below, and knowing this the native hunters would patrol the beaches each morning to pick up the freshly killed animals that were often partly eaten.

This type of hunting was within tribal law; as a native explained, 'Food killed by dingo belongs to man.'

This is interesting, because food killed by other creatures, as for instance the eagle, was taboo, and sickness, such as leprosy and other skin complaints, was accounted for by the fact that the sick person ate such a food.

Even with inland tribes, 'dingo kill was blackfellow tucker,' and the greatest insult one could hurl at a person was to call him 'robber of eagles.'

Regarding the animal itself, and away from all bias, it is truly regal. Domesticated, it shows utter disdain for the yelping curs that surround it in the blacks' camp, and when hunting for itself it has an ability that is uncanny.

At Jensen's pineapple plantation, Darwin harbour, a dingo would pull down a banana from the low Cavendish plants and after peeling it on the ground would slowly eat it, then trot away, and this it did whenever it was hungry. The dingo's method of hunting fish from the sea was to trot along the shore near the surf, and observing a movement in the waters, it would bound in to catch the small sand-sharks that swam near the beach. On many beaches the turtle eggs are scented out and dug up by the dingoes, even though they may be up to three feet beneath the sand.

Dingoes are often loyal to each other; doggers have often remarked that they rarely tackle one of their kind in a trap, or when they are wounded upon the ground; and often when one is poisoned the others will try to decoy the sick one away to the bush and safety.

Useful in the past as a friend and hunter for the aborigines, the dingo is to-day hunted down as a pest, yet many of the early pioneers in the Northern Territory know that their resistance to bad conditions and poor markets in the past was helped considerably by the aborigines' trading to them the dingo scalps that were converted into food and supplies to enable them to carry on and thus open the land.

A Desperate Rescue

Geoff Hudspeth (as told to Tim Bowden)

The story of a young timberman's trek to get help for a man with a nearly severed foot is recounted to Tim Bowden by Geoff Hudspeth, former General Manager of the Mt Lyell mine in Tasmania.

They were working for the Hydro-Electric Commission cutting a track out on the Andrew River. Keith Morrison was the eldest member of the party and Georgie Martin, who'd be about 19, and a boy of about 14. This accident happened at 9 o'clock on a Saturday morning. Keith put an axe clean through his foot and almost severed it. He was a bushman of considerable experience. He got a tourniquet round the pressure point on his groin and lay on his back and they wrapped his foot up in a blanket.

Then Keith told Martin that his only hope of survival was for Martin to walk to Gormanston to get help. Morrison was an old friend of mine. He wasn't working for us, he was working for the HEC but he said: 'If you can find Geoff Hudspeth and get a helicopter there's some chance that I might get out of this.'

Now there are no tracks on the Andrew River to Gormanston. They'd been dropped in there by helicopter. Martin said: 'How the devil do I find my way to Gormanston?' And Morrison said: 'You climb that hill up there, you'll see Mount Owen now. Make a beeline for it. Sooner or later you will hit the old North Lyell railway and when you do, turn right and walk up the railway to Linda and into Gormanston, and get me help.'

So Martin set off at 9.30 on Saturday morning and he arrived at my house at one o'clock on Sunday, and we got busy straight away.

I got the field engineer and the helicopter pilot and we had to put Martin into the helicopter to show us where his mate was and I suppose it was two o'clock before we got away.

So we flew out and we circled the area and there were fires going. The boy had the wit to light fires and make smoke, and he had tried desperately to cut a landing area. Now to get a big helicopter down you want a circle of at least . . . 120 feet, the boy had one of about 50 feet. He was only a kid.

We had no hope of landing in it so Max Holloman, the pilot, put the helicopter into the Andrew River. There was a shingly bank in the middle of the river and he said, 'I'll put it here, and stay here flying it,' 'cause he'd be washed down the river otherwise. So he was flying it in a stationary position with its wheels on the shingle.

We swam ashore and Martin had an axe with him. We found the start of this track and we walked a bit over two miles with a stretcher and there was Morrison – lying on his back with his foot up in the crook of a tree.

The little boy had walked some miles back and brought a tent up and built it over him. Keith Morrison had a fire just behind his head and fire either side of him, to keep him warm, and the boy had done everything he possibly could, plus tried to cut a landing ground.

Well, Morrison was the colour of parchment, very faint pulse and he had lain there, letting that tourniquet go every 20 minutes, someone had told him every 20 minutes it had to be released. He'd wait until the blood soaked through the blanket via his foot and tighten it up again.

He was able to talk and welcomed us, and he grinned at me and said: 'I knew you'd come, Geoff,' and that's about all he said.

Anyway, we did what we could with his foot and got him onto the stretcher and tore up some blanket strips and tied him into it, because we had to haul him over logs and that.

And then when we got back to the Andrew River, there was the trouble of ferrying a man on a stretcher out into the middle of the river, deep and running fairly fast. So Georgie Martin, who's done all this walking for some 30 hours, felled a King Billy Tree and split us some logs and we made a rough raft and we floated Morrison out and got him into the chopper, which had been hovering there for about two hours, engine running, just slowly.

By the time he was in the chopper there was just room for him and me, and we had to leave Georgie Martin and the boy and my third engineer behind, and we went into Queenstown.

When we got Morrison into the helicopter, I thought he was gone, his pulse was so slow. He was a shocking colour. We did something the textbook says is all wrong, we put a great slug of rum into him – and you could feel his pulse back up.

Anyway, we flew to Queenstown. He held my hand all the way and we got him into hospital and then we went back to get the three people we left behind, including Georgie Martin, who was the real hero of the thing with all his walking.

I suppose it was about six o'clock by the time we got there and we had to land in the middle of the river again, and they swam out and we put all aboard and home we came.

I had a car waiting to take Georgie Martin to Strahan, where he lived. 'Not on your life!' he said. His job was up in the hospital. So we delivered him up to the hospital and he sat all night with Keith Morrison, sat up by his bed. He'd been without sleep for about two and a half days, you see.

And Monday morning, when they pronounced that Morrison was now out of danger, Georgie Martin said, 'Alright, now I'll go home to Strahan,' and that's what he did.

There were three notable people in this – Georgie Martin, the boy who had enough wit to light fires and look after Keith, and Keith Morrison, who managed to stay alive. I think I would've given up the ghost, you lie there for 30 hours, bleeding to death, with very little hope of any rescue.

Patrolling the World's Longest Fence

Arthur Upfield

The Number One Rabbit Fence, designed to keep rabbits out of the Western Australian wheat belt, ran for 1130 miles from the southern ocean to the north coast when Arthur Upfield decided to accompany the fencing patrol through the wastes of the inland.

If it please you, accompany Millie and Curly and me on a patrol of one section of 163 miles of the longest fence in the world, the Number One Rabbit Fence, Western Australia. The purpose of such a fence, of which there are many in Australia, is to stop the migration of rabbits to the wheat belts. This particular fence begins at the edge of a water-washed rocky jetty facing the Southern Ocean, near Hopetoun, and it runs northward for 1130 miles to end at a salt-water creek near Banningarra, on the North-west coast.

Millie and Curly are camels, almost akin to the elephant in intelligence, swayed by the human emotions of joy and anger, controlled by a 'homing' instinct almost as strong as that of the pigeon, at times placid and at other times as petulant as children. They are harnessed in tandem to a large, covered dray, which, when not drawn by them, is kept level with drop-sticks to provide the boundary rider with a one-room house on wheels.

At the northern extremity of the section, from which end the monthly patrol is made, is the Government Camel Station named Dromedary Hill, so called from the twin-backed, stony hill in the vicinity of the homestead. The man in charge comes with us the short distance to the fence through which we must pass to reach the narrow track flanking the fence on its east side, for many hundreds of miles. Millie, the team leader, turned to the south and, when clear of the gate, the dray is stopped while *au revoirs* are exchanged by men who may not see another human soul for ten days or a fortnight.

Here we are able to view the fence and the track that form what is known as a cut line – a line first surveyed and then cleared to a width of twenty feet, the fence being then erected two feet west of the centre. Northward the cut line dwindles to infinity in the dark mulga scrub. Excepting for a few angles to escape 'break-aways', the cut line is rule-straight. Southward, the line narrows to a ribbon at the summit of a long rise nearly two miles distant, and beyond that rise, 161 miles away, is the small wheat town of Burracoppin on the main railway line from Perth to Kalgoorlie, which marks the southern extremity of this section. The fence runs a further 218 miles beyond the railway line to the Southern Ocean, whilst in the opposite direction it shears through the bush to the Indian Ocean, 750 miles distant.

We have to cover 326 miles before once again we see Dromedary Hill. Twenty-eight days the journey will occupy, and we will travel with the time-table regularity of trains. Down in Burracoppin, or wherever he may be, the inspector will know every evening where his riders are, or ought to be, camped.

Millie swings along, her tread cat-like and silent, placidly chewing her cud and quite resigned to the month's exile from all her friends and relatives at the station, but Curly, between the shafts of the dray, is not so resigned. He is, in fact, openly rebellious. He vents throaty growls, and endeavours to turn himself into the letter S in order to look back at those of his comrades that have come to the fence to watch us away, for be it understood that he wears winkers like an old dray horse.

Soon the homestead and the barren hills behind it are shut out by the bordering scrub. On the long slope, the wheels hiss softly in the deep, dry sand. The everlasting fence-posts slip by in endless procession. We pass our first wooden mile-peg marked M/162 with the broad arrow beneath the numerals. Looking back and down the straight track, we can see a tiny dot midway between us and the vanishing point of the cut line. That dot is the Camel Station overseer, watching us until we disappear from his sight over the rise but a short distance ahead.

On the summit of the rise, the sand on the track is replaced with surface ironstone rock. Here the scrub trees thin out and give growth to the soft, pearl-grey flannel-bush, the salt-bush and the blue-bush, and the world-famed Western Australian everlasting flowers.

Round then the first angle of the fence at the 161-mile peg, to continue a further mile when the fence in turn forces us a trifle eastward. There is no obvious reason why these angles should be made, but in all cases the real reason is that they are made to escape the precipitously-faced break-aways. The dray wheels rumble hollowly over the surface rock, giving Curly a grand excuse to pretend to be frightened. As he is easily able to pull the dray himself without exertion, the brake is applied and he is given work to do.

To our right, through a veil of tree-branches, looms the sheer face of a Western Australian break-away caused in some far geological age by the subsidence of wide sections of the earth's crust. From here the track falls sharply at first, and then more gently in a perfectly straight line across comparatively open country to stab the heart of the bush spreading to the level, knife-edged horizon. The break-away cliff of red ironstone rock sweeps in a giant arc westward and then southward, appearing like the face of a great quarry, its summit fringed with scrub trees, its foot put down on white sand dotted with salt-bush. On the track, and out from the bordering bush, particles of mica reflect the sunlight from a billion points coloured white and gold and amber.

Down the stony slope, with hand on brake and eyes on the fence to detect a broken wire or a rent made in the netting by kangaroo or emu, we are hurried by the impetuous Curly, who would so like to break into a tearing gallop for a full mile – and then lie down for two or three days to get over it. When level ground is reached, the brake may be left alone, but never beyond jumping distance. It is astonishing how quickly a camel can spring into a gallop from a slow walk.

At length we reach the dense scrub, where no longer do the light of day and the reflection of the sun by the mica particles make buoyant our spirits. On both sides of the cut line, shadows fall between the trunks of living trees to the trunks and debris of dead timber. Save for a few crows that will follow us from camp to camp for many miles, and the ever-watching wedge-tailed eagles, mere specks against the sky, the world seems empty; it seems so, but is not really so.

Having of necessity left the Camel Station late this morning, we select our camp near the 156-mile peg, where the scrub provides a variety of food for the camels. A camel will not long eat of one kind of bush or tree leaf, and it will never eat grass, which is as well, because we shall see no grass until the farms are reached. It demands variety, and, if variety is not to be obtained, it will go hungry. Its habit is to wander from bush to tree, snatching a mouthful here and there and ignoring fodder on either side.

The dray is drawn just off the track. The wheels are chocked and the drop-sticks let down to ensure its level position after Curly is taken from between the shafts. Having been unharnessed, the camels are short-hobbled and permitted to roam.

This section of fence is the hardest of any for animals expected to live on the country. Its northern end at the Camel Station reaches the southern extremity of the pastoral country proper, and between that place and the salmon-gum country, first entered at the 60-mile post, extends a hundred-mile-wide belt of desert scrub, of low, tough bogeta and broom-bush, whereon no camel or horse or donkey will long maintain condition. As there are no cross fences from one end of the section to the other, and as the camels will ever make back to the land of their birth, once they get away from the rider, he will be lucky to overtake them before they reach the Camel Station gate.

As they cannot be trusted to camp for the night at even one of the few good camel camps, it is necessary along this section to cut bush and drag it to selected trees, to which they are secured with long neck ropes that permit them to lie down. At one time a rider lost his camels at the 69-mile peg and was obliged to walk back to the 163-mile peg to get them again.

One eats from a drop table in the dray to escape the ants. Save only when it rains, one sleeps on a Coolgardie stretcher set up beside the dray. At dawn, when the camels simultaneously get up, the clatter of their bells announces the new day. Before we dress, the mound of grey fire ash is broken open to reveal the red wood coals, on which is placed the billycan containing the remains of last night's tea; and, when the camels have been freed to find their breakfast, ink-black tea is sipped and a cigarette smoked. The sky is ever of interest as a weather prophet, excepting during the winter months when rain-bearing clouds often sweep across the clear sky without a heralding sign.

After a simple breakfast of bacon and damper and milkless tea, we pack all gear into the dray, and then, perhaps, a couple of posts are cut to replace posts which have become rotten. Every year hundreds of new posts are put in.

To-day we cross a spinifex plain – semi-globes of spiny bush covering the brown earth like large, green meat-covers. Beyond the plain, we again enter the mulga timber, with the track and the fence dwindling to infinity ahead until we are able to see the blank wall of scrub at the angle marked by the 148-mile peg. Time drags before we reach the turn, and, having swung round it, we again see the fence dwindling to infinity amid the silver leaves of the broad-leafed mulga.

There is work to be done south of the 144-mile peg, where there is a rain-shed – a simple roof of corrugated iron from which rain-water is piped into two large receiving tanks beneath it. There are several of these rain-sheds on this section constructed for the fence-rider and his camels, and sometimes thoughtless and unauthorized travellers leave a tap running with the consequent waste of hundreds of gallons of precious water on which life itself depends.

Curly makes known his desire for a drink when within a quarter of a mile of the rain-shed. He strains against braked wheels, his haste objected to by Millie, who vents low rumbles of protest. Two hundred yards from the water, the dray is drawn off to the side of the track, because round about the rain-shed there is no wood for cooking and there is a super-abundance of ants.

At five-thirty the two drinking buckets are taken from the dray with purposeful noise. At once the bells strapped to the necks of the camels feeding deep in the bush cease their pleasing tinkle. The buckets, continuing to be loudly rattled, are taken to the water tanks, when from a distance again comes the rhythmic tinkle quickly becoming louder until the two grey shapes appear at the edge of the scrub to hasten to the filled buckets as quickly as hobbled feet will permit.

Some twenty gallons of water they drink between them. For a little while they stand with legs wide apart, eyes bright, long, split upper-lips waggling. They begin to chew their moistened cuds with vivid enjoyment, content for an hour, but for an hour only, when the desire to return 'home' will seize on them.

They have wandered half a mile before they are brought back to the supper prepared for them against the trees to which they are to be tied for the night. Millie is little vexed at being thus frustrated. Curly is angry and stubborn. Now and then he lies down and bellows like a small child who refuses to walk another yard. Tempers, however, are banished by sight of the prepared supper, when Millie wants to kiss the driver and Curly wants to jump on him.

Routine governs life on the fence. Mental cobwebs cannot be spun. One may take chances with horses or bullocks, but one cannot take chances with camels and long survive. Millie may be trusted a little. Curly may be trusted not to kick with his hind feet and strike with his fore feet, but, when he is being harnessed, his head must be roped close to a tree trunk, and when at work he must not be trusted for a second.

In answer to the oft-put question: 'Are you not terribly lonely?' one must answer: 'There is no time to be lonely.' In one week a fence-rider will read more than the average city man will read over a full year, which his reading will be infinitely more varied. The only part of the life that palls is those windless periods, when for days and nights not a leaf stirs in country where there is but little bird life and no animal life. When the wind is first heard in the distance, roaring across the top of the scrub, one feels inexpressible relief.

Once I had a dog for a companion; but it picked up an old strychnine bait and, despite all efforts, it died in my arms. At another time I took with me a cat that I came to love very much, and then Curly stamped on her when she only wanted to rub herself against his dinner-plate foot. I took a young galah. It used to ride all day in the dray and it never knew the bars of a cage. At night, when reading or writing in the dray by the aid of a hurricane lamp, should I be irritated by the visit of a tree moth or a fluttering bat, the galah perched on one shoulder would murmur sleepily: 'You old devil!' Then one morning, when returning to camp with the camels, I heard a scream of defiance, and, on looking up, was in time to see my bird in the talons of a swiftly-rising hawk. After that I gave up companions on a rabbit fence. Their loss incurs too much heartbreak.

At the 135-mile peg the timber is scattered and the ground is a vast, unbroken carpet of white and gold and blue splashes of colour made by the myriads of wild flowers. Each nodding head is supported on a long stem rising from tiny leaves lying flat on the ground. Weeks after the leaves have perished the flowers remain. In this amazing garden we camp for noon lunch, and while we are eating it in the dray, a bird settles on a fence post to watch us. The world is hushed, and the only sounds are made by the cud-chewing camels and a few blowflies. Presently, at a great distance, one hears belled camels coming our way. The bells grow ever louder exactly as though the camels, or it might be bullocks, are being brought into camp. Done by the entertaining ventriloquist on the post – the bell-bird!

At the 96-mile peg there is a rain-shed and hut combined. Here, in the centre of the great belt of desert bush is an oasis of salt-bush, wait-a-bit, and native peach trees, growing between gnarled red gums. From this splendid camp we go on to the 82-mile peg where the fence and track passes through a wide gap in a line of break-aways about which the lightning plays its tricks. A poor camp this. There are many deviations in the fence between this peg and the 69-mile peg from where we turn off into the bush to reach a small hut built in a natural clearing. The clearing is surrounded by wattle trees blazing with heavy, yellow bloom, and the ground on which they grow is snowed deep beneath the white everlasting flowers. A garden, a bush garden, that imperishably burns itself on the mind.

We are in the salmon-gum forest when we pass the 60-mile peg. The tall, straight, lovely trunks of these trees gleam pale against the dark-green background of the lesser bush, and like all gum-trees they shed their bark in preference to their leaves.

We come now to the northern wheat farms in process of creation. The 'chop-chop-chop' of biting axes and the whirr of tractors distract us. A mighty heave at the dray, and we are off at a gallop, the rider clinging to the brake-handle protruding from the rear of the vehicle. A settler's wife and children are running through the bush to see their first camels outside a zoo – and the camels are made fearful by the coloured, swaying skirts to which they are quite unaccustomed.

I *should* glory in Australia's development. Alas, the sound of thudding axes and the splintering crash of falling forest giants both anger and sadden me.

Day by day we pass the endless fence-posts, repair broken wires, and patch the netting torn by the farmers' machines and trucks. In one day we have emerged from the bush proper to the farming districts, where we meet modern road traffic and where it is never silent. We have no place in the world of machinery, this world of cleared spaces not natural to our beloved bush. Perhaps of the three of us, Curly dislikes it least, for it provides him with unlimited excuses to play the fool. At the 25-mile peg we cross the loop railway line at Campion, and thereafter travel nine miles over an established wheat-belt to reach, and pass through, poor ironstone country until, finally, we step on to the main highway from Perth to Kalgoorlie skirting the railway.

The line, of course, breaks the fence; but here it crosses over a deep pit that presents as great a barrier to rabbits as does the fence itself. Beyond the line the mile-pegs begin again at Number One, and across the line we bump and clatter to reach the Government hay farm, where the camels will rest for two days. One mile west lie Burracoppin and the boarding house, where may be eaten fresh yeast bread and butter, celery and red steak for which the body craves after a month's subsistence on tinned food, bacon, and baking-powder bread.

Neither the driver nor the camels are happy here at Burracop-pin, and we are emphatically pleased when our faces are again turned northward. Even the desert bush country to us is better than this.

Reaching at last the summit of the rise at the 161-mile, there, fall-ing away from us in a straight line, lies the track to the Camel Station. The sedate Millie voices her pleasure, and Curly tugs at the trace and wants, oh, so much! to do the last mile and a fraction at express speed. Down there, where the track appears to be no wider than a small girl's hair ribbon, moves a little black dot. It is the station overseer, who knows the day of our arrival and almost the hour.

How the minutes do drag! We are at the bottom of the slope. Now above the western scrub rise the summits of Dromedary Hill. Then two lonely men are talking like excited women. Five minutes later Curly and Millie are running towards the hill in search of their comrades, free of the wretched hobbles for four days.

Then I am sitting at a real table beneath a house roof. We drink scalding hot tea in the homestead kitchen and shout above the cacophony of two gramophones and the wireless all going at the same time.

They love noise, whose ears have been strained day and night to hear any kind of sound.

Close to Nature

John Landy

In a year of observation at his family farm and in the surrounding bush near the Southern Highlands, John Landy created a unique record of the passage of the seasons and their influence on plant and animal life. The result was the bestselling book Close to Nature.

I woke again to heavy fog. I browsed around the garden and heard a noisy pair of Yellow-tufted Honeyeaters. If they are looking for flowering plants they won't find too many here, although insects are said to be their principal food.

Later in the morning, as the fog began to lift, I could vaguely see a flock of birds flying around the dam. They proved to be Welcome Swallows, displaying their forked tails and erratic yet graceful flight patterns. At first glance one might think they were looking at their own reflections, but swallows have a particular interest in insects associated with water – mayflies, gnats and mosquitoes – and are noted for their skill in catching them on the wing. I watched for half an hour or more and never once did they land, wheeling in tight circles, occasionally touching the surface of the water with their feet or with one wing and creating little ripples.

After lunch the sun finally broke through the fog and I set out along the edge of Welumba Creek, making for the lower end of the

Greg Greg Fire Trail. On the way I noticed a flock of Eastern Rosellas. They are beautiful birds, apple green, red and yellow, with flashes of blue. They livened up the sombre, misty scene as they fed on the seed heads of Saffron Thistles, which also seem attractive to cockatoos.

The Welumba Creek area, where the Greg Greg Fire Trail begins its abrupt ascent towards the snow-line, is a mosaic of rocky outcrops dissected by deep gullies with damp shrubby patches on the southern aspects. Dramatic changes in vegetation take place in the space of a few metres.

One of the forested areas was thickly carpeted with native grasses. Here, in a green dell among the trees, I discovered a curious fungus, commonly known as a 'vegetable caterpillar'. This particular species, found at the base of wattles, was *Cordyceps gunnii*, yellow-green in colour with a dark, almost black tip. The whole of the fruiting body stands about 7 centimetres above the ground and is long and club-shaped. I dug it up and 5 centimetres below the fruiting body it was attached to a dead swift moth caterpillar. A year or so ago the fungus would have invaded the caterpillar, its fungal threads proliferating and digesting the internal tissue of the caterpillar before the fruiting body emerged from the soil.

In mediaeval times, when witchcraft was rampant, vegetable caterpillars were seen as a manifestation of the belief that animal matter could change spontaneously to plant matter. Here was a caterpillar from which sprouted a growing plant. It was not until the late 18th century that biologists were able to explain that fungi invaded the caterpillar while it was alive and ultimately produced a spore-forming body above the ground. In most species the fruiting body is formed on the larva or pupa, but in some it appears on the adult insect, although to my knowledge this has not been observed in Australia.

An interesting feature of the fungus is that certain species select particular larvae of moths, beetles or wasps to parasitise. In the tropics cordyceps have been found growing from the head of adult wasps. In the 18th century these were something of a collector's item and were known as vegetable flies.

I quietly crept towards a bird calling further up the hill. Although I did not see it, I am sure it was a lyrebird. It was not producing the range of mimicry so often heard from the male bird, but was making the characteristic 'choo' sound which is its territorial call. I had not expected to find lyrebirds here as it seemed too dry and stony. However, on closer examination I found disturbed ground where grasses, herbs and mosses had been worked over extensively – typical of lyrebird scratchings as it searches for small crustaceans, insects and worms.

Later in the afternoon I encountered the communication systems that exist between kangaroos. As soon as the first kangaroo saw me it seemed noiselessly to transmit its concern to its neighbours, although the alarm system is said to be a cough. Their disquiet was relayed to the cattle as well. The stock feeding near by quickly became aware that the kangaroos were looking at something and also turned their heads, seeking the source of agitation. At another stage, as I traversed a small valley, I heard some heavy thumping on the ground from the tail of a large old man kangaroo about 100 metres away. This quickly alerted all the others for a long way around and prevented me from getting too close. Finally I did get a picture of a group immediately below me in a grassy gully. They were unaware of my presence, while those further afield could see me but seemed unable to communicate with them.

Coming home in the semi-dark I walked through an area of the introduced pasture plant phalaris, in a place fenced out from cattle and sheep. The seed heads stood on dry stalks over a metre high. Phalaris, introduced to Australia from the Mediterranean region, is a valuable pasture grass which is sown widely in south-eastern Australia.

It is deep rooting and able to tap sources of underground moisture even when the surface is very dry.

In a prolonged hot summer here the leaves dry up but the plant survives by means of subterranean dormant buds which obtain water from the soil through the deeply penetrating roots. In my view phalaris is clearly the best pasture grass for the rising country of quick-drying granitic soils. It survives where more nutritious species such as Perennial Rye Grass die out, and provides vital winter feed and protection against soil erosion.

Phalaris has been the subject of much research by the CSIRO, which has produced more vigorous and drought resistant strains. It has also developed varieties with a lower alkaloid content, because one of the problems with phalaris is that at certain times of the year, particularly in the autumn following the first rains, its content of these chemicals can be sufficiently high to poison stock.

With all its great capacity for growth and adaptability to our environment, phalaris has one surprising weakness. It produces millions of tiny seeds per hectare yet few survive in the competitive environment of the paddock. Once established there one can almost guarantee that the plants will never increase in number. Paradoxically, it may proliferate along the side of roads where the fertility level is sufficient for the phalaris but does not encourage competitors.

Walking on Water

Bill King

A pioneer of outback tour operations, Bill King was constantly searching for new experiences for his 'punters' as he established his famous Bill King's Northern Safaris. He found himself in dangerous waters on the Roper River, Northern Territory.

The next initiative was to establish a barramundi fishing camp on the lower end of the Gulf of Carpentaria, and to that end a bloke in Alice Springs approached me to bring our people to this hunting and fishing camp he was going to set up at the old Port Roper site, near the mouth of the Roper River – 'A little piece of tropical paradise,' he told me, 'rich in wildlife and game.' Well, that may have been true, but the Roper River was then and still is a crocodile-infested waterway, so Val and I went with him for a look, Val and I in one Toyota ute and this bloke and his girlfriend in the other, both heading off down to this 'tropical paradise' at the mouth of the Roper.

Now it was certainly not the most welcoming place I had ever been to. There were big stretches of wet black soil country to negotiate, and somebody had warned us that we might have to run the gauntlet with a rogue bull buffalo. He was known as 'One Horn' for the obvious reason, and he hated motor vehicles. He had attacked a Land Rover once and all but tipped it over, with one horn jammed through a side panel. It was only when the horn snapped off that the

Landy came back to rest. Anyway we saw the nasty old bastard and he was bloody huge, pawing the dust, throwing his head about and moving forward threateningly, but he never came after us.

At disused Port Roper the floods had washed away the piles of the old jetty that were hanging out of the bank at a crazy angle. There was a big steel-framed shed that had lost half the sheets of iron off its roof and sides in some cyclone, and the sheets that had blown off were lying all over the place, twisted and torn. It was just on dark when we got there, so I just rolled our swag out on the concrete floor of the shed under what was left of the roof and after a bit of grub we turned in. I woke up in the early hours, anxious to dispense with what had awakened me and return for more sleep, and there in the moonlight was some of the wildlife. Bloody hell, there were snakes everywhere – not at our end, though. They were lying on the warm part of the concrete that had been in the sun.

The buggers were just relaxing there moonbaking. I quietly had my pee and wriggled back into the swag, making sure not to disturb Val and the snakes, otherwise we would have been spending the rest of the night sitting up in the front of a Toyota. I reasoned that if I minded my business the snakes would mind theirs. Humans were not prey for little reptiles. I must say, though, I did not get much sleep, keeping one eye open in the direction of our little visitors.

The snakes had slithered off as the concrete grew cold, so I arose early and walked over to the river. It was a sight to behold in the morning sunlight. There is 80 kms of water between the mouth of the river and the high tide mark at Roper Bar, and when it turns, as was happening that morning, it really comes down with some force, a head on collision, with the waves coming in from the gulf creating a foaming mass of currents and counter-currents. What is more, there was a feeding frenzy in progress, a couple of dorsal fins wheeling and diving in and out of the swirling water, hunting the food coming down with the tide. I would not have fished there for all the coffee in Colombia.

It was about that moment I saw it. I was standing on a small beach in the middle of a slither mark. It was nearly a metre wide with claw marks as big as dinner plates where the thing had dragged itself into the water. Bloody hell, he was a monster. What is more, the claw marks in the wet sand just under the water were visible with little clouds of silt still floating around them. The crocodile must have either heard me coming or by pure coincidence decided to go for breakfast just a minute or two before I arrived.

I never looked back, I can tell you. I scampered up the bank on all fours. I have never moved so fast. With the hair on the back of my neck still bristling I threw our stuff in the back of the ute and Val into the front seat, then fled that Godforsaken place, vowing never to return. 'I'm off!' I yelled at this fool who took us to this 'tropical paradise' and the site of his mooted fishing camp among snakes, sharks and crocodiles. The idiot was still in his swag, and I discovered later he had never been there before either. He had sucked himself in with his own bullshit.

Val and I went and saw Ray Fryer at Urapunga Station, and we came to an arrangement to set up a camp on the Wilton River, which bordered his station lease. It was a tributary of the Roper and we set out a campsite a couple of kms up from the junction.

We bought two boats with Mercury outboards and a heap of fishing gear that we could keep in a shed on the station, so we were all set up and ready to go. We packaged a 10 day Roper River barramundi fishing safari out of Katherine with Ansett.

It was a great fishing spot; we could fish the Roper down as far as Kangaroo Island, the Hodgson River, and of course the Wilton. We each had our favourite fishing spots and boasted to one another about river knowledge and the like. But this, of course, was governed by where you caught your last decent fish. I tried the tributaries and didn't like them much. That Hodgson was bloody spooky. It was really still water and you could literally feel the eyes looking at you. It was real crocodile territory and you could smell the rotting flesh. I couldn't relax in that waterway. Ian 'Sticko' Weatherly liked it because he caught some good fish there.

I preferred the Roper near the mouth of the Wilton. That's where Val caught her big one. It was about 4 o'clock in the afternoon and we were idling along the north bank when Val hooked a snag, or what we thought was a snag, because the line anchored and the boat spun us around, 'Ease it off a bit and I'll try and unhook it.' I said, grabbing hold of the line, and I no sooner got hold of it when it moved around to the other side of the boat. 'Shit, you've hooked something.' I said, as her rod nearly bent in two. 'Ease the bloody reel off!' I was giving all this advice. Anyway, whatever she had hooked had gone to the bottom, and we were idling in this circle around it. 'Bloody crocodile.' crossed my mind. Then it took off, with Val hanging on for grim death. She had the reel set right, so the 'thing' was using the run.

Then it stopped and she started to reel it in. This struggle went on for about an hour, and when I looked over the side, there it was, a big 'barra'. I dived for the gaff – there was no bloody gaff, always a problem with many people using gear, so I hung over the side and grabbed it in the gill, hoping to Christ that no croc. was eyeing it off for supper and took my arm with it. I gave the thing a heave and in it came, bloody hell, it was the biggest 'barra' I had ever seen and there they both were, all 19.5kg of fish and all 49.5kg of 'Herself', both lying exhausted in the bottom of the boat.

And what was it like to eat? It was absolutely delicious. One of the station hands had his own 'secret recipe' for barra, and it fed the mob at the station for dinner and there was still enough for a breakfast. Is there a better eating fish than fresh barramundi? I doubt it.

Sticko was fishing the Hodgson, and on this particular trip he had a young honeymoon couple on board and they were really keen 'fisherpersons.' Anyway, they were quietly moving up the Hodgson – putt-putt-putt – quietly, quietly, catchee fish. Sticko took the boat under the lee of a huge fallen tree sticking out from a clump of pandanus on the bank. 'A likely spot for a bite,' he muttered, when all of a sudden – SPLASH. The bloody crocodile must have been basking on the log, camouflaged by pandanus. It heard the boat coming too late and had to crank its heart rate up to get some movement, and by that time the boat had arrived.

Anyway, the crocodile shat itself and rolled off the log just as the boat passed underneath, and it landed full length, half in, half out. Now this thing was nearly as big as the boat and it was only by some miracle that it did not land on anybody, but it flipped the boat up in the air, whipped its tail around, and by the sheer weight of its tail took Sticko down with it. Well, did I say the crocodile shat itself? Spare a moment for Sticko. Imagine being submerged on the bottom of the bloody Hodgson with a monster crocodile. Anyway he broke surface and made the few metres to the bank, relieved to see his honeymoon couple hanging on to one another, their faces ashen to match his own. Now here is the miracle. Sticko swears the couple was bone dry. 'How did you get ashore?' he asked.

'Don't know,' they replied. Sticko said it was weird, they really didn't remember how they got ashore and his theory was that they either did a Jesus – their feet moving at such great speed that when they hit the water they ran across the top, or when the boat flipped it did so with enough force to throw them to the bank. Either way, they were dry.

Crocs were not a problem where we camped, although the little black kids from nearby Ngukurr, who swam in the Wilton at 'Flat Rock', as they called it, never took any risks. 'Flat Rock' was a huge sliver that protruded well out over the river a short distance upstream from our camp. They told us that a big rock dropped on top of the sliver echoed like thunder underneath, so they always dropped a couple to frighten the crocs away before diving in. Their ancestors had probably been doing that for thousands of years.

Sticko tells the story of the bloke who set up a small mixed farm on the river near Katherine. He hung a sign out the front 'Pigs for Sale.' It sounds like good idea for a BBQ, he thought. He was heading toward Darwin at the time, so he saw the bloke and picked out a pig in the pen to have it all dressed out and ready to cook on his return.

He rigged up this spit out of a couple of fence droppers and wire, but the pig took much longer to cook than he estimated, and by the time it was ready the punters were eyeing one another off as food. In the meantime the cooking smells had been wafting off down the river for hours, and when they were sitting around eating their meal in the silence that occurs when the guests are desperately hungry, Sticko heard crocodiles barking down by the river. He grabbed his torch and there they were: four sets of red eyes. The sneaky devils had followed the scent up the river and were all lined up on the bank eyeing off their dinner. Sticko threw some firewood at them and they took off, the punters slept in the Desert Cruiser and on its roof that night.

Settlers and Snakes

Miles Franklin

Miles Franklin's memoir, Childhood at Brindabella, *posthumously published in 1963, reveal a warm love for the countryside where she grew up, in the Monaro District of New South Wales. In this extract she writes of the menace of snakes near a household.*

I am thankful that I have not had to reside in those parts of Australia where pythons or carpet-snakes are valued as mice-killers and kept in store-rooms as pets. A Queensland friend told me she was so fond of her carpet-snake that when she found it coiled on a flourbag in its residential quarters she would stroke it in passing as one does a cat . . .

Ours were of the shy variety, clever as conjurors in disappearing. They never attacked unless molested or cornered. I know of few horses or dogs that died by their fangs and fewer human beings who have been bitten. When picnicking we would sometimes find their last year's sheath, a complete replica, even to scales and eyes, in what looked like cellophane.

So unrelaxing was the war against snakes that the settlers would nearly tear their houses down to dislodge one from the foundations or the caves where they like to take refuge. It was disconcerting to see a snake's head come through a crack in the veranda or protrude beside your legs if sitting on its edge. A settler near us one day saw a deadly tiger snake extrude its head onto the doorstep, whereupon she got the carving fork and firmly spitted him to the board. The reptile coiled around her arm but she kept the head nailed through a roasting summer afternoon till her husband returned from work to rescue her . . .

Many women were courageous and adept in snake-killing and kept a snake-stick at hand. This was often a sucker, that had sprouted tough and supple from a stringybark or gum stump, with a knobby end to smash the delicately articulated spine of the snake. One of my aunts, finding herself in the entrance hall when a snake came to call, took the loaded shotgun which stood in the corner ready for orchard or chicken marauders, and blew the intruder to pieces on the hardwood floor and found it very like an exploded fish . . .

One day later, during my farewell sojourn in paradise, my youngest aunt yielded to my plea to go for a walk to pick flowers. I had not outgrown the greedy desire of children to grab flowers suffocatingly in their fists. No native flower was then used in house decoration. Their elfin grace could not compete in favour with the imported riches of the garden plots. The cattle paddocks were bright with bloom, and, seeking variety, we followed one of our swiftly running home creeks, lovely as a fountain, through several fences to the hills. A big black snake lay full-length at his ease beside the water in the thin fringe of maidenhair ferns that were sprouting after winter retreat. The creature's forked tongue flickered rapidly in and out; his new skin gleamed blue-black with peacock tints; a little of his underside was showing like blended scarlet and pomegranate. I stood a fascinated moment and fled to my aunt. She went back seeking the snake but it had dissolved, leaving no trace.

The experience was not startling, merely surprising. Then why should that snake have persisted in my consciousness for over thirty years? As I have sat in some great congress in one of the major cities, or in a famous concert hall, or eaten green almonds on a terrace in

Turin in the early morning, or worked amid the din of the Krupp guns on an Eastern battle-front, or watched the albatrosses in stormy weather off Cape Agulhas, or have been falling asleep in an attic in Bloomsbury, that snake has still been stretched in the ferns beside the creek, motionless except for that darting tongue.

An Angel in the Queensland Floods

Tony Wright

Amid all the accounts of bravery, tragedy and amazing escapes from the January 2011 floods in Queensland that swept through the Lockyer Valley and took seventeen lives before inundating much of the city of Brisbane, journalist Tony Wright found an inspiring story of survival in the shattered town of Grantham.

'This,' says Marty Warburton, 'is my angel in silhouette.'

Linda Weston seems an unlikely angel. She climbs down from a ute and bustles towards us, the energy in her small frame seeming to bleed the oxygen from the air. She turns that air blue as she vents her opinion of officialdom and its latest plan to cut off her wrecked town from the media and all outsiders for the next seven days.

'The bloody world will forget about us in seven days, for Christ's sake,' she declares. 'And then where will we be?'

'Yes,' grins Warburton, 'This is the lady who saved my life. The lady in silhouette. Now she's saving everyone else.'

There are uncounted stories about tragedy and astonishing escapes in the floods that have ripped and rolled and seeped through communities from Queensland to Victoria over recent weeks, but few tell quite so simply of the human capacity for survival and the spirit of plain generosity that characterises what happened between Marty Warburton and Linda Weston during the night that destroyed the little town of Grantham on January 10.

It was a night when Weston was nothing more than a silhouette in candlelight, her spectral presence urging a man clinging to a roof to hang on, to live when others were dying.

Grantham is – or was – a hardscrabble Queensland bush settlement 100 kilometres west of Brisbane, home to perhaps 250 souls. It sits astride a railway line that cuts it in two. To the west, a street or two of homes and a small school that sits on a rise; to the east, the main part of the community hunkers down on a floodplain. More correctly, it did. Now it is a sodden mess of destruction, as if some giant malevolent raven had ripped apart a rubbish tip and strewn its contents over a square kilometre. Mattresses, shipping containers, sheds, upturned boats, refrigerators, clothing, splintered furniture and battered cars lie in muddied paddocks along with miles of torn plastic. Worse things are out there in the mud, too, which is why, almost two weeks after the deluge tore apart Grantham, police and Queensland authorities have locked it down against outsiders.

While armies of workers clear mountains of debris from Brisbane, Ipswich and Toowoomba and return those cities to a semblance of normality, the only work at Grantham is the search for bodies. Twenty people are known to have died in Queensland's great flood. Seven perished in and around Grantham. More are missing.

While far down the valley politicians argue about the future of Brisbane and whether suburbs should be rebuilt in flood-prone areas, Grantham is frozen in its immediate hideous past.

Warburton knows about the missing, and believes there are more than the 10 that authorities say there are. He watched as several of them were sucked into the raging waters just beyond his reach. He's a rangy, tough example of rural Australia, a self-described 'busted-arse shearer' who is also a floor sander by trade and the owner of Grantham's service station, but his eyes are filmed with a peculiar sheen and shift out of focus as he speaks of grabbing a hand reaching out of the water and being unable to keep a grip on it.

Floods are not uncommon in the lower streets of Grantham. Sandy Creek, one of numerous tributaries fed by water tumbling off the eastern face of the 700-metre-high Toowoomba Range 40 kilometres to the west, backs up when it reaches Lockyer Creek and lacks the energy to nose its way into the stronger stream. Denied passage, the creek breaks its banks and edges into the town's streets. No one much minded before January 10. Here, the locals boast that their labour is spent on the salad bowl of Australia, scratching a living picking vegetables for the big packing plants. The old-timers welcome floods, knowing they renew and fertilise the valley's soil.

Warburton knew a flood was coming – he only had to look at the darkening sky – but he was not too fussed until mid-afternoon, when his mobile phone lit up with weird messages from mates upstream. Areas were flooding that seemed to make no sense. Water was in a neighbouring village pub where it hadn't gone before. A wall of water was coming from the south. He'd never heard of such a thing. It had simply ignored a bend in the Lockyer Creek and taken off cross country, smashing everything in its path.

After weeks of heavy rain – Grantham had experienced three floods since Boxing Day – storm cells had punctured a massive bank of rain clouds up on the Great Dividing Range. More than a tenth of the Toowoomba Range's average annual rainfall of 900 millimetres would be dumped that day, most of it – 63 millimetres – between 1pm and 2pm. It roared off the eastern face of the range and into the sodden valley, while more spilt off the western slopes to drown the Darling Downs and the Condamine system.

The messages were urgent and Warburton trusted his mates. He waded to his service station, shouting warnings. The water was to his knees when he got into his office but quickly it rose to neck height and he had to hang from a beam overhead to get a breath of air before he could dive through the door. When he surfaced, he slid on to the awning of his business. Water hurtled by, turning logs into missiles. Then a car, floating with two people screaming and waving on its roof.

'If they weren't doing 80 kilometres an hour I don't know what I'm talking about,' Warburton says. 'Suddenly, the car and those people were sucked straight down and I didn't see them again.'

It was then that hands of more of the damned thrashed to the surface right next to the awning. 'I reached out and grabbed a hand, but I couldn't hold on,' he says, and then falls silent.

Across from Warburton's service station, Weston stared in disbelief. A house from the end of the street sailed past, and she saw people inside, crying for help.

Weston and her partner Paul Armstrong live in a fine old home in the style known as the Queenslander, high off the ground to catch a cooling breeze. They grow zucchinis, pumpkins, cucumbers, silverbeet and tomatoes. Their house was spared, though their sheds were crushed by debris. The floating house wedged itself against a steel structure in their paddock. Weston kept watch, calling encouragement from her window until a rescue helicopter lowered a saviour by winch and hauled into the sky an elderly couple and their dog, just as the evening light began to fade.

Warburton, praying that his service station wouldn't collapse beneath him, had retreated to the highest part of his roof. He knew he was in for a hard night, and Weston knew it, too. She wasn't about to let her neighbour suffer alone.

As night fell, she lit candles and placed them on her kitchen window sill. She stood there, hour after long hour.

Comforted by her silhouette in the candlelight, Warburton took to firing up his cigarette lighter every few minutes to signal he was alive. Near wore out his thumb, he says.

Fatigue crept upon him and, fearful of falling asleep and rolling into the flood, he lifted the edges of a couple of sheets of roofing iron and clipped himself to them with tool hooks he wears on his belt. But still he drifted off, and each time he did so, Weston, alarmed by the absence of cigarette-lighter signals, roared at him to shape up. Around 3am, with Weston still at her vigil, Warburton unclipped himself and edged down the roof to check the water level. He cannot recall what happened next, but he washed up on a neighbour's second-floor verandah several doors down.

Weston, seeing no more flashes of light from the service station, sat down to a breakfast of cold chips and chicken.

At dawn, traumatised survivors began emerging and climbing to the high, dry side of town over the buckled railway tracks. As the last of the floodwaters rolled down the valley towards Ipswich and Brisbane, Weston took charge, herding folk into the schoolhouse and scurrying around town urging help. Pantries were raided, dry blankets and clothes appeared, children were comforted and the community began its own, unofficial recovery program before most of the valley realised the tragedy that had taken place. Warburton went home to see his wife and young son – they live out of town on high ground – snatched an hour's sleep and returned. He's chairman of Grantham's community recovery committee.

They have seen a Prime Minister, a Premier and bureaucrats come and go in the days since, but they speak well only of Governor-General Quentin Bryce ('an amazing, wonderful person,' says Warburton) and Melbourne trucking tycoon Lindsay Fox. Fox sat down, asked what was needed, got on the phone and ordered a 22-seat mini-bus and 12 shipping containers pronto. 'He hasn't forgotten where he came from,' Weston declares.

As she speaks, thunder rolls through and lightning dances from every ridge. We shelter in Weston's borrowed caravan, rain pummelling its roof. She pays no heed. She's seen storms before, and this is nothing.

About the Authors

Patsy Adam-Smith grew up in the Depression years, the daughter of a railway fettler. The lonely life beside the tracks was interspersed with the excitement of the bush pursuits of rabbiting, yabbying and rare social occasions. Always there were books to be read, a habit sustained through wartime days and later life as a radio officer on coastal ships. The story is taken from the first of her two volumes of autobiography, *Hear The Train Blow*.

W.W. Ammon was among the tough breed of men who drove the wool trucks from the inland stations of north-western Australia to the coast at Carnarvon, taking on the job in 1925. The trucks were 'little high-pressure-tyred vehicles always grossly overloaded . . . pitted against those hundreds of miles of rutted wheel-tracks, endless loose sandhills, washed-out river crossings, tropical deluges and a pitiless sun.'

C.E.W. Bean was a barrister turned journalist for the *Sydney Morning Herald* when he garnered material for *On the Wool Track*. He won an Australian Journalists Association ballot to become official correspondent to the Australian Infantry Forces and accompanied the first convoy to Egypt in 1915. He became celebrated as Australia's Official Historian of World War 1, and was instrumental in the establishment of the Australian War Memorial in Canberra. He was a founder of the Parks and Playgrounds Movement of New South Wales, which aimed to establish country-style parks for city children.

The Tasmanian wilderness photography of **Chris Bell** follows in the tradition of Olegas Truchanas and Peter Dombrovskis with its astonishing beauty and clarity. He works from his Hobart studio and publishes privately through Laurel Press.

Geoffrey Blainey is one of Australia's best known and most significant historians. He taught Economic History at the University of Melbourne and was Chairman of the Australia Council from 1977 to 1981. His books include the bestselling *The Tyranny of Distance*, *Triumph of the Nomads* and *A Land Half Won*, as well as *A Shorter History of Australia* and his study of everyday life in an earlier Australia, *Black Kettle and Full Moon*.

Tasmanian-born broadcaster **Tim Bowden** is a household name in Australia, not only for his long-running ABC presentation of *Back Chat*, but also for his many books, including *One Crowded Hour*, *The Way My Father Told It*, *The Silence Calling* and his autobiography *Spooling Through*.

Robin Bromby began his career in journalism in his native New Zealand before transferring to Australia and becoming a senior writer with *The Australian*, specialising in finance. His long interest and expertise in the field of railway history led to a number of books, including *Ghost Railways of Australia*.

Gordon Wentworth Broughton was a New South Wales government surveyor and engineer, and his early life as a station hand and drover gave him the background needed for the task of leading a team to survey the Murray River for the installation of locks along a 700 km stretch of the great river. This was no weekend fishing trip, but one packed with danger and incident over many months.

While cutting logs for a living, **E.H. Burgmann** received his theological licence through part-time study. He then had to return to Taree High School to matriculate before studying at St Paul's College, University of Sydney. After a time in London he became travelling secretary to the Australian Board of Missions, and then warden of St John's College, Armidale, before becoming Bishop of Canberra and Goulburn. He was a prolific social commentator mainly through his letters to the Diocesan paper *Southern Churchman*. 'A Bishop's View of Bullock Driving' is from his book *The Education of an Australian* (1944).

Louisa Clifton was one of fourteen children of Marshall Clifton, who was lured by the post of Chief Commissioner of the new town of Australind, a town created by a London company to be formed on the Western Australian coast. Utopian dreams were fed by descriptions of abundant nature and a town of quays, streets, squares, markets and public gardens. The dreams dissolved in the antipodean heat and dust, but Louisa stayed in W.A. as the wife of the resident magistrate of Leschenault, George Eliot.

Tom Cole came from England to Australia in 1923, at the age of seventeen. He spent two decades working as a drover, station hand, crocodile hunter and buffalo shooter in Queensland, the Northern Territory and New Guinea. His autobiography *Hell West and Crooked* is a vivid account of a period in Australia which has been lost in modern times.

Bernard Cronin was dux of Dookie Agricultural College and became a cattle farmer, but he devoted his spare time to writing fiction and this, supported by journalism, became his profession. He wrote many novels as well as short stories and plays.

Adventurer and crocodile hunter **Malcolm Douglas** set off with his friend David Oldmeadow in 1964 to traverse the top of Australia. The experience bore a highly rated documentary, the book *Across the Top* and years of adventures, culminating in the establishment of a crocodile farm in Broome.

Geoffrey Dutton, poet, author, academic and the grazier scion of an old South Australian family, delved into the family archives to recount the improbable success of his father in being the first to traverse Australia by car.

A.B. Facey's memoir, *A Fortunate Life*, published when he was eighty-seven, records the cruelty he endured during childhood, his survival at Gallipoli, the loss of his farm during the Depression and subsequent personal losses. Throughout his life he remained steadfast in his acceptance of both the good and the bad.

Richard Flanagan is considered to be one of Australia's finest writers, and is the author of the acclaimed novels *A Terrible Beauty*, *Death of a River Guide*, *The Sound of One Hand Clapping*, *Gould's Book of Fish* and *The Unknown Terrorist*. Flanagan, born in Tasmania, lives in Hobart.

Internationally acclaimed scientist, explorer and conservationist **Tim Flannery** was named Australian of the Year in 2007. The former Director of the South Australian Museum, he is now Chair of the South Australian Premier's Science Council and head of the Australian Government Commission on Climate Change. Flannery is widely recognised for a host of books and articles which have made natural science accessible to the lay reader.

Miles Franklin (1879–1954) achieved fame at the age of twenty-two with the publication of her novel *My Brilliant Career*, which was based on her country upbringing. It had been rejected in Australia, but was published in England with the aid of Henry Lawson. Franklin published many more novels, but never achieved the same success. Her struggles, including restless travel and bouts of ill health, were revealed in *My Career Goes Bung* (unpublished until 1946), but she became successful again with a series of novels written under the pseudonym of 'Brent of Bin Bin'.

Alan Frost grew up in North Queensland and finished his school years at Salisbury High School in Brisbane, before taking an Arts degree at the University of Queensland and then a PhD at Rochester University, New Jersey. After lecturing in English at La Trobe University he switched to history and became Professor of History. He is Director of the La Trobe Institute for Advanced Study. His books include *Voyage of the Endeavour: Captain Cook and the Discovery of the Pacific* and *The Global Reach of Empire: British Maritime Expansion in the Indian and Pacific Oceans*. He is a fellow of the Royal Historical Society, London, and of The Australian Academy of the Humanities.

Mary Fullerton was born in a bark house at Glenmaggie, Victoria, where the Great Dividing Range drops down to the Gippsland Plains.

She produced a wide variety of poetry and prose, and set down her childhood memories in *Bark House Days*.

Jonathan Green found his way in journalism, first as a subeditor with his hometown *Canberra Times*, and eventually as a columnist and then keynote writer with the *The Age*. He was editor of the influential online news sheet *Crikey* and is now editor of *The Drum*, the Australian Broadcasting Commission's online opinion site. He decided to take his column and his family around Australia in 80 days, sending his reports from far-off places on 'the loop' around Australia.

Bill Harney grew up in outback Queensland and spent most of his life under the stars as a station hand, rouseabout, fencer, drover and rough rider. He became famous for his radio memoirs, including the simultaneously hilarious and moving *Bill Harney's War*, which became one of his many books. His understanding of the traditions of the Indigenous people of Central Australia made him the ideal choice as the first Commonwealth Government Ranger at Uluru.

In his thirty-five years in journalism, **Gary Hughes** has been European correspondent for the *Herald Sun*, Victorian editor of *The Australian* and head of the investigations unit of *The Age*, where he won three Walkley Awards. He also won the Gold Walkley Award in 2009 and that year was named the Graham Perkin Australian Journalist of the Year. Among many other awards he has also won two Melbourne Press Club Awards and two Commonwealth Media Awards.

E.M. 'Mick' Kelsall was in his seventies when, at the urging of his children, he sat down to write about his remarkable earlier life in Murray River towns, during which time he had many jobs, including a paddle-steamer 'bargee' and a timbergetter with his errant father and uncle. The result was the uplifting and hilarious book *A Riverman's Story*, which gave rise to a television miniseries titled *Ratbag Hero*.

Bill King is a doyen of outback tour operators. He established his Bill King's Safaris in the 1970s, taking visitors on camping tours in Central Australia. The business, with many setbacks and tough bush experiences, grew to capture both the European and American markets as well as an ever-growing Australian clientele. Bill King became a major figure in Australian Tourism development. His influence remains in the firm AAT-Kings.

Born and raised in Queensland, **Henry G. Lamond** attended the Queensland Agricultural College and then worked on stations for twenty-five years. Later he bought the Molle islands in the Whitsunday Passage and lived for ten years on South Molle Island, writing novels and articles based on Queensland pastoral life. His first book, *Horns and Hooves*, was followed by such novels as *Dingo*, *Big Red*, *Kilgour's Mare* and non-fiction works like *An Aviary on the Plains* and *Etiquette of Battle*. He was a prolific contributor to *The Bulletin* and *Walkabout*.

John Landy achieved worldwide fame in the 1950s as an athlete, setting world records for the 1500 metres and the mile and winning Commonwealth and Olympic medals. Behind the fame was a man whose interest in natural history directed his scientific and business career and led him to excel as a nature photographer. He is a Fellow of the Australian Institute of Agricultural science. John Landy was Governor of Victoria from 2001 to 2006.

Chronicler of Australian bush life **Henry Lawson** is best known for his short stories, sketches and poetry, including such classic stories as 'The Loaded Dog' and 'The Drover's Wife', and the poem 'Past Carin'. His instances of pure reportage were few, but they carried the same seemingly effortless colouration of the bush and its people. Lawson was born at Grentell in New South Wales, but his mother, Louisa, broke from the struggling bush life and achieved success in Sydney. Her positive influence on Lawson's literary career was somewhat offset by his broken home life and the wanderings and failed relationships which wore him down, even while his prose and poetry were acclaimed.

C.T. Madigan, a robust geologist and explorer, was born in South Australia. His career was closely entwined with that of his good friend Douglas Mawson. He was selected by Mawson as meteorologist for the Australian Antarctic Expedition of 1912–1913. He then went to England as a Rhodes Scholar and, with the interruption of war service, took first class honours in geology while also gaining blues for rowing and boxing. His epic crossing of the Simpson Desert was one of his many geological expeditions in Australia. Like Mawson, his base was as a Professor of Geology at the University of Adelaide.

Alan Marshall was born at Noorat, Victoria. He contracted polio when he was six and from that time on walked with crutches. His story of his childhood endurances and triumphs, *I Can Jump Puddles*, was translated into twenty-four languages. He received both an Order of the British Empire (1972) and an Order of Australia (1981).

Jock Marshall was expelled from Kogarah High School for his practical jokes and academic laziness. He later lost his left arm after a shotgun accident. His investigations of bush fauna around Sydney brought him to the notice of Professor Alec Chisholm and the connection led him to a worldwide academic career which culminated in his appointment in 1959 as foundation Professor of Biology at Monash University, Melbourne. He was outspoken, at times aggressive, and idolised by his students. A journalist described him as a literate, latter-day version of the Wild Colonial Boy.

Queenslander **Roger McDonald** is the author of seven novels, including *1915* and the internationally acclaimed *Mr Darwin's Shooter*. His account of his travels with New Zealand shearers in the Australian outback, *Shearers' Motel*, won the 1993 National Book Council Banjo Award for non-fiction.

Ros Moriarty, formerly a journalist with Radio Australia, specialising in Indigenous affairs, women's issues and the environment, is designer and managing director of Australia's leading Indigenous design studio, Balarinji, a business she established with her husband, John Moriarty, in 1983.

A celebrated political adviser to the emerging Chinese Republic and *London Times* correspondent in China, **G.E. 'Chinese' Morrison** was a lifelong adventurer, traveller and long-distance walker. As a youth he walked from Geelong to Adelaide, and after a period in northern Australia he decided to walk from Darwin to Melbourne. He later was wounded in New Guinea, gained a medical degree in England, and worked and travelled around the world, before writing a book about his experience of walking across China.

Gerald Murnane spent his childhood in country districts of Victoria. His seven books of fiction are often evocative of country Australia. Reviewers and critics differ sharply over Murnane's work. *Tamarisk Row* (1974) was described by *Nation Review* as the finest novel to appear in Australia for years, while another reviewer found it unread-able. His most widely read book, *The Plains* (1982), was called by one critic 'a classic of our literature', and by another 'nonsense'. Murnane won the Patrick White award in 1999, when none of his books were in print in Australia.

Les Murray is considered by many to be Australia's most important living poet. He grew up on his grandfather's farm at Bunyah, New South Wales, and now lives in Bunyah again with his wife, Valerie. He has published thirty books, received an Order of Australia and an Honorary Doctorate of Literature, and won the Queen's Gold Medal for Poetry and many other literary awards.

D'Arcy Niland left his Glen Innes, NSW, school at fourteen, deter-mined to be a writer. He published his bestselling novel, *The Shiralee*, twenty-four years later. Over the years he had been a copy boy, rail-way porter, shearer and odd-job man, but he always wrote and after he married Ruth Park in 1942 they settled down to make a living at the game. The success of her novel *The Harp in the South* kept them going in their literary struggle, and with five children to raise. Various successes led Niland to a Commonwealth Literary Fund and gave him time to write *The Shiralee*. A string of novels followed – the last, *Dead Men Running*, completed two days before Niland's death from a heart attack in 1967.

A.B. 'Banjo' Paterson, a solicitor turned writer and poet, is the author of the words to arguably Australia's best known song, 'Waltz-ing Matilda', and the famous poem 'The Man from Snowy River'. He grew up on his father's property in the Yass District, New South Wales, and was educated in Sydney. He contributed poems to *The Bulletin* and his ballads became famous. He gained the post of Boer

War correspondent for the *Sydney Morning Herald* in 1899, and then went back to the land before distinguished service in World War 1. After the war he resumed a career as a broadcaster and writer.

Richard Piesse, conservationist and bushwalker, was a representative in America for the Australian National Travel Association, which owned the magazine *Walkabout* until 1971, and later became Director of the Australian Conservation Foundation. He was associated with the establishment of the Great Dividing Trail, a 280 km public walking trail straddling the Great Dividing Range.

Eric Rolls was a farmer, an environmentalist, a food and wine expert, and the author of many books. His *A Million Wild Acres*, first published in 1981, has been a bestseller and published in many languages. Among many prizes, the book won the *Age* Book of the Year, the C.J. Dennis Prize and the Braille Book of the Year. He was a Fellow of the Australian Academy of the Humanities and an Australian Creative Fellow, and held an Honorary Doctorate from the University of Canberra.

Edward S. Sorenson was born at Dyraaba, a river town in northern New South Wales, and soon took to the road, working as a stock-rider, drover, shearer, wool classer and gold fossicker. His main education was through constant reading. He later 'settled down' to become a small farmer and then a publican, and a constant contributor to journals like *The Lone Hand* and *The Bulletin*, before 'retiring' to Sydney. *Life in the Australian Backblocks*, first published in 1911, was described by Geoffrey Blainey as 'a wine-like book which has become extremely palatable with age'.

Douglas Stewart, poet, journalist and editor, brought his love of fishing from his native land of New Zealand. A country newspaper editor at twenty-two, he travelled to Australia in 1938 and became literary editor of *The Bulletin* from 1940 to 1961. He was later literary advisor at Angus & Robertson publishing house and did much to encourage Australian writers and poets. Many collections of his poetry were published as well as his memoir, *Springtime in Taranaki*, and his fishing book, *The Seven Rivers*.

Brian Taylor spent most of his life in the outback reaches of Queensland cattle country, working in all sorts of jobs that required his talents, as a horse tamer, blacksmith, fencer, saddler, stockman and drover – to name a few. He recorded his stories in *A Swag of Memories*.

Arthur Upfield created Australia's best known fictional detective, Napoleon Bonaparte (known as Bony), who featured in many of his novels. He was the first foreigner to be made a full member of the Mystery Writers of America. Upfield was sent from England to Australia by his father at the age of nineteen, served in World War 1 and then spent many years working in the bush. He later became a feature writer for the *Melbourne Herald*.

Edna Walling studied horticulture at Burnley College, Melbourne, and started work as a jobbing gardener in 1917. Asked by an architect to plan a garden, she succeeded so well that she soon built a flourishing design practice. On large estates her designs included grand architectural features in a formal setting, but she always included a 'wild' section. Big or small, her gardens were a series of 'pictures', featuring a mastery of plants, and of space. She created Bickleigh Vale Village, a series of cottages and gardens around her home at Mooroolbark, Victoria. She published four books, including *On the Trail of Australian Wildflowers*, which was released posthumously in 1984.

A triple Walkley Award winner, **Keith Willey** worked on newspapers all around Australia. He was the author of twenty-six books on Australian travel and life, and a prolific contributor to magazines. He taught at the Darling Downs Institute of Education, and after his death his family set up the Keith Willey Award, which annually recognises the top journalism student at the University of Southern Queensland.

Tony Wright is the National Affairs Editor of *The Age*. He has been based in the Canberra Press gallery for over twenty years, working for the *Canberra Times*, the *Sydney Morning Herald* and *The Bulletin*. He has won several UN Media Peace Prizes and has five times been a finalist in the Walkley Awards for outstanding journalism.

Editor's Note

This collection of non-fiction bush writing is drawn from the colonial past to the present day. The prejudices sometimes presented have perforce been left to stand. While some views might be considered offensive today, they might also be seen to give a valuable understanding of the attitudes of the writers and their times.

While much of this collection is drawn from a time when European settlement was spreading, it does not seek to dismiss the great tragedy of the dispossession of Australian Aboriginal people of their land. While Aboriginal understanding has a rich oral tradition, passed on through generations, there have been collections of Aboriginal literature of modern times – history, memoir, fiction and poetry – which provide an entirely different aspect of 'bush writing' from this presentation. They are thought to be better read in their context, than in any passing gesture that might have been attempted here.

The selection of a considerable amount of material from the colonial past reflects a 'golden age' of the Australian bush, when it was seen as a far-off place of wonder and danger, of pioneering life and struggle. It was a time when magazines like *The Bulletin*, *Smith's Weekly* and, later, *Walkabout* presented material which was fascinating to those who would never get into the distant farmlands, stations and the outback, to whom the Red Centre and the great Australian deserts were notionally as distant as the moon. Even into the mid-twentieth century there was a steady stream of books about experiences in 'the bush', but they have tended to dry up in modern times. Today's conveniences of aircraft, four-wheel drive, bitumen and caravan parks have made the bush accessible, and have reduced most modern 'bush writing' to travel writing. There are many exceptions, but the evocation of an old Australia has been part of the pleasure of assembling this collection.

Acknowledgements

The editor acknowledges The State Library of Victoria and Yarra Libraries (Richmond Branch), and the unfailingly helpful and professional service provided by library staffers.

The editor and publisher are grateful to the following writers, agents and publishers for permission to reproduce their articles. Some writers are out of copyright, while the copyright information or assigns for a few pieces have, despite extensive investigation, remained untraced. The publisher would be happy to have any information on copyright, and remains ready to honor the terms and conditions of permission as set down by the Australian Society of Authors.

'The Landscape of the Imagination' by Gerald Murnane, introduction to *Wimmera*, Thames & Hudson, 2002. Reprinted by permission of the author.

'The Romance of the Swag' by Henry Lawson, from *The Romance of the Swag*, Angus & Robertson, 1907.

'Land of the Delicate Scrub' by C.E.W. Bean from *On the Wool Track*, Cornstalk Publishing, 1927. Reprinted by permission of Mr E.B. LeCouteur and Mrs A.M. Carroll.

'Scorpions by the Thousand' by W.W. Ammon from *Wheel Tracks*, Angus & Robertson, 1967.

'Breakdown' by Jonathan Green from *Around Australia in 80 Days*, Craftsman House, 2004. Reprinted by permission of the author.

'The Waaia Races' by Patsy Adam-Smith from *Hear the Train Blow*, Penguin 2003. Reprinted by permission of Noeleen Megay for the estate of Patsy Adam Smith.

'A Transcontinental Ramble' by G.E. 'Chinese' Morrison from *Across the Australian Continent on Foot, The Leader*, Melbourne, 1883.

'Bush Pubs – Oases on the Plains' by Jock Marshall, from *Journey Among Men*, Hodder & Stoughton, 1966.

'Bugger Australia Altogether' by E.M. 'Mick' Kelsall from *A Riverman's Story*, Lothian, 1986. Reprinted by permission of Hachette Livre Australia.

'The Big Forest of Wang Wauk' by Les Murray from *Gone Bush*, Bantam, 1990. Reprinted by permission of the author c/o Margaret Connolly Literary Agency.

'The Long Drought' by Geoffrey Blainey from *A Land Half Won*, Macmillan, 1980. Reprinted by permission of the author.

'The Sugar Lands' by Alan Frost from *East Coast Country*, Melbourne University Press, 1996. Reprinted by permission of the author.

'First Time in the Bush' by Louisa Clifton from *The Diary of Louisa Clifton, 1840–1841*, held in the Battye Library, Perth.

'An Old, Old Country' by Douglas Stewart from *Meanjin*, 1962. Reprinted by permission of the Curtis Brown Literary Agency.

'A Bishop's View of Bullock Driving' by E.H. Burgmann from *The Education of an Australian*, Angus and Robertson, 1944. Reprinted by permission of St Mark's Library, Canberra.

'In a Wet Season' by Henry Lawson from *While the Billy Boils*, Angus & Robertson, 1896.

'The Rising of the Fish' by Eric Rolls from *The River*, Angus & Robertson, 1974. Reprinted by permission of Elaine Van Kempen.

'Bushman Junior' by Edward S. Sorenson from *Life in the Australian Backblocks*, Whitcombe and Tombs, 1911.

'Storm over Ayers Rock' by Richard Piesse from *Walkabout*, March, 1966. Reprinted by permission of the author.

'Bathhurst' by D'Arcy Niland from *Walkabout*, August 1965. Reprinted by permission of Tim Curnow Literary Agency.

'Borroloola' by Keith Willey from *Walkabout*, February 1967. Reprinted by permission of Joanna Willey for the Willey Estate.

'Cross-Country Caravan' by Alan Marshall from *These Are My People*, Cheshire, 1944. Reprinted by Permission of the Curtis Brown Literary Agency.

'Birds and Snakes' by Gordon Wentworth Broughton from *Men of the Murray*, Rigby, 1966.

'Crossing the Dead Heart' by C.T. Madigan from *Crossing the Dead Heart*, Rigby, 1946.

'Lost in Friendly Territory' by Roger McDonald from *Shearers' Motel*, Picador, 1990. Reprinted by permission of the author.

'The Way of Wild Pigs' by Henry G. Lamond from *Walkabout*, January 1951.

'Across Australia by Car' by Geoffrey Dutton from *Pegasus no 28.*, *Mobil Services Ltd.*, 1985. Reprinted by permission of the Curtis Brown Literary Agency.

'The Flowers of Kosciusko' by Edna Walling from *Walkabout*, March 1951.

'The Old Bush Fence' by Bernard Cronin from *Walkabout*, April 1951.

'The Trouble with Merinos' by A.B. 'Banjo' Paterson from *A.B. 'Banjo' Paterson: Complete Works*, Sydney, 1983.

'Timbergetters and Scrub Dwellers' by Eric Rolls from *A Million Wild Acres*, Nelson, 1981. Reprinted by permission of Elaine Van Kempen.

'Cheating the Flames of Death' by Gary Hughes, *The Australian*, February 9, 2010. Reprinted by permission of the author.

'The Piners' Life' by Richard Flanagan from *A Terrible Beauty*, Greenhouse Publishing, 1985. Reprinted by permission of the author.

'Head Stockman at Wave Hill' by Tom Cole from *Hell West and Crooked*, Collins, 1998. Reprinted by permission of Harper Collins Publishers Australia.

'Fettlers – A Particular Breed' by Robin Bromby from *Ghost Railways of Australia*, Lothian, 2006. Reprinted by permission of Hachette Livre Australia.

'Crocodile Hunters' by Malcolm Douglas from *Across The Top*, Rigby, 1972. Reprinted by permission of New Holland Publishers.

'Games of the Bush Children' by Mary Fullerton from *Bark House Days*, Melbourne University Press, 1921.

'The Brumby Mare' by Brian Taylor from *A Swag of Memories*, Hachette Livre Australia, 2008. Reprinted by permission of Hachette Livre Australia.

'The Horse Will Save You' by Leo Rosten (as told to John Ross) from *Voices of the Bush*, ABC Books, 2001. Reprinted by permission of Harper Collins Publishers Australia.

'My Wild Life' by A.B. Facey from *A Fortunate Life*, Fremantle Arts Centre Press, 1981. Reprinted by permission of Penguin Books Australia.

'The Brightest Place on Earth' by Tim Flannery from *Country: A Continent, A Scientist and a Kangaroo*, Text Publishing Australia, 2004. Reprinted by permission of Text Publishing Australia.

'Ceremony' by Ros Moriarty from *Listening to Country*, Allen & Unwin, 2010. Reprinted by permission of Allen & Unwin.

'Wilderness – A Personal Account' by Chris Bell from *Tasmania: Primal Places,* Laurel Press, 1990. Reprinted by permission of the author.

'The Dingo' by Bill Harney from *Walkabout*, July 1951.

'A Desperate Rescue' by Geoff Hudspeth (as told to Tim Bowden) from *Voices of the Bush*, ABC Books, 2001. Reprinted by permission from Harper Collins Publishers Australia.

'Patrolling the World's Longest Fence' by Arthur Upfield from *Walkabout*, March 1935.

'Close to Nature' by John Landy from *Close to Nature*, Currey, O'Neil Ross, 1985. Reprinted by permission of the author.

'Walking on Water' by Bill King from *King of the Outback*, 2011, Allen & Unwin. Reprinted by permission of the author.

'Settlers and Snakes' by Miles Franklin from *Childhood at Brindabella*, Angus & Robertson, 1963.

'An Angel in the Queensland Floods' by Tony Wright from *The Age*, January 22, 2011. Reprinted by permission of the author.

The Penguin Book of Australian War Writing

EDITED BY MARK DAPIN

From the cliffs of Gallipoli, through the jungles of Vietnam, to the deserts of Afghanistan and Iraq, Australia's short history is a story of war. The battlefield has shaped the way we define ourselves – the Australian values of mateship, courage under fire, larrikinism – but few of us have witnessed these scenes firsthand. Soldiers writing from the front and journalists on the ground have formed the way we think about war and so formed the way we think about ourselves.

In *The Penguin Book of Australian War Writing*, author and journalist Mark Dapin has gathered together the finest of these accounts. Starting with Watkin Tench's observations of an Aboriginal war party, we see the terror, confusion and occasional heroics of the front line through the eyes of some of our best writers, including AB Paterson, Martin Boyd, Patrick White, Alan Moorehead, Kenneth Slessor, Peter Cundall and Barry Heard.

These remarkable letters, journals, memoirs and reports remind us of our history, and of our responsibility in recording and remembering what happens in the wars we send our soldiers to fight.

THE PENGUIN BOOK OF THE OCEAN

EDITED BY JAMES BRADLEY

Ever since the first travellers reached the coast of Africa hundreds of thousands of years ago, the ocean has been one of the wellsprings of the human imagination. Its restless immensity has given us new horizons to cross, new possibilities to explore, and inspired wonder, heartache and heroism.

In *The Penguin Book of the Ocean* bestselling author James Bradley presents a dazzling selection of writing exploring this grandest of obsessions, combining fact and fiction, classical and contemporary, to create a collection like no other.

From Rachel Carson's luminous account of our planet's birth to the story of the wreck that inspired *Moby-Dick*, from Ernest Shackleton's harrowing account of his escape from Antarctica by open boat to Tim Winton's award-winning dissection of the dark side of surfing, *The Penguin Book of the Ocean* is a hymn to the mystery, beauty and majesty of the ocean, and to the poets and explorers it has inspired.

THE PENGUIN BOOK OF THE ROAD

EDITED BY DELIA FALCONER

Australia is a nation of drivers. We spend more time behind the wheel than almost anyone else, on fast highways, lonely bush tracks, jammed city lanes and suburban streets. The road is the place where the great dramas of our lives unfold, the route to our greatest pleasures as well as our worst nightmares. It is sexy, dangerous and unnerving.

In this landmark collection, acclaimed novelist and essayist Delia Falconer brings together some of our very best writing on every aspect of the road.

Lovers, lost children, bushrangers, killers. From the classic to the modern, from the outback to the beach, *The Penguin Book of the Road* is an entertaining ride into the heart of Australia.

'A savvy and diverse collection'
Weekend Australian